The aim of the *Earth Quest* series is to examine and explain how shamanic principles can be applied in the journey towards self-discovery
– and beyond.

Each person's Earth quest is the search for meaning and purpose in life – it is the establishment of identity and the realization of inner potentials and individual responsibility.

Each book in the series examines aspects of a life science that is in harmony with the Earth and shows how individuals can attune themselves to nature. Each book imparts knowledge of the Craft of Life.

Other Books in the *Earth Quest* Series

ANIMALS OF THE SOUL
Sacred Animals of the Oglala Sioux
Joseph Epes Brown

BEAUTIFUL PAINTED ARROW
Stories and Teachings from the Native American Tradition
Joseph E Rael

THE CELTIC SHAMAN
A Handbook
John Matthews

THE DRUID WAY
Philip Carr-Gomm

EARTH LIGHT
The Ancient Path to Transformation
Rediscovering the Wisdom of Celtic and Faery Lore
R J Stewart

EARTH MEDICINE
A Shamanic Way to Self Discovery
Kenneth Meadows

LETTERS FROM A WILD STATE
An Aboriginal Perspective
James G Cowan

THE MEDICINE WAY
A Shamanic Path to Self Mastery
Kenneth Meadows

POWER WITHIN THE LAND
The Roots of Celtic and Underworld Traditions
R J Stewart

SHAMANIC EXPERIENCE
A Practical Guide to Contemporary Shamanism
Kenneth Meadows

SINGING THE SOUL BACK HOME
Shamanism in Daily Life
Caitlín Matthews

TRACKS OF DANCING LIGHT
A Native American Approach to Understanding Your Name
Joseph E Rael and Lindsay Sutton

WHERE EAGLES FLY
A Shamanic Way to Inner Wisdom
Kenneth Meadows

Rune Power

Kenneth Meadows spent more than 30 years of his life seeking answers to some of life's most perplexing mysteries: Who am I? What am I? Why am I here? What is life's *purpose*? He explored the world's great religions and was offered *beliefs*. He considered the philosophies of learned men and gathered *opinions*. He examined the theories of materialistic science only to find that many are based upon *assumptions*. At a crucial point of abandoning his search, Kenneth came in touch with the simplicity of native American spirituality and of a wisdom which had been conveyed through oral traditions. He discovered that the Medicine Wheel, far from being the sacred preserve of North American Indian tribes, was a catalyst providing a means of bringing all ancient traditions into harmony and unity for the benefit of humanity.

Kenneth was given the name *Flying Horse,* implying the communicator of information, and 'commissioned' to construct a 'lantern' of books on what he had learned. *Rune Power* is Kenneth's fifth book – the fifth component of that 'lantern'.

A Leeds University-qualified teacher and a former Lecturer in Further Education, Kenneth is Director of Studies of the Faculty of Shamanics, an educational enterprise founded in 1994 to further the development of *Shamanics*, the unique process of personal development and life enhancement derived from a distillation of shamanic wisdom from cultures and traditions worldwide. Other books by Kenneth Meadows include *Earth Medicine*, *The Medicine Way*, *Shamanic Experience* and *Where Eagles Fly*.

EARTH QUEST

Rune Power

The Secret Knowledge
of the Wise Ones

KENNETH MEADOWS

ELEMENT
Rockport, Massachusetts ● Shaftesbury, Dorset
Brisbane, Queensland

Text © Kenneth Meadows 1996

First published in Great Britain in 1996 by
Element Books Limited
Shaftesbury, Dorset SP7 8BP

Published in the USA in 1996 by
Element Books, Inc.
PO Box 830, Rockport, MA 01966

Published in Australia in 1996 by
Element Books Limited
for Jacaranda Wiley Limited
33 Park Road, Milton, Brisbane 4064

Cover illustration and Cover design by Max Fairbrother
Text design by Roger Lightfoot
Typeset by Footnote Graphics, Warminster, Wiltshire
Printed and bound in the USA by Edwards Brothers, Inc.

British Library Cataloguing in Publication
data available

Library of Congress Cataloging in Publication
data available

ISBN 1–85230–706–4

Contents

Rune-work

Illustrations

Acknowledgements

MY ABUNDANT THANKS – TO THE Runic shamans in Sweden who shared with me knowledge of the Runes that has been obscured in spite of the so-called Runic revival, and who were the first to motivate me into writing this book so that the Runes can be used with love and concern.

To my principal mentor, Silver Bear, who has kept me to the task that has bridged several years; to my other teachers who in various ways have guided me; and to my helpers in the spiritual ecology who have supported me.

To Rod Nicholson who enabled me to connect with my ancestry.

To my students who have explored the wonders of the Runes with me and allowed me to share in the excitement of their own discoveries and to watch the beneficial changes that have been wrought in their lives through the power of the Runes.

And to my wife, Beryl, my partner and companion along the way, for her patience and encouragement.

Preface

SHAMANISM IS THE OLDEST FORM of spiritual expression known to humanity for it has its origins in prehistoric times and so predates all of the world's religions. Among all races and traditions a person who possessed an unusual ability to perceive what others cannot see, experience realities other than ordinary physical life, and communicate with the intelligences of other life forms and of other realms of existence, was known by some as a *shaman*.

The word *shaman* (pronounced 'shah mahn') is derived from the language of the Tungus people of Siberia. It can be interpreted as 'one who knows' or 'a wise person'. More precisely the word means 'one who knows *ecstacy*' – a person who has transcended the body and the mind and undergone a profound spiritual experience. A shaman of whatever race or culture was usually a man or woman who had completed a long and often painful process of 'apprenticeship' and, perhaps, suffered from some physical disability. Though an honoured member of a tribe, he or she was usually socially separated.

This book is concerned with the insights and understandings of a particular kind of shaman – the *Runic* shaman – who existed among the indigenous peoples of northern Europe, Scandinavia and Iceland, and was familiar with angular patterns called Runes. This Runic knowledge had close similarities with the spiritual perceptions of North American Indians and with the Taoist wisdom of the Orient, for it formed part of a *universal* shamanism. Though suppressed through religious intolerance and political tyranny, this knowledge was safeguarded within oral traditions. Long hidden, it is now being reclaimed so that access to it can enable individuals to make better sense of the world and find meaning, purpose and fulfilment in their lives.

Runic shamans were men and women with a working knowledge of Runes – angular shapes written on a smooth surface, carved in wood, or engraved on stone or on personal belongings. Some people considered them to be a secret code which in a mysterious way unleashed a power to manifest what was desired, restrain those who intended harm, or reveal what the future held.

The Runes have been much maligned by associations with the occult, magick and sorcery, and with the sinister forces of Nazism, which used certain Runic patterns as its insignia. In this way they became defiled as people came to associate these patterns with racism, terror, and destruction. The so-called Runic revival in the latter part of the 20th century has been largely a re-awakening of the craft of those who perceive the Runes as a magickal tool for satisfying desires and obtaining that which is wanted through exercise of the Will. Others have regarded the Runes with reverence as a means of restoring the pre-Christian Odinic religion. Still others have trivialized them as lucky charms and tools-in-trade of fortune-tellers.

The Runes, however, were never revealed for selfish, sinister or religious purposes, or as a means of discovering one's Fate. They were given as a gift to humanity and as a blessing to mankind – a mission that sadly has been overlooked for all too long. It is in this context that they are revealed in the pages of *Rune Power*.

This book is about understanding the true nature of the Runes. Through such an understanding we can comprehend more fully the wonders of Nature and the natural environment and strengthen our motivation to respect and protect them. Through understanding the true nature of the Runes we can also come to know ourselves more fully and to determine the underlying purpose of our own life.

In past times, 'mystery' cults, which flourished underground during periods of oppressive state religion, were a means of obtaining 'secret' information that was denied to all but a privileged few. When used in connection with magickal spells and incantations, the word *mystery* was a distortion of its original meaning of 'secret information'. This was an oral method of obtaining arcane knowledge by direct contact with spiritual forces inherent in the different aspects of Nature – powers which some called 'gods' because their intelligence appeared to transcend that of humans. The 'secret information' was knowledge which could be obtained only through a process of initiation – that is, through direct personal contact with what was desired to be known. In other words, it was *experienced* knowledge – knowledge which could be obtained only as a result of the very act of *performing* it. The whole process of such an initiation took candidates seeking enlightenment through experiences which themselves comprised different stages of personal development and various levels of conscious awareness. The individual was finally brought to a recognition that the spiritual quest to discover Truth can never be found in the world 'out there' or the heavens 'up there' – however pure the motive, however genuine the desire, and however persistent and courageous the endeavour – but was accessible only from *within*. This was the meaning behind the words inscribed above the Delphic temple in ancient Greece: 'Man, know Thyself'.

Those of us who have searched the highways and byways of religious thought and sought to find answers to some of life's most perplexing questions from spiritual leaders and gurus, from philosophers and from learned institutions, have done so because we have all been conditioned to look *outside* ourselves. We have been taught to regard knowledge as truth, whereas it is only information – and much of it is based upon speculation, assumption and, sometimes, blind belief.

The Runes can teach us the importance of looking *within* and experiencing for *ourselves* the relationship between the physical and the spiritual, the manifest and the unmanifest, the outside and the inside. By so doing we come to a realization that the physical, mental and spiritual are not separate and divided, but different *facets* of a total, composite wholeness.

With the dawning of a new millennium, humankind has reached a critical phase in which there is a clear choice. In spite of the great inventions of materialistic science and the wonders of modern technology, our world is heading for a great crisis. Either we can choose spiritual bankruptcy and degeneration – expanding further the forces of Chaos which can overwhelm humanity and bring destruction to the Earth – or we can choose to extend human consciousness into higher levels of awareness and by so doing grasp the multidimensional nature of Reality and create a new Golden Age.

According to modern physics, the basic substance of matter is at subatomic level, beyond atoms and molecules and where matter and energy is interchangeable. This basic unit of matter and energy has been called a *quantum* – an invisible signal or fluctuation which precedes both impulses of energy and particles of matter. It is at this most subtle level that the greatest potential energy exists, and it is here that the Runes have their origin.

The Runes are not, therefore, as historians, anthropologists and others have led us to suppose, the product of the human mind – though certainly they have been *manipulated* by the mind. Nor are they mere symbols that represent something else. Each Runic character is a pattern or carrier of an energy-potency that *precedes* substance. It is a vessel of a basic constituent activity within Nature and within ourselves which, when activated and released, generates *movement*. So Runes indicate the possible movement and transformational change of potencies within Nature and ourselves. In other words, Runes are themselves forces that empower *activity*. We have also been misinformed about Nature. Nature itself is not an object, though we have been conditioned to treat it as such. Nature is a *process*. Nature is a process by which manifestation from invisibility into physical form is enabled to take place as an *expression* of spiritual 'substance', so that Spirit itself may be cultivated and developed.

Such an understanding helps us to recognize life's purpose, which is 'to thrive and endure' – that is, to produce and go on developing. Produce what? Produce that which has form, of course! An essential purpose of human life is to manifest emanations of ourselves *from our own substance*! The natural act of reproduction teaches us that! Offspring are produced through the merging of seed with substance. A fruit, a newborn animal, a human infant – each is a fulfilment of that union. The words I am writing are made up of letters which together manifest my thoughts in physical form. The book you are holding in your hands is thus a manifestation of my own mental and spiritual substance, brought into being through the physical task of expressing that substance in words – symbols that can be understood – and committing those words to paper by means of a word processor. The publisher then devises a design to embrace those words into a product that can be manufactured, distributed and made available worldwide to whoever wants to share my thoughts and experience my mental universe. Similarly, Runes are components of a Cosmic language that can reveal to us an inner knowledge of the physical Universe and of ourselves, for the natural laws that govern the Universe function also within ourselves. Each of us is, therefore, a mini-universe!

When the Runes are thus approached for understanding and in an attitude of honour and respect, rather than as a means of manipulation and exploitation, they are able to bring you in touch with the powers of your own innermost being and enable you to discover how your choices and actions create energy-patterns that determine your own reality and fashion your future and destiny.

When we understand the Runes, we understand both the environment and ourselves. Understand the Runes and we understand the Earth and the Universe. Understand the Runes and we understand both the outside and the inside, the manifest and the unmanifest, the physical and the spiritual. That is the true purpose of Runes. That is the purpose of this book.

The Runes were never intended as a tool for sorcery or for any sinister purpose. They were given as a gift to humanity and intended as a blessing to mankind. It is in that spirit that they are revealed in this book.

1 Whispered Secrets

THE NORTHERN TRADITION COMPRISES THE SPIRITUAL attitudes, beliefs, customs and practices of the indigenous peoples who populated an area of northern Europe, including the British Isles, Scandinavia and Iceland, before the Christian era. These pagan peoples were not the savages we have been led to suppose from distorted history and the sensationalism of Hollywood movies. Their living conditions were very basic compared with our own and their environment was harsh for they were conditioned by more primitive methods of survival than those of so-called 'advanced' nations today. However, they shared a deep love for the Earth and a recognition of the need to respect the natural environment and the other life forms that shared it with them. Although there was a variety of religious themes and philosophical concepts, and variations in customs and practices between different communities, there was a similarity of essential principles. These embraced a common realization that the creative forces that exist in Nature and within human beings can be directed either positively and constructively, or negatively and destructively. These people sought to be in balance with Nature and with themselves by coming into harmony with the pulse and rhythms of the Earth. Great emphasis was placed upon personal freedom and independence. No truth was considered absolute. Other people's understanding of the mysteries of birth, life and death were taken not as threats to their own beliefs and experience but rather as different viewpoints of multifaceted Truth. So there was toleration and respect.

Religious ideas were not forced upon people, as was the case

1

in later times when, under monotheistic influence, religion became more formulated and institutionalized. Some took their religion seriously and tried to live out its principles in their everyday lives. Others treated it more casually and got involved only on festive occasions. Many took no interest whatever in religious ideas and practices. Equality of the sexes prevailed, not in the sense of men and women performing similar work, but in that both were accepted as of equal worth – as complementary 'opposites' in a partnership in which each contributed what the other needed or lacked. After all, the Cosmos itself was observed to be an outworking of the masculine and feminine polarities inherent in all things. The whole atmosphere was thus quite different from one in which a universal and exclusive truth was claimed by those who sought to convince and dominate and to suppress or prohibit whatever appeared contrary to their own perception: persecuting and punishing – sometimes by death – anyone whose understanding of Truth differed from theirs. Such power and dominance over human lives has diminished in more recent times through the spread of democratic principles, the widening of the freedom of the individual, and the rise of materialistic science which disproves or undermines previously held dogmatic concepts.

The gods and goddesses of Odinism, the principal Northern religion, were personifications of the invisible intelligences perceived to be behind the creative, formative and dispersing forces of Nature and the Universe. Personalities and behaviour traits were attributed to them simply because these invisible forces seemed to behave like humans. These gods and goddesses were not hallucinations, figments of a religion-inspired imagination, or even symbolic representations. They were *real* because they were expressions of how mighty natural forces behaved, and they provided a 'tangible' means of enabling human beings to come into a meaningful relationship with them in spite of their invisibility. Each of the gods and goddesses personified qualities which the individual human being could comprehend, so they were approachable like a father, mother, brother, sister, lover, friend, companion, comrade, advisor or teacher, depending on personal needs at the time. In other words, there was a human-ness about their divinity. It was as if the deities themselves had been through every facet of human experience and, therefore, had an empathy towards mankind and understood what it must be like to be 'human'.

The principal deity was perceived as an imposing patriarchal figure who was acknowledged not only as a chief among gods but as the All-Father – meaning the Originator who had 'seeded' everything that had come into existence. The name given to this deity was Odin. The name *Odin* is derived from an Old Norse noun 'od', meaning 'wind', or 'all-pervading spirit' in which everything lives and moves and has its being – similar to the Great Spirit of Native American cosmology. The word is also derived from a Norse verb meaning 'to walk' implying an active presence on an Earth 'journey'. Spirit is likened to air – wind – since its presence cannot be seen but only felt. Air was also likened to the way thoughts flow through the mind. So Odin was associated with the power of the mind and of inspired and creative thought. Perceived as the All-Father who originated the Universe, Odin was associated with the family unit and with the wisdom, guidance and protection that arises out of loving concern. According to oral myths, Odin, the All-Father, was known by 49 names, indicating that mortals of different languages, cultures and traditions used different names for the same deity, based upon their own attitudes and beliefs.

Dictionaries define 'walk' as 'a journey on foot' and 'to make progress on the ground'. So Odin signified both a means of making progress on Earth – on the 'ground' of practical, every-day reality – and a divinity that was in the experience *with* human beings, sharing their Earth 'walk'.

Odin was often portrayed as riding on an eight-legged horse – symbolic of Time – which conveyed him between the realms of Spirit and matter.

The Runic shaman did not necessarily share the religious beliefs of Odinism, but did respect them as a way of giving recognition to the existence of a non-ordinary aspect of reality to which he or she had access. He or she – and it is likely that the majority of Runic shamans were women – did not *worship* Odin and the other gods, but shared a desire to emulate them in a process of self-development. Indeed, the days of the week were dedicated to the Northern deities because each day was considered to embrace a quality of Time which expressed characteristics and attributes of the deities.

Sunday was dedicated to the Sun – the source of light and life and representative of the Ultimate Source out of which everything comes and is enabled to manifest.

Monday was dedicated to the Moon – the deity Mani – and the fluidic power that ebbs and flows, affects and emotions and influences the body fluids.

Tuesday was the god Tyr's day and emphasized the protection that comes from honest work and endeavour, and the application of law, order and justice.

Wednesday was Woden's day – Woden being a Germanic name for Odin, the All-Father and Originator who was in the Creation with us and is therefore indicated in the midst of the weekly cycle; in the midst of Time.

Thursday was Thor's day and is associated with fertility, productivity and the transformation that comes from growth and development.

Friday was the goddess Freyja's day and is associated with the power of love and compassion, the warmth of friendship and freedom of the individual.

Saturday was related to the three Norns – or the three aspects or qualities of Time, often regarded as Past, Present, and Future – and signified the need for rest and refreshment.

These pagan people thus recognized divinity in all things, with all things in existence being interdependent. Human life was perceived as an expression of alive-ness which was required to be lived out to the full in practical ways in the Here-and-Now. Death, as observed in Nature, was not regarded as an end of life but as part of it. Birth, growth, maturity, death and rebirth were perceived as a continuing phenomenon of development, change and transition. Odinism's festivals were not memorials of incidents in the life of a deity, but celebrations of the rhythms of life and the cycles of Nature. Incidentally, the word 'pagan' does not mean 'godless', as is generally implied. Its original meaning was 'in harmony with the cycles of Nature'. And that meant the cycles of Time, also.

The religious connotations of Odinism – possibly variations and departures from the original shamanism – became the principal faith of the peoples of northern Europe and Scandinavia before the Christian era. Their development into a religion may have occurred through a need by many to have someone in authority to make decisions for them, and clear rules and conditions to live by. This had happened also in China, as Taoist shamanism branched into both a religion and a philosophy. With the move away from the original shamanic principles of guidance from the forces of Nature and inner promptings to a religion that demanded obedience to a priesthood, there was less emphasis on personal responsibility.

The name Odin was assumed by the chieftain of a tribe which emigrated from the Caspian Sea area in the first century of the Christian era, after a mystical experience in which the god Odin featured. According to legend this chieftain, whose original name was Sig, led a wandering tribe through northern Europe, including parts of Russia, the Ukraine, Poland, Germany, Denmark and Sweden, eventually establishing a settlement in southern Sweden. There are fascinating comparisons between this historical Odin and the legendary King Arthur of Camelot, for Odin's rulership also was with the assistance of 12 elders, each representing a sign of the zodiac. After his death, this Odin was deified by his followers. A mound where his body is thought to be buried is located near the site of an ancient Odinist temple at Uppsala in Sweden, where a Runic school is said to have been founded.

After Iceland was colonized by Scandinavians, its ruler was not called a king but a 'Lawspeaker'. He, too, had 12 assistants called magistrates, who were local administrators. In Icelandic courts a magistrate was accompanied by two others so any verdict was by tripartite discussion and agreement. In Northern mythology the Odin of prehistory is often depicted with two other gods to form a divine triad, indicating that the Universe in coming into being was divided into zones of Cosmic Fire and Cosmic Ice – the Yang and Yin of Taoist shamanism – and a centre where these Cosmic forces were in balance. This civil arrangement was thus a reflection of an earlier Odinic understanding.

There was also a third Odin – a mystic who was a rather formidable figure. He was described as tall and slim with long grey hair that hung down to his shoulders, and was portrayed as wearing a dark blue cloak with a hood or a soft wide-brimmed hat pulled down over one side of his face as if to cover a missing right eye. His left eye was a piercing blue-grey. In his right hand he carried a blackthorn staff from which dangled a collection of objects – bones, shells, stones, feathers and fur. At the top of the staff were carved Runic patterns. With him were two ravens and a wolf. This Odin was a master shaman who travelled far and wide and whose abilities and exploits were so remarkable and seemingly miraculous that he acquired a reputation for having the god-like powers of the celestial Odin.

Medieval tales associated the shaman Odin with trickery and deceit, but such stories were distortions of the concept of a 'trickster' fulfilling a divine mission – identified by Native American Plains Indians as 'Heyokah', whose sacred task was to teach people to laugh at their mistakes and minor misfortunes. The shaman Odin fulfilled a similar role. The sacred trickster did not use lies and deception; rather, he prompted people into wondering why they accepted what they said and did. In other words, he provoked them into thinking for themselves rather than accepting without challenge the crutch of wobbly beliefs proffered by others. He was also able to make them smile at their own stupidities, for by so doing they could reclaim their sacred space. By medieval times the sacred trickster had a counterpart in the role of the court jester, whose jokes and antics were often attempts to induce members of the audience not to take life too seriously but to enjoy the experience of living.

Each of these versions of Odin is essentially true, but in the telling has merged in with the others to form not a misrepresentation but a continuity of truth. There was a shaman to whom the Runes were revealed when he was in an altered state of awareness; there was a political figure who ruled with fairness and justice to maintain the right of the individual to live in peace and harmony; there was a Creative Source who fathered the Universe and all that is in it.

The Runes were experienced by Odin the travelling shaman as a revelation of the Creative Source – from Odin the celestial Originator to Odin the terrestrial communicator. This is implied in the line 'Myself an offering to myself', from the Viking Eddas, the poems and songs of the skalds who were the storytellers and conveyers of the ancient myths.

Whether regarded as a god, an influential chieftain, or a travelling shaman, Odin is associated with the Runes. Each Runic 'character' had its own unique identity and its pattern was referred to as a 'stave'. A stave may be defined as a pole or batten used to support and sustain a shape or structure. For instance, wood that was curved to form the sides of a wooden cask was called a stave. The word is very appropriate because Runic shamans who had been schooled in the 'language' of the Runes considered that they were dealing with potencies that actually supported and sustained the Universe!

The word 'stave' also describes the parallel lines on which a note is placed in musical notation to indicate its pitch and the quality of sound. Sound is a sensation produced in the ear by vibrations in the air and their dynamic power. Since everything in existence vibrates, everything produces its own sound. The sound, however, may be on a frequency beyond the range of human hearing, or even beyond the range of the most sophisticated scientific equipment. In olden times the Runes were sung – or, rather, *sounded* – as a way of activating their potencies.

The word *rune* is derived from an Old Norse word *run*, and from the Old German *runa*, meaning 'whisper' or 'secret'. In Old English the word meant 'mystery'. So a more complete definition of a Rune might be 'a whispered secret mystery'. Dictionaries define a whisper as 'a vocal sound conveyed without vibrating the vocal cords, in order to communicate quietly and confidentially'. It is interesting to note that beneath the dome of St Paul's Cathedral in London is a circular chamber called 'The Whispering Gallery'. The Cosmos might be regarded as a circular chamber, not unlike the Whispering Gallery, in which – because of its spherical, acoustical design – it is possible for a sound to be conveyed from one side to another, from the inside to the outside, and from the outside in, through soft *quietness*. The ebb and flow of the tide of a calm sea on a shore of shingles on a warm, sunny day might be likened to the whispering of Cosmic sound.

The Cosmos is the entirety of existence. It is larger than the Universe of science because as well as all that is manifest it contains Time and Space and that which is formless and unmanifest. The Unmanifest has no size or place. It is larger than immense, yet smaller than minuscule. Simultaneously it is both here and there, everywhere and nowhere. The Unmanifest is neither depleted nor extended by the act of Creation, because Creation is derived from the Unmanifest and both contains the

Unmanifest and is contained by it. The Cosmos is separated from Chaos, where random forces prevail, by the laws which govern its own existence as well as that of all life forms within it. These laws hold it in being, just as a perimeter determines the existence of a circle.

Anciently, Runic sounds were never vibrated and resonated. That concept was introduced by sorcerers who treated Runic names as magickal words to invoke powers which could be manipulated in order to obtain what was desired. Runic shamans, on the other hand, *whispered* the sounds.

A secret may be defined as a message that is concealed, revealed only to those who have been prepared to receive it. Not only was the secret of the Runes conveyed in whispers, but the knowledge was regarded as so sacred that it could be communicated only to those whose minds, hearts and spirits had been suitably prepared to receive this inner message.

A mystery can be something more than just a secret lore shared by certain people. It may be defined as that which transcends the intellect and can be known only through direct personal experience. This is at the heart of the life-enhancement process of self-development and personal guidance derived from the essence of universal shamanism which I have called *Shamanics*. Understanding comes primarily through the experience of doing.

Misunderstanding has been caused by presenting the angular patterns – the staves – as the Runes themselves. The Runes are a *process* by which the fundamental potencies are enabled to be conveyed. Let me repeat that:

The Runes are a *process* by which the fundamental potencies of Nature may be carried or conveyed.

This is why Runic shamans perceived the Runic images as *vessels* – carriers and transporters of the potencies. Knowledge of the Runes and the Runic patterns provided them with a means of access to invisible realities and to different levels of existence.

Let us understand what a potency is. A potency may be defined as a power or force that is capable of expression but is not yet in motion. In other words, it is a capability to perform what is inherent within it, but that ability requires to be released before it can function. This leads us to a further understanding about the true nature of a Rune-stave.

A Rune-stave is an energy-pattern that is inherent in Nature and within ourselves.

Each stave contains a potential *quality* or *vitality* which, once released, acts intelligently to effect changes in the material world. That is why the Runes were associated with deities – because they function in 'god'-like or 'miraculous' ways.

A Rune-stave might, therefore, be regarded as the *signature* of the potency it represents.

The true Runic sounds were known to only a few and this knowledge has all but died out now as a result of religious persecutions and political and social changes in the fabric of society. These sounds, or 'whisperings', were sonic combinations that operated at all levels of existence and could be reproduced by the human voice only through specialist training. Each Rune was thus regarded as a signature tune or call-sign of a process of natural forces – and also of a quality of the Soul, because these same universal processes function within us on a spiritual level.

Since Runes contain the potencies of natural processes and also indicate qualities of the Soul, they can be regarded as having an ecological aspect that applies both to the external world around us and the internal world within. They function beneficially for both mundane and spiritual purposes when approached respectfully and caringly. The sinister image associated with the Runes was attributed to them by medieval priests as a means of frightening people away from an alternative form of spirituality. By outlawing their use, people were cut off from an ancient wisdom that was inherent in their racial ancestry. In modern times a bizarre representation of the Runes has been perpetuated by the imaginings of writers of supernatural fiction and horror movies.

The reality is that the Runes were fashioned in Love and given as a gift to humanity and a blessing to humankind.

2 The Origin of the Runes

SOME HISTORIANS SAY THAT THE Runes had their birth among the Teutonic tribes of northern Europe as long ago as 500BC. Others are of the opinion that the Goths of Scandinavia adapted the Greek cursive script during their contact with the Hellenic culture around 200AD. Still others speculate that they originated in northern Italy much later and were derived from the Latin alphabet. And there is a view that they were invented during the Viking civilization of around 800AD. But although there are differences of scholastic opinion about when Runic writing began, there is general historic agreement that Runes were used by pagan tribes over a vast area of northern Europe. Many of these tribes were descendants of Teutonic peoples whose mythology and theology became encoded in later texts known as Eddas. These loosely related poems, songs, and texts were collected together in the *Codex Regius* (Royal Manuscript), so named because it was a treasured item in the Royal Library at Copenhagen until 1971, when it was returned to its native Iceland. This 13th-century manuscript was compiled more than 200 years after Iceland was converted to Christianity.

What is today known as the *Elder Edda* is a collection of poems and songs derived from Vikings who settled in Iceland around 800AD, compiled by a Christian priest called Saemund. The *Younger Edda* or *Prose Edda* was written much later by an Icelandic historian, Snorri Sturluson (1179–1241). Although these historical writings describe Runic characteristics, they do not reveal the power of the Runes or explain how to use them. Some present-day Runologists who approach these texts as if they are sacred scriptures do not seem to recognize that their authors were not compiling an authoritative work on the Runes. Sturluson was himself a poet and his principal purpose was to provide a handbook for budding poets, as Professor R L Page of Cambridge University, England, makes clear in his book *Norse Myths*. In analysing certain texts, Professor Page questions whether some are genuine accounts of Norse mythology or mockings of deities despised by Christians and thus intended to throw scorn. Certainly both compilations may well have been influenced by Christian attitudes of the time and therefore not entirely objective accounts of earlier pagan concepts. The Eddas were attempts to preserve in writing the spoken works of earlier poets, who had made great use of allegory in presenting facets of the perpetual struggle between the beneficent influences of Nature and the injurious forces of Chaos. What seems not to be generally recognized is that incidents described in these texts were concerned not so much with the *origins* as with the *rebirth* of the Runes, comparable perhaps with the modern Runic revival. Their 'revealing' was but a rediscovery and a reclaiming of what had been 'lost' for, according to oral traditions, the Runes go much further back than historical speculations appear to indicate.

The Viking civilization which thrived from the 6th to the 12th century made extensive use of Runes. The word *Viking* is derived from a Nordic word meaning 'adventurer' or 'explorer', for what characterized these Scandinavian people was their maritime achievements in exploring vast areas of waterways and uncharted seas in their elaborately built wooden sailing boats. Travelling shamans accompanied many of these vessels, so with them went knowledge of the Runes and myths and legends regarding their *origin*. Myths are attempts to explain in allegorical stories how life began and developed on this planet and how events that took place in past Ages had a subsequent effect on the human condition. They were conveyed to illiterate peoples by word of mouth and passed on orally from generation to generation.

Mythology is an unscientific way of explaining how the Universe came into being and the interrelationship between the fundamental powers of Nature and how they function. A myth expresses in poetic or narrative form underlying principles rather than literal truths, and thus appeals to the intuitive rather than the logical senses and stimulates feeling rather than the intellect. The difference between a myth and a legend is that a myth usually relates to a non-ordinary reality – an Otherworld – whereas a legend is concerned with human activity in ordinary reality. It is possible that myths were part of a racial memory of an earlier 'civilization' and presented in a form which the descendants of the survivors of a worldwide natural ecological catastrophe could relate to. Indeed sacred writings also contain references to a civilization of prehistory which was destroyed by an ecological disaster. Noah's flood in the Old Testament is an example.

Runes are presented in the myths of the Eddas as no invention of the human mind, but as something already in existence, awaiting only to be re-discovered and revealed. What is not clear from these mythological accounts is whether the Odin who recovered them was a celestial or an extraterrestrial being, or a shaman who was later deified as a result of his achievements. The relevance of the accounts, however, is not affected by whichever of these alternatives is believed.

The poem *Havamal* (meaning 'Song of the High One') in the *Elder Edda* describes how Odin, in an attempt to gain something of value for mankind, experienced a self-imposed ordeal by hanging upside down on a tree for nine days and nights without food or drink pierced by his own spear. During his suffering he lost an eye but found the Runes, which were revealed as a gift to humanity from the non-ordinary reality of shamanic experience. They provided a means of acquiring knowledge about the hidden forces of Nature and the processes which enable manifestation to take place. They enabled the development of perception to reach out beyond the range of the physical senses – a 'seeing' with the Spirit through the opening of 'inner' eyes, and a 'listening' to unheard sounds through the opening of 'inner' ears. Personal transformation was possible because the Runes themselves are great transforming powers.

The following poetic account of Odin's experience is taken from the *Poetic Edda* (1200AD), translated from the Old Norse.

> Down to the deepest depths I peered
> I know I hung on that windy tree,
> Swung there for nine long nights
> Wounded by my own blade
> Bloodied for Odin.
> Myself an offering to myself

Bound to the tree
That no man knows
Wither the roots of it ran.

None gave me bread.
None gave me drink.
Down to the deepest depths I peered
Until I spied the Runes.
With a roaring cry I seized them up
Then dizzy and fainting I fell.

Well-being I won
And wisdom, too.
From a word to a word
I was led to a word.
From a deed to another deed.

Why did Odin hang upside down on the tree? This question is largely ignored by writers of books on the Runes, yet Odin was clearly endeavouring to convey some important knowledge.

The account of Odin hanging on a tree has similarities with the Crucifixion story. Indeed, Christianity became acceptable to the Nordic people partly because Jesus's suffering on the cross reminded them of Odin's ordeal and that he too had been pierced by a spear. But one difference was that Odin was suspended upside down!

Hanging upside down on the tree may be regarded as the action of a martyr willing to sacrifice his own life in furtherance of the truth, and as sign of readiness to put aside the Ego in order to receive a greater wisdom. Facing downwards on the tree and looking towards the roots may be interpreted as symbolic of seeing into the depths of the Unconscious, where lies hidden the potential of everything that is manifested – or an expression of Death, or transition of awareness from the external activity of physical existence to that of rest and renewal as a preliminary to rebirth. Odin's sacrifice of the Ego-self for the greater good of the Higher Self may have provided the power to spark that sudden flash of inspiration – that insight, that inner seeing which enabled a vision of the Runes to be experienced. But there was more to it than that. Let us consider further.

Although there is an affinity between humans and trees, their characteristics and functions are reversed. For instance, the leaves of a tree take in carbon dioxide from the atmosphere and give out oxygen. The lungs of a human being, on the other hand, breathe in oxygen and exhale carbon dioxide. Trees have their roots in the earth and their reproductive system – their flowers and fruit – at the top of the trunk. The human reproductive system is at the base of the trunk and the 'stem' and 'roots' are in the head, for whilst nourishment of the physical body comes from the Earth, the source of life – which is in the Spirit – is from the Universe, and it is in the head that consciousness is nurtured and individual personal development is realized. Micho Kushi, in *The Book of Macrobiotics* writes: 'It is more accurate to say that we hang down from heaven than stand on earth.'

So Odin, through his shamanic experience, was demonstrating that our roots are the brain cells, and our structure and constitution, though physical, are essentially spiritual, but we are suspended between the two. Odin was thus conveying an understanding of the energic nature of human life and teaching us that the purpose of human life is to harmonize the forces of Heaven and Earth so that body, mind, Soul and Spirit function harmoniously and in unison. His experience was to indicate that whilst, in physical reality, growth is outward and expanding, in the non-ordinary reality of the Spirit, growth is inward towards its own seed and source, until the physical and the spiritual become integrated.

The tree on which Odin was suspended is called in Northern mythology 'the Tree of Yggdrasil' (pronounced 'Yag-drill') which symbolized the Tree of Life. The Old Norse word *Ygg* is said by some writers to be another name for Odin, but I understand that a better translation is the word 'I' – the identity of the essential Spirit within. The word *drasil* can be translated as 'steed', but its sense is that of a carrier or transporter. So 'the steed of I' is the vehicle that conveys the essential Spirit – the shaper and creator – through a journey of life and experience within a multidimensional Reality in order that it may be cultivated to transcend that which is human. The Tree of Yggdrasil is thus the Tree of I's Existence, in and out of Time.

Before I describe how the Runes were revealed to Odin and what it was he experienced as he looked down into the hidden depths of the Unconscious, I should explain that a Caucasian shaman in the Northern tradition was also known as a 'staff carrier' or 'staves carrier'. A staff might be likened to a walk-

Figure 1 A female Runic shaman, dressed formally, with a drum and her staff with its horse's head representation and bands of Runes

ing-stick, and sometimes the features of a horse's head were carved into its top or attached there. Indeed, a child's hobby-horse is an adaptation of the shaman's staff, which some believed was the means by which travel into other dimensions of existence – into realms beyond 'ordinary' physical and mental reality – became possible. It was the forerunner of the witch's broomstick. In times of persecution ordinary household items served as substitutes for shamanic tools. The broomstick stood in for the shaman's staff. It had, however, no magickal power in itself but was a symbolic representation of different levels, planes or conditions of existence, and boundaries in between – root, stem and branch.

For special occasions a female Runic shaman is said to have worn a dress with embroidered hems and a necklace of amber beads, plus bones or shells. She also wore a shawl which hung in nine tails – one for each of the nine levels or enclosures of reality. Her headdress contained the antlers of an elk or reindeer and she was shod with soft leather, fur-lined boots like moccasins. In addition to a drum and rattle she carried a staff topped with a representation of a horse's head and banded with Runes. The staff was not only a symbol of office but also a representation of the Tree of Existence – Yggdrasil. Other women Runic practitioners or seers wore similar outfits, some had cloaks made from animal skins with a hood lined with fur which could be pulled down over the eyes for ritual purposes.

Although there are two distinct ways of working with the Runes – either for one's own benefit and empowerment, even at the expense of others, or as a means of personal development, in harmony and balance with the forces of Nature and the Universe – the two became less defined as practitioners pursued their own individual paths. The distinction could only be discerned in the way Runic practitioners operated, and in the effect of their workings – for good or ill – in their own lives and in those of others whom they influenced. I have used the term 'Runic shaman' to distinguish those who worked with the Runes in their *natural* sequence – which I shall describe in detail later in this book – rather than in the so-called 'traditional' Futhark order adopted by the Runic magician.

Runic shamans regarded the Runes as 'a gift of the divine', not simply because of the way they were revealed to Odin but because, like any form of writing, they were a means of imparting knowledge and wisdom. The Runes were thus understood to be a divine revelation, given in love, and intended to bring benefits to humankind through an understanding of how Nature functioned and how the patterns that are within Nature are also within human beings.

Nine staves were often carried or obtained to remind the shaman of the Zero to Nine Cosmic Law of Creation by which matter came into manifestation out of invisible energy, and Form ultimately reverted back to energy. Out of the Zero – from the invisibility of the abyss of 'Nothingness', the 'Ginnungagap' of Northern mythology – came everything that exists. Out of the Great Mystery of this Nothingness came the singular Unity – the One which contained within itself the dynamic duality of polarities. The merging of the Two produced the Three, which set into motion action and reaction and a structure of infinite possibilities. Nine is the sum of three threes and indicated the primal Cosmic pattern of matter and the sequen-

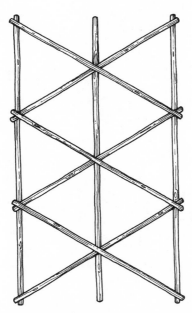

Figure 2 The nine staves, which had been cast on the ground, formed a pattern in which Odin observed 24 Runic shapes

tial process of Nature, the Universe, and of humankind – all combining to form a completeness. Nine staves or sticks represented to the shaman the Cosmos – the totality of existence – structured in nine 'worlds' or 'enclosures' of reality in which the 'alive-ness' of Life could be experienced.

In his willingness to 'sacrifice' his Ego in order that his Soul's purpose could shine forth and bring ultimate benefit to humanity, the shaman Odin would have taken his nine staves and cast them onto the ground as he hung upside down on the tree. During the later stages of his ordeal the cast-down staves appeared to form patterns within their vertical and diagonal lines. One, then two, three, four, five, six angular patterns appeared within the formation of the staves – and then more and more until they totalled 24. Twenty-four Runes were thus revealed to Odin.

These 24 shapes later became known as the Common or Elder Futhark because the phonetic characters F-U-Th-A-R-K comprise the first six staves featured in the earliest writings of oral Runic poems and songs about the Runes – the Eddas – and are thus the prototype from which all other Runic systems were

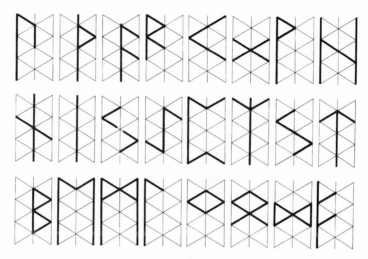

Figure 3 The 24 Runic shapes observed in the pattern of nine sticks

derived. However, it should be borne in mind that the sequential arrangement given in the Eddas may not necessarily have
been the order in which they were revealed to Odin. It has been
common practice, in order to keep information accessible to
only a select few and to 'hide' its true meaning from others, to
use allegory, symbolism or some method of displacement so
the message is obscured from those considered to be unpre-
pared, unwilling, or even unworthy, to receive the truth it contains. However, the number of Runic patterns – 24 – embraces
several relevant shamanic principles.

Twenty-four is in accordance with a Cosmic Law of Har-
monics – an arrangement in octaves or eights like musical
notes. These Runic octaves – a threefold division of eights –
coincide with motion on vertical and horizontal planes of
higher, middle and lower levels and outer, centre and inner
planes. They also relate to three principal conditions of existence: physical, mental and spiritual. Also, 24 can be arranged
into two groups of 12. Twelve is qualitatively the number of
organizational arrangement and stability at an organic level,
whilst Two represents the duality of active and receptive forces
complementing each other within the dynamics of the holistic
unity of the Cosmos.

Additionally the 24 Runes can be arranged in four cubes,
each of which contains three pairs of complementary opposites.

Four indicates equilibrium and harmonic balance, and Three the creation of patterns of change arising from the merging of the masculine and feminine polarities indicated in One and Two. This 24-character Rune series was used by all Teutonic peoples and north European tribes, according to Professor Sven B F Jansson, a leading Swedish Runologist. His book, *Runes in Sweden*, states that of the 3,500 inscriptions on stones and artifacts found within the present-day borders of Sweden, the vast majority are in this archaic 24-Rune arrangement. Professor Jansson and other historical researchers have concluded that in most cases the Runes were not used for the sinister purpose of magick and sorcery, although magickal intent may explain why some inscriptions are so obscure. The point I am advancing is that whilst Runes were employed by those who sought power over the invisible forces of Nature and over other people for purposes of self-will, they were never revealed for such purpose. In Sweden, the presence of so many Rune-stones and Rune-inscribed artifacts of everyday life is evidence that a benevolent purpose prevailed and that Runes were used in various ways: to enhance life, to seek protection against disease, and to bring people in harmony with Nature and with themselves.

As with all natural forces, Runic power can be used beneficially or adversely. Fire, for instance, can be used to provide the heat to warm a home and the energy to cook a meal, or it can be used destructively to consume or destroy whatever it is applied to. Nuclear energy can be used to power huge factories and to light great cities, but in a weapon of war it can be used to bring death to tens of thousands and lay waste everything in its path. The end result– healing or harmful – is determined by the intention of the one who activates the force and gives it direction. It is the same with Runes.

Manipulation of the Runes for purposes of self-interest or for sorcery to work harm on others was called 'woe' working. Beneficial use of the Runes for the welfare of oneself and others was called 'weal' working. But even 'weal' working could have an adverse effect on the operator if it deprived others or resulted in self-glorification. The consequences might not be immediate but were regarded as sure. The Runes, then, must be approached with discrimination and discernment and a great deal of respect.

The truth is that essentially the Runes are *not* magickal

symbols or a cryptic code. Each one is a container of a transcendental potency and process inherent in Nature and ourselves and is an indication of the qualities and characteristics of forces that affect what is coming into being, what is in manifestation, and what is going out of physical existence. Similarly, as qualities of the Soul, Runes are expressions of what is coming into our human experience, what is affecting our life now, and what is in the process of transition and transformation.

Since Rune-staves are made up of only two simple components – vertical and diagonal lines – they are simple to write, cut with a knife or sharp instrument, carve or burn on wood, inscribe on leather, or engrave on stone or metal. Runic shapes were inscribed on rings, bracelets, belts and personal belongings; on shields, swords, daggers and other weapons; on staffs and shamanic tools; and on amulets and talismans. Large stones inscribed with Runes, serving as memorials and landmarks, were especially popular in Scandinavia. Runic patterns were also worked into the arrangement of beams in half-timbered buildings, and this became a feature of German architecture. Runic writing was also incorporated in merchants' signs, in trademarks, in monograms, and was even concealed in heraldic coats-of-arms. In other words, Runes were very much a part of everyday life.

During the times of religious persecutions in the Middle Ages and later, the Runes were maligned along with the old pagan religions, and those who perpetuated them were accused of every kind of perversion. Attempts were made to destroy the Runes and the lives of those who seemingly had regard for them, for the knowledge the Runes revealed threatened the dogmatism of the 'new' religion which sought to convert all in its path. Rune-masters, Rune-writers, Runic magicians and Runic shamans were imprisoned, murdered and executed, or simply driven underground. Within a few generations knowledge of the Runes had apparently been vanquished.

Rune-work: Assignment 1 Connecting with the Tree of Existence

---

During his nine days and nights on the tree, Odin was demonstrating that before we can truly 'find' ourselves – discover who and what we truly are – and give more fully of ourselves to others, we need first to give of ourself to our Higher Self – the highest and most noble aspect of our composite being. This involves the giving of our 'little' self (our Ego or 'temporary' personality self) to our Greater Self (the permanent self of the Spirit). The Greater Self will then respond by giving of Itself for the benefit of the 'little' self.

Go outdoors to a place where you can be alone and undisturbed for a few minutes. Take a notebook and pen with you. Face the North – the direction of the North Star which is the pivotal point around which the Universe appears to revolve – and stand with your feet together. Raise your arms upwards at an angle of 45 degrees so your stance is in the shape of the Z-Rune, ALGIZ ᛉ.

Focus your attention on connecting with this Rune and for the Rune itself to connect you to the Tree of Existence, and by so doing heighten your awareness. Whilst retaining this stance recite the following words, which you will need to learn before you undertake this assignment.

> In connecting with the Tree of Existence
> I give *myself* to Myself
> And in taking up the Runes
> I am motivated by Love and Harmony
> So that I may be nourished with understanding
> And those whose lives I touch
> Shall receive blessings also.

Pause to reflect on the words you have spoken. Then wait for a response. The response may come by way of i) sensations, ii) mental images, or iii) feelings, or a combination of all three. After the response, lower your arms, relax, and take a few deep breaths and make a note of your experience.

Afterwards, consider carefully what you have experienced and seek an understanding that will come from within yourself. That understanding may not come at once. It may come later and unexpectedly, and this understanding should be recorded also. I want to encourage you to keep a written record of your personal experiences of Rune-work in a 'special' book. Treat yourself to a special notebook that you can use as your Journal of Self-Giving and in which you can freely describe your Runic experiences and your innermost thoughts without concern about how others might react. This book will be private to you – it will be part of your Sacred Space – and a means of helping you to recognize where you are, where you have come from, and to see more clearly where you are going, from a shamanic perception. Good stationers generally stock attractively bound notebooks with ruled pages and cliplocks on the side. Your notes and findings from this Assignment should then be transferred into your Journal; they will be the start of your Runic quest – a journey to discover your own self-identity.

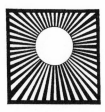

3 The Runic 'Revival'

THE ORIGINS OF 20TH CENTURY Runic revival are to be found in the occult organizations that existed in Germany around the turn of the century and which had an influence on the rise of Nazism. The revival stemmed from the creation of a system devised by Guido von List, a German occultist, who claimed that originally there were only 18 Runes. His 18-Rune system, which became known as the Armanic Futhark, was based upon a misunderstanding of part of the Eddic poem *Havamal*, in which Odin tells of 18 'galdrar'. Odin, however, was referring not to Runes but to shamanic power songs, which were sung for various purposes. Many present-day teachings of the 'traditional' 24 Runes are based upon von List's occult theories and methods.

The Runic revival has presented the Runes as essentially a system of magick – a means of manipulating Runic powers to bring about one's wants and desires, and also for predicting the future. They have thus become a tool of the Will to exert control, rather than as aid to the Spirit in furthering an understanding of the Universe and ourselves, enhancing our lives through coming into harmony with the natural forces, and advancing our own individual evolutionary development.

Guido von List was born in 1848 in Vienna, the son of a leather merchant, and from an early age showed a deep interest in German mythology, mysticism and folklore. This interest was further stimulated in the 1890s by the first flush of Theosophy – through the publication in German of Madame H P Blavatsky's *The Secret Doctrine* – and the subsequent occult revivalism which followed. He earned a living as a journalist

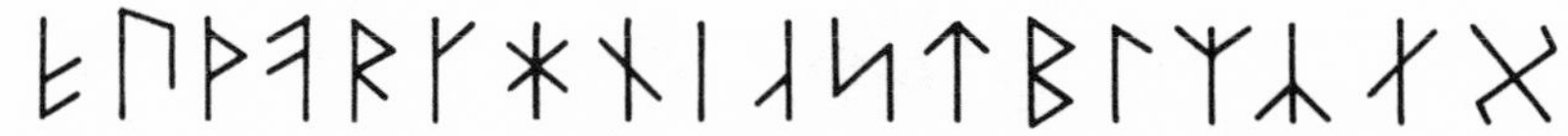

ᛒᚾᚹᚨᚱᚴᚷᚼᛁᛃᚴᚾᛏᛒᛚᛃᚼᚾᚷ

Figure 4 The Armanic 18-Rune alphabet which Guido von List claimed was revealed to him during a visionary experience

ᚠᚾᚦᚨᚱᚢᚷᚹ ᛋᛃᛃᛋᛁᛏᚺᛏᛒᛖᛗᚨᛚᛟᛞᛦ

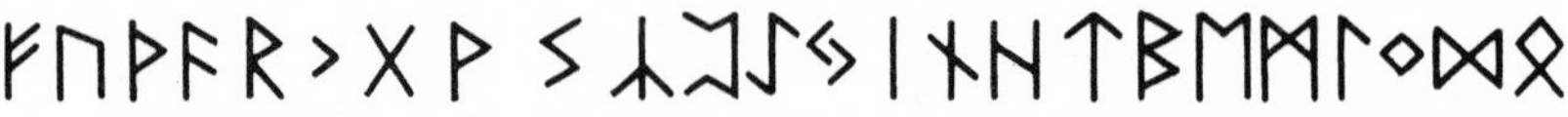

Figure 5 The Futhark Runes, so called because the related letters of the alphabet – F-U-Th-A-R-K – comprise the first six of the series of 24

and author, but in his later years devoted his full attention to Runic occultism. Von List suffered from an eye disease and in 1902 underwent surgery for the removal of cataracts, a risky operation in those days. For almost a year he was blind. During that time he had a visionary experience during which he claimed that the Runes had been revealed to him in their original form and as an 18-character system. He perceived this experience as a mystical initiation and the big turning point in his life. As a result of this experience he presented the Runes as a magickal system. In 1908 the first of his eight esoteric books was published – *Das Geheimnis der Runen* (The Secret of the Runes). Von List's system called the 'Armanic' Futhark because it was connected with the theories of Armanism, a mythological, cultural and racial ideology, later became the 'traditional' one in Germany.

Linking this 18-Rune system with the Eddas – especially the *Havamal* stanza, which is associated with Odin – provided it with almost 'scriptural' authority, and appeared to give confirmation of a deity. As I have already indicated, the Eddas were not the dictats of deity but the work of poets – who were the professional entertainers of an illiterate society – and travelling shamans.

Patricia Terry, Adjunct Professor of Comparative Literature at the University of California, San Diego, and translator of the *Poems of the Elder Edda*, makes it clear that this collection is an incomplete and partial sampling of an ancient poetic tradition, and that the *Codex Regius* is itself marred by gaps and discrepancies. Professor Terry indicates that the characters in these poetic writings are clearly legendary rather than historical.

Von List became a prolific writer on the occult, on Aryan symbols and customs, and on the magickal use of Runes. *Aryan* is derived from a Sanskrit word meaning 'noble' and refers to supposed racial ancestors of the European family of peoples. He founded a Guido von List Society in 1908 to support his occult research work and to extend his teachings. Between then and the outset of the 1914–18 War he wrote extensively about his Armanic Runes system.

His interest in German nationalism led him to form the Thule Society, which was both an esoteric Order and a right-wing political club. The Thule Society encouraged a sense of Teutonic superiority and of a pure and ideal racial ancestry. Adolf Hitler, Rudolf Hess, Hermann Goering and Heinrich Himmler were said to have been amongst its later members and influenced by von List's teachings. It needs to be recognized that Nazism developed out of a nationalist resistance to Communist 'internationalism', which was becoming prevalent in Germany and other parts of Europe in the wake of the 1914–18 War and the Russian Revolution in 1917. The 'internationalism' then being projected implied an obliteration of nationalities and of national traditions. National Socialism was a political attempt to defend national identity, which had been severely damaged as a result of military defeat and the economic chaos which followed the First World War, and to revive national pride. There is a warning message in this piece of history, for attempts to form a federal Europe would, if successfully accomplished, lead to a great corrosion of national identities – which many people might go to extreme lengths to defend.

Von List died in 1919, but when the Nazis came to power in 1933 and created a state religion out of nationalism and racial superiority – Germany over all – their basic dogma had its roots in occultism. The Nazis' use of Runic emblems was based upon von List's 18-Rune system and meditative aphorisms, but they also introduced a new symbolism emphasizing struggle, control and dominance, thus inflicting artificial meanings on the Runes. For instance, *Sol*, the S-Rune ⚡, was adopted as the insignia for the dreaded SS and for mastery, *Tyr*, the T-Rune ↑, for the Hitler Youth movement and courage, and *Hagal*, the H-Rune ᚺ, was applied to the 'salvation' of racial purity – all of which misapplied the Runic expressions. Similar ideas have been inflicted on the 24-Rune arrangement. It was from occult teachings, too, that the Nazis learned how to trigger a release of emotional energies as a means of controlling the masses.

Von List's esoteric writings and his teachings that Runes could be made use of for magickal purposes thus influenced others after his death. One such person was Friederich Marby (1882–1966), an occultist who was convinced that the Runes were a language of a prehistoric antediluvian civilization which sank beneath the waves of the Atlantic Ocean some 12,000 years ago. Indeed, the word *Thule* – meaning 'a far northern land' – when used in an occult context referred to the origins of a super race which had been destined to rule the world. Thule is a mythical island which is said to have existed somewhere between Scandinavia, Greenland and the Arctic Circle. It is purported to have been destroyed by a natural disaster, possibly when the extended polar ice-cap began to melt, with a subsequent rise in sea levels. The name *Thule* also means 'the place of turning back' because it was located near the edge of the world in the days when scholars and theologians conditioned people into believing that the Earth was flat and that mariners who went on long voyages of discovery in their sailing ships risked being cascaded down into the depths of an Abyss if their voyages took them too far! Ancient maps often carried a warning about these unknown waters, with the inscription 'here be Dragons' to indicate the approaches to 'the place of turning back'. After archaeological research on a remote island in the Hebrides, north of Scotland, some years ago, it was suggested that the earliest people to arrive in Britain after the Ice Age came from the North! From the legendary land of Thule? Thule was believed by some occultists to be the spiritual home of the Aryan race of noble, 'pure blooded' white-skinned people who were descended from the 'gods' and, therefore, the rightful rulers of mankind! This was the hidden influence that underlined the Nazi intent to establish a 'master race'.

Marby promoted an Anglo-Frissian 33-character system and a method of Runic gymnastics which was developed into a kind of yoga. He authored a number of books and founded a League of Runic Researchers. Although he at first sympathized with Nazi nationalistic and racial ideology, he was arrested in 1936 and committed to a concentration camp. Accusations made against him were apparently unclear, although it was

*Figure 6 The swastika (left) is the ancient symbol of the Wheel of Life, indi-
cating the motion of the Sun and the four cardinal and four non-cardinal
directions and the four seasons of the year. Its reversal into a Nazi emblem
(right) turned it into a symbol of death, destruction and chaos*

implied in post-war years that he had been interned to keep
him quiet about the involvement of certain Nazis in occult
work. Marby was freed from Dachau in April 1945. He continued his Runic work until his death in 1966.

Another occultist, Siegfried Kummer, founded a Runic school near
Dresden in 1927. He developed a system of Runic yoga, based
upon von List's 18-Rune Futhark, which is still prevalent today.

When the Nazis came to power in 1933, esoteric lodges,
occult organizations and schools of magick were banned, but
some occultists within the movement continued to have a
powerful influence. Rune magick was apparently an interest of
Himmler, whose chief advisor, Karl Weisthor, was familiar
with the magickal application of Runes and designed Runic
rings which were worn by some members of the SS.

The swastika was adopted as the official emblem of the
National Socialist movement in 1920 at the suggestion of Adolf
Hitler himself, who chose it as an emblem of the revival of
national life in Germany. It was later to become the most feared
symbol of the 20th century. Significantly, the emblem was a
mirror-image of an ancient symbol which was regarded as a
representation of Life and Light arising out of the Source
within its centre and whose 'arms' followed a clockwise direction emulating the apparent movement of the Sun around the
Earth and the division of the solar year into four seasons. It
indicated a spiralling upwards and the expansion outwards of
organic growth and development. Hitler reversed the symbol,
believing he was using two S-Runes ς, one superimposed
over the other, indicating the drawing power of the Source of
Light and Life. The Nazi emblem, however, was set anti-
clockwise, indicating a devolutionary movement and a break-
ing-down of organic processes.

When a positive potency is activated and its natural flow reversed through the application of external pressure, instability sets in and the flow becomes turbulent and chaotic and negative forces are unleashed.

The word 'swastika' is said to be rooted in two Sanskrit words, which together mean 'well-being'. Perhaps this is why the swastika appears widely on amulets and talismans, in pre-Christian mosaics, and on some ancient coins.

There are eight lines on the swastika, indicating a Figure of Eight, which itself is a symbol of infinity and the movement of Force into Form and matter reverting back to energy – of that which is invisible becoming manifest and reverting back to invisibility and of Life and Death, Yang and Yin, being complementary polarities of the one continuous movement which constitutes the Whole. As an ancient solar symbol, the swastika indicated not only the motion of the Sun, but the four divisions of the year into seasons, and the four cardinal directions. So it was that it became a symbol of the Wheel of Life. When reversed by the Nazis, it turned into the opposite – a symbol of death, destruction and chaos. This may not have been what the early Nazis intended, but when the pattern was manipulated into their party's emblem, this is what they set in motion.

Since the 1939–45 War the presentation of the Runes has been based largely on the principles and techniques of Rune magick introduced by von List, Marby and others, although racist features have been excluded.

The Odinic Rite, an organization established in 1980, is respectful of the Runes from a religious perspective and regards them as a feature of the 'old' religion. It, too, uses the 24-Rune Futhark arrangement and leans heavily on interpretations of the Eddas as its authority.

There is at least one instant in the Eddas to indicate that one can be misled by the Futhark. In *Egil Skallagrimsson's Saga* there is an episode in which Egil, a Runic shaman, arrives at a farm where the daughter of the family is lying gravely ill and nobody has been able to cure her. Egil discovers a sliver of whalebone under her bed. On it is a Runic inscription. It had been written by a young man as an attempt at love magick. The young man had apparently used the Futhark to try and win the girl's heart, but had instead created a heart condition. Egil scraped away the Rune-staves that had been written on the sliver of bone and wrote new ones. The girl recovered from her illness.

The Futhark arrangement, which is generally regarded as 'traditional', is essentially an arrangement to hide the natural order and to provide a magickal code. The time has now come

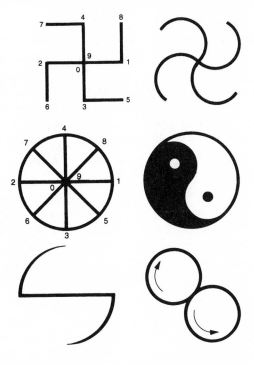

Figure 7 The ancient swastika symbol (top left) served as a teaching 'wheel' for the Zero to Nine Law of Creation. Indicated within it is the circular, cyclical, spirallic, and infinity movement of the Life-force of the Universe (represented by the top right symbol) which can be compared with the Medicine Wheel of Native Americans and the eight-spoked Circle of Power of other traditions (centre left). The Chinese Taoist symbol of the Supreme Ultimate (centre right) contains the complementary polarities of the Yin and Yang and the process of change that is inherent in all physical manifestation. The Wakan-Tanka symbol of the Plains Indians of North America (bottom left) was a representation of energy manifesting as form and form reverting back to energy, as indicated also in the infinity movement of the Figure of Eight symbol (bottom right). All these ancient symbols, apparently derived from different parts of the world, are thus shown to be closely connected and to indicate not only a unity of teachings but also a common origin

for the Runes to be revealed in their natural and organic sequence so that once again they may be used with love and concern and for the benefit of humankind.

Rune-work: Assignment 2 Where You Have Come From?

Having acquired a writing book in which to record your Rune-work, you can now make a start on your Journal of Self-Giving. As I explained in Chapter 2, this Journal is more than a personal diary. It is a piece of your Sacred Space that is private and special to *you*. It is a safe place where you can reveal your innermost thoughts without fear of how others might react.

Your first entry is to describe your experience of coming into connection with the Tree of Existence, as outlined in the first Assignment. This should now be followed with brief summaries of the Paths you have explored – and possibly abandoned – in your searching and seeking: each philosophy, religion, sect, cult or concept. Take each in turn, if there is more than one, and preferably in the sequence in which they were experienced. What led you into it? What was its principal appeal? What were the doubts you had? What did you gain most from the experience? What did you suffer most? What principal lessons was each path endeavouring to teach you about yourself?

Don't attempt to complete the task all at once. It is best done thoroughly, a piece at a time, over several days.

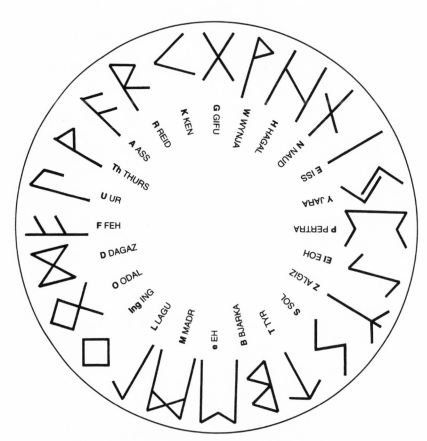

Figure 8 The Runes in their circular and cyclical order

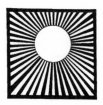

4 The Natural Order

THE ALPHABETICAL ARRANGEMENT OF the Runes in Futhark order was primarily to *disguise* their original sequence. According to an oral tradition in present-day Sweden, the original order began with UR, the U-Rune ⊓, and was completed by FEH, the F-Rune ⊧, at the end of the sequence. Actually 'began' and 'ended' are misnomers because the Runes were originally a circular or spiral arrangement rather than a linear one. So the 'last' came directionally next to the 'first'. Each Rune had a sequential value. FEH ⊧ might be likened to the Ace in a pack of playing cards, which may be given the highest or lowest numerical value according to the nature of the game being played. The Uthark arrangement may be compared to a card game in which the Ace is low, so UR counts as one and FEH as 24. Many who have studied the Runes under the Futhark system may have puzzled, as I did, over why the first Rune should be associated with the culmination of wealth and possessions, whilst the second Rune in the sequence should be associated with primal essence or potential. Misplacement of the sequence makes this apparent. In the *natural* order, UR ⊓ is the primal potency from which all follows, and FEH ⊧ is the Rune of fulfilment, as I shall shortly demonstrate.

There was also magickal significance in presenting the Runes as a Futhark, dividing them into three sets of Eights, and introducing a binary code to indicate in which Eight a Rune appeared and its placement in that set (see *figure 9*). In other words, it was an arrangement which put the Mind in control in order to exert the power of the Will and bring about required changes that would satisfy the Ego.

Stave	Nordic name	Alphabetical letter	Phonetic sound	Sequential number
ᚢ	UR	U as in *urn*	'er'	1
ᚦ	THURS	TH as in *the*	'thers'	2
ᚨ	ASS	A as in *ace*	'ace'	3
ᚱ	REID	R as in *ride*	'ride'	4
ᚲ	KEN	K as in *kettle*	'ken'	5
ᚷ	GIFU	G as in *gift*	'geefoo'	6
ᚹ	WYNJA	W as in *win*	'win-yah'	7
ᚺ	HAGAL	H as in *hail*	'har-gool'	8
ᚾ	NAUD	N as in *nut*	'need'	9
ᛁ	ISS	E as in *seed*	'ees'	10
ᛃ	JARA	Y as in *yes*	'yah-rah'	11
ᛈ	PERTRA	P as in *pair*	'pert-rah'	12
ᛇ	EOH	EI as in *height*	'yo'	13
ᛉ	ALGIZ	Z as in *Oz*	'all-giz'	14
ᛋ	SOL	S as in *sun*	'sole'	15
ᛏ	TYR	T as in *time*	'tire'	16
ᛒ	BJARKA	B as in *birth*	'be-yarkah'	17
ᛖ	EH	E as in *end*	'e' as in end	18
ᛗ	MADR	M as in *man*	'marder'	19
ᛚ	LAGU	L as in *lake*	'largoo'	20
◇	ING	ING as in *sing*	'ing'	21
ᛜ	ODAL	O as in *Odin*	'owed-all'	22
ᛞ	DAGAZ	D as in *day*	'dargaz'	23
ᚠ	FEH	F as in *fee*	'fe' as in fetch	24

Figure 9 The Uthark arrangement: the 24 Rune-staves with their Nordic name, alphabetical letter, phonetic sound, and place in the natural sequence

It is the Uthark order that is the natural and original system and the one that reveals the actual process of the creation of the Universe and all the different qualities inherent in it, for its emphasis is on the activities of the Spirit.

The Runes, then, reveal the very process of creation and the qualities inherent in Nature and within ourselves.

This is why Runic shamans always approached the Uthark arrangement with respect and loving concern, and explains why the motive of the Runic shaman was Love and Harmony. The Runic shaman co-operated with the powers of the Runes; the overall intention was to bring harmony, balance and orderliness into a situation and to do no intentional harm, regardless of whether the Runes were consulted for him- or herself or on behalf of another. The core purpose of what we might call 'personal development' was perceived as the cultivation of the Spirit – the innermost Self – and the well-being of the total individual.

So let us have a brief look at the Uthark arrangement and how it describes the old Nordic worldview before we examine each of the 24 Runes in some detail.

At the 'beginning' is the U-Rune, UR ᚢ, because in the beginning of all things was a great primeval Void which the Norse peoples called Ginnungagap ('gin-oon-guh-gap') and which was the 'space' between two polar opposites or extremes – Fire and Ice, Yang and Yin. UR represents the Void – the primal creative essence. Its stave is shaped like a cow's horns pointing downwards as it grazes, for the Rune is also a symbol of the sacred cow of mythology, Audhumbla ('ow-dhumb-luh') – the name means 'nourisher' – the powerful, primeval shaping force created from the first mingling of Cosmic Fire and Ice, Yang and Yin. It was in the 'womb' of Ginnungagap that, in mythology, an androgynous giant called Ymir ('Uem-r') was born. In the myths, Ymir is nourished by Audhumbla's milk. This act represents the alchemical process of evaporation, condensation and purification which is the work of the power of UR.

The Th-rune, THURS ᚦ, is the primitive force which shaped and fashioned Ymir. The name THURS actually means 'giant' or 'strong one'. In the myths Ymir is the father and mother of the 'gods' – the intelligences that control and direct the Cosmic and natural forces that arise in an organic process of gradual development.

The A-Rune, ASS ᚠ, is the power of creativity. In the Northern myths the three gods Odin, Vili and Ve, overcome Ymir and from his body create the physical Universe as we know it. The word ASS means 'god' and in Anglo-Saxon it also meant 'mouth'. So this Rune is the power breathed into the 'Word' or sound that brought the physical Creation into existence. It is the power to make the unmanifest manifest.

The R-Rune, REID ᚱ, is the power of movement and orderliness that brought in the Four Directions and the Four Elements – which is why it is the *fourth* Rune. In legends it was regarded as the Rune of Thor, the god of thunder and lightning, because Thor represents the Cosmic intelligence that actually prevents the Cosmic order from reverting back to Chaos. It is thus the protector of orderliness and the 'maker' of laws. The R-Rune is the illuminating power that is in lightning and brings that sudden 'flash' of illumination. It is also the power of direction and movement that concluded the first phase of Creation.

From lightning comes fire, and the K-rune, KEN ᚲ, is the spiritual creative fire that is clear and bright like the flame of a torch, with which it is sometimes associated. This Rune is the illumination of the Spirit which lights the way. It is the power of a light that comes from an 'inner' fire and makes achievement possible.

Sixth is the G-rune, GIFU ᚷ, which marks the Six Directions and the centre of the Universe. It is the power of harmony and balance. The stave shape is the embodiment of an equal exchange of energies held in perfect balance. It is the divine gift of Life – the giving and receiving of the Life-force.

The W-rune, WYNJA ᚹ, is the power in the joy which arises out of an exchange of energies. It is the joy of satisfaction and fulfilment that follows orgasm – which is one reason why it is also the seventh Rune, for seven is the mark of perfection.

The H-rune, HAGAL ᚻ, represents the rainbow – the 'bridge' between the worlds. Now we are getting closer to our material world as this Rune is the completion of the first octave and there is a transcendence to the next. It is the Rune of the primal crystal, which produces all the colours of the spectrum and bears the message of materialization, like the DNA code within a single cell. The stave may also be shaped like the snowflake symbol ✳ indicating the Eight Directions: front, behind, left, right, above, below, centre, and within. So it is rightly the eighth Rune.

With the N-rune, NAUD ᚾ, the intelligences that weave the Web of the Universe and spin the thread of everyone's life, enter in. These influences were represented in myths as three goddesses called Norns: Urd (that-which-is), Verdandi (that-which-is-becoming) and Skuld (that-which-should-be). The Norns have been commonly identified as Past, Present and Future. But it needs to be recognized that Time, in the sense of a division into past, present and future, is historically a concept of Western culture under Greek and Roman influences. Anciently, shamans had a quite different concept of Time; they saw it as an *interwoven unity*, an ever-changing Now flowing from that which has been to that which is coming into being. This understanding believes that all that has happened is still *active* and thus influencing the present in which the future is being shaped. The stave shape of the N-rune is similar to two sticks being rubbed together to kindle a fire and is indicative of the power of friction and the need for resistance, which is inherent in this Rune.

The tenth Rune – the E-rune ISS | – is the force that slows vibrational energy to a denser state and causes the 'solidity' of inertia. It possesses the qualities of clarity and solidity, which is why it is likened to ice.

These first ten Runes indicate primal Creation and the forces that make up the *inner* spiritual structure of the Universe. The next ten Runes relate to the physical and the manifest.

It is with the Y-Rune, JARA ᛃ, that we first enter the world of 'ordinary' reality. The word *jara* means 'year', for the Rune is cyclic power and the power of giving birth and keeping alive. The stave shape represents the seasons as two half-years, summer and winter, which interact with one another continuously. Summer's harvest is winter's food, and the seeds that are hidden in the Earth at the beginning of winter sprout as summer comes near. The Y-rune is thus the power of bringing into being tangible results.

The three Runes that follow are concerned with the Mineral, Plant, and Animal Kingdoms.

The P-Rune, PERTRA ᛈ, is the transformational power within Earth minerals – such as iron, which can be transformed and absorbed into thousands of things yet still remains iron. It is the *holding power* which retains the solidity and stability of things.

The EI-rune, EOH ∫, is the power of growth that supports wild plants. It is the inherent power in spinal fluid that gives strength to the backbone. It has the quality of patient and sustained endurance.

The Z-rune, ALGIZ Ⴥ, is the instinctive, protective power that is prevalent in wild animals. It is that which provides the determination to survive.

Next comes the S-Rune, SOL ⟨, which means 'Sun-power'. It is the power of the spiralling *Life*-force and the vibrational *Light*-force – the energizing power behind the 'light' of consciousness in the process of individuation.

Then enter human beings.

The T-Rune, TYR ↑, is masculine power as expressed in courage, determined action, forcefulness and might. The stave is shaped like a spear – symbolic of determination and the will to succeed.

The B-Rune, BJARKA ß, is feminine power, which is nurturing, nourishing and protective. It is the mothering Earth-force which is the power to care and support unconditionally. The stave is shaped like female breasts – symbolic of love, beauty and nourishment.

The EH-rune, EH ᛗ, can be regarded as the communication or joining together of the masculine and feminine. It is the power that is inherent in ecstasy. It is also the energy experienced in a shamanic 'journey' – an altered state of awareness which enables other realms of reality to be explored. This is why this rune is sometimes associated with the horse, because in Northern mythology it was Odin's steed, Sleipner, that conveyed him to other realms. Inherent in this Rune is the power of cohesion.

With the M-rune, MADR ᛘ, this cohesive power moves more deeply. It is the adhesive quality of co-operative sharing that brings about integration and harmony. This same power is what brings together right- and left-brain activity to be mutually supportive so that both the intellectual ability of reason and the insight of intuition are enabled to develop together in unison and harmony.

The L-rune, LAGU ᚾ, is the power of fluidity. It is the fluid power that moves the lunar tides and energy streams of all kinds. It is the fluidity inherent in water which is clear and life-giving. The L-rune marks the end of another cycle in the Runic sequence.

The Ing-rune, ING ◇, is considered to be a fertility Rune, but it is an impulse that has moved from physical existence to the Cosmic. It is a conceptive force – the power to conceive something 'new' from what has gone before.

The O-rune, ODAL ✕, is the power that has made us what we are as individuals. It is a power that is passed on through ancestry and that we have brought with us from previous lives. It is sometimes associated with inheritance and with the security that is found in the home and in tradition.

The stave for the D-rune, DAGAZ ⋈, looks like a butterfly and symbolizes the power to reach beyond what we are now – like a butterfly which crawls out of its cocoon and is then transformed so that it can experience a greater existence. This Rune contains the transformational power of enlightenment that brings into being a new dawn of spiritual realization.

With the F-rune, FEH ⊦, we reach the fulfilment of Creation. It is the power to fulfil what we have come into existence to accomplish in this lifetime. It is a conclusion, but when we reach it we find that it is not an ending but a new beginning, because the F-rune stands in close proximity to the U-rune ⋂, and both have the cow as their symbol.

In the next chapter we shall continue our learning process by considering each Rune in turn – recognizing its stave shape, comparing it with a letter of the common alphabet and its phonetic sound, examining the nature of its potencies, and its characteristics and behaviour.

Rune-work: Assignment 3 Self-evaluation

A principal purpose in coming into an understanding of the Runes is to further our own individual personal development and cultivation of the Spirit. As a preliminary to working with the Runes we need first to work on *ourselves*. And it is essential also that we work on ourselves *before* we can become qualified to counsel others. There is great shamanic truth in the admonition that we should take the beam out of our own eye before we can be ready to help to remove a splinter from someone else's! So here is further work to do for recording in your Journal of Self-Giving.

First, make a list of all the things you *like* about yourself. The positive qualities you have. The things you are good at. The tasks that give you pleasure and a sense of achievement. List them all under the heading 'My Bright List'.

Next, list the things you *dislike* about yourself. Your faults, weaknesses and bad habits. The chores that cause you displeasure. The things you have to do but cannot do well. The qualities you lack but would like to have. List all of them under the heading 'My Murk List'. Be frank. Hide nothing from yourself.

Assignment 2 was a consideration of where you had come from and what had led you to where you are now in the 'school' of Life. So the third task is to assess your Present. Make a Bright List of all your assets – mental as well as physical – and the conditions that are supportive of what you consider to be your best interests. Then compile a Murk List of your liabilities and what is holding you back from being the sort of person you would like to be and the circumstances of life you would like to enjoy.

Next, consider the Future. Compile a Bright List of your hopes and aspirations. The kind of person you would like to become. Your ambitions and the things you would like to have in your life. Then compile a Murk List of what you would prefer to *avoid* but is likely to happen unless you make changes in your life.

Finally, when all four sets of lists are completed to your satisfaction, spend a little time considering them in their entirety, recognizing how your life is made up of things that are advantageous to the direction you would like your life to take and those that are disadvantageous and impediments to your progress. From this final consideration, ascertain those areas in which your life needs to be changed in order for you to come into harmony with the 'Bright' Future you would like to have.

This Assignment should not be hurried. Do not attempt to complete it in a single session. It is best compiled over a period of days. Do not minimize its importance. When it is completed you will have a valuable Self-evaluation which is private and entirely personal to you and which will be of help in reshaping your life.

5 The First Phase of Creation

ALTHOUGH, AS WE HAVE SEEN, the Runes as a whole are an organic process, each has individual qualities and characteristics which we need to understand in order to work with them effectively. We shall examine each Rune in accordance with its place in the Uthark sequence, its Nordic name and phonetic sound, the nature of its potency and principal qualities, and how the Rune might help us in practical ways. How each individual Rune might 'challenge' us is also given as a further opportunity for personal growth. My commentary on each Rune is in accordance with the understandings of Runic shamans and teachings I have obtained shamanically on inner planes. A shamanic perception of the Runes is one of direct personal experience.

The sequence of the Runes in their natural order differs from the so-called 'traditional' arrangement not only by the movement of FEH ᚠ to the culmination, but also that of some other Runes. PERTRA ᛈ and EOH ᛇ change places. So do ODAL ᛟ and DAGAZ ᛞ. The reasons are explained in the process of their unfoldment.

The first four Runes – UR ᚢ, THURS ᚦ, ASS ᚨ and KEN ᚲ – are the potencies which are activated in the first phase of the creative process and work at the deepest levels of the Unconscious to generate the creative forces which bring things into manifestation in our lives.

1 UR, the U-Rune – The Beginning of Everything

UR, the U-Rune ('er'), is the potency that exists within the Void or Abyss – the 'Space' between two polarities. In Nordic mythology it is the 'space' between Cosmic Ice and Cosmic Fire. This 'space' is not 'nothing' as we might assume it to be. It is filled with numinous power, called in Old Norse *ginnung*. The *ginn* part of the word is similar to the 'be' in becoming – meaning that which is in being *before* formation and manifestation take place. So the Nordic word *Ginnungagap* means 'a vital unordered essence waiting to come into being as either force or form'. The UR is the power of that essence. It is *in* the 'space'. UR *is* the 'space' between two opposites in which a magnetic power of attraction arises as the two polarities are attracted to one another and a great force is released as they come together and merge 'in the middle'.

Before anything can come into being it has to be charged with the power to *be*. It needs to be energized. UR is both the space – the Unmanifest – in which to forge or fashion something out of 'nothing', and the initiating power that makes visibility or manifestation possible. It might be likened to a charge of electrical energy that 'jumps' between the filaments of an electric light bulb when it is switched on. The electrical charge moves rapidly to and fro to provide new light and to keep it in being.

The Light that came out of the darkness of the Unmanifest 'in the Beginning' was not bright like light from the Sun to sharply define what could be observed. It was more like the silvery softness of moonlight, which has a gentleness that hides its tremendous power. Behind the pale light of the Moon, for instance, lies a power so tremendous that it moves mighty oceans – great masses and weights of water – and is so transforming that it regulates the cyclic flow of life within all Earth forms.

Many writers on the Runes have suggested that UR is a symbol of a ferocious but now extinct bison-like ox called an Auroch, which stood over 2 metres (7 feet) high to the shoulder – a north European equivalent of the buffalo – and was prevalent until around the 17th century. This idea is a misunderstanding of the oral tradition. The Runic character is shaped like the horns of an animal with its head to the ground, but it is not symbolic of a bull but a cow – Audhumbla, the holy cow of Northern mythology who was the Cosmic Mother of Manifestation. Indeed, the name *Audhumbla* means 'nourisher' or 'source of sustenance'. The quality behind the Runic pattern is not the potential power of a charging bull but that of a feeding cow! Its power is like the action of a pump drawing up water from deep subterranean wells.

The comparison with the Auroch gave another meaning. To the American Indian the buffalo was a totem of the Great Provider – 'That Out Of Which Everything Comes'. The buffalo provided meat for food, sinews for thread, bones for implements, and skin for clothing and shelter. A buffalo skull in the centre of a Native American Medicine Wheel was a reminder of the Great Spirit in manifestation. The Auroch had a similar meaning to the ancient Northern peoples.

UR, then, is a potency which is at the beginning of everything. It contains within it the potential for anything that can become manifest. An artist begins with a virgin canvas or a clean sheet of paper. It has nothing on it or in it. It is simply 'space'. Yet it is from this 'emptiness' of space that the artist will bring forth ideas into manifestation where they can be seen. From 'nothing' he thus creates a work of art.

In lateral thinking, 'space' might be defined as 'the distance between two points' or 'the distance between two polarities'. But the 'space' was already there before the two polarities provided the means for the space to be comprehended! UR, then, is the potency that enables something to come seemingly out of 'nothing' once it is released by *movement*.

Although UR is often associated with strength and endurance, it is not the force of might. It is the gentle but powerful power that causes rain to fall or draws up moisture from the ground so that it can descend again to nourish the Earth and allow new forms to appear. UR is what enables form to appear, but it is not a form itself. It is the vital virility evident in Nature just before new growth appears in bud and foliage.

The diagonal stroke of the UR stave might be likened to the Hidden Self – the silent, subconscious intelligence within a human being which links the conscious Ego-self (represented by the vertical line) with the Higher Self of the Soul, which is 'the Watcher Within' (represented by the descending line). A fourth 'spirit' – what I have called the Body Self – is the intelligence of the physical body, which serves as a vehicle or 'temple' of the other three 'selves' and is rooted in the shallow soil of mortality. This can be represented by a stemline on which the Rune-stave rests. UR thus indicates by its stave shape that everything experienced can be perceived in three ways – physically, mentally, and spiritually – through the vehicle of the physical body, and only then can it be comprehended in its totality.

POTENCY: The 'space' out of which everything comes into being

KEY QUALITIES: Limitless potential, infinite possibilities, sustained strength, renewal, release of energy, untamed power, sudden change

PRACTICAL USES: UR is the release of creative power that brings about sudden change. It is the power that precedes a new cycle of activity. It is helpful, therefore, where there is scope for new ideas, a fresh start, a change of circumstances, or an immediate boost in morale.

CHALLENGE: Have the courage to let go of things you no longer need. Then you will allow new possibilities to arise.

The U-Rune can help you to:

- ground your ideas so they may become practical realities
- revitalize yourself and find the determination to start new projects
- find the inner strength to put the past behind you and start afresh
- shape circumstances to form more fulfilling situations

- become more productive
- increase your resolve and have the courage to assert yourself

2 THURS, the Th-Rune – Clearing the Way

THURS ('thers') was the power that cleared away the random forces of Chaos so that the Cosmos could appear. It might be likened to a clap of thunder for it is that which results from a clash of polarized opposites. THURS was the destroyer of the forces of Chaos hostile to Cosmic order, and is the power that protects the Cosmos from reverting to Chaos. So although its power can be destructive – cutting away what has existed or is still there so that something better may take its place – it has a protective mode, and as such is a defender of Law and Order. As thunder heralds the rain, so the power of THURS makes possible new beginnings.

THURS has the potential to clear a way to make order where disorder existed. It is like clearing a neglected garden of weeds and undergrowth so that valuable shrubs are not damaged and a place of great beauty may appear. It might be likened also to having a clear-out or a spring-clean but taking care not to dispose of what is of value. Its stave shape is a reminder of an axe that is used to cut down what is unwanted, and can be used also as a defence against harmful influences. Indeed, the axe is THURS' emblem.

'Thurs' is a Nordic word that means 'giant' or 'mighty one', indicating the brute force and aimed strength that is needed to break down barriers. Because THURS has been traditionally associated with the frost giants of Northern mythology, some

writers have attributed evil undertones to it, but this is a misunderstanding, both of the truth behind the myths and the
Runic power itself. Part of this misunderstanding arises from
the translation of the Icelandic word for 'giant' into 'demon' – a
deliberate attempt by religious propagandists to eliminate previously understood knowledge and to assign moralistic intent
and a barrier of fear. The giants of mythology represented the
random forces of Chaos, of raw uncontrolled energy before the
Cosmos appeared. THURS was a cosmic power that kept them
at bay and protected and defended the Cosmic order. The
destructive power inherent in the Rune is thus towards that
which is hostile to orderliness and threatening to mundane
existence and what is presently in manifestation.

Another explanation for the implications of evil assigned by
the translators of Runic poems is that the stave Þ is shaped
like a thorn and thus has phallic connotations. The sex act
itself, until modern times, was considered evil by much of the
Christian priesthood, except for the purpose of procreation.

THURS is a carrier of the potency of a masculine creative
energy, just as the penis is a channel for the life-giving seed. It
is shaped like a thorn, which anciently was a symbol of man's
'mortality', whilst the rose, which the thorn 'protects', was a
symbol of the 'immortality' that is implied in the feminine principle, for everything comes into physical manifestation through
the female aspect. The fairy tale 'Sleeping Beauty' is rich in
such allegorical symbolism of ancient truths, with the hero
having to force his way through a barrier of thorns to reach the
heroine who had slept for a hundred years after pricking her
finger on a spindle. The thorn as a phallic symbol indicates the
rushing power that wields the seed of life. It is not the life-
giving force itself, but its conveyor that breaks down opposi-
tion and releases projected energy to enable new beginnings to
be made. THURS might, then, be regarded as an 'awakening'
power, bringing into conscious awareness that which existed in
the regions of the unconscious, although its prime purpose is in
making order out of chaos.

The thorn shape of the stave also suggests the testing nature
of the Runic potency to overcome fear, for in picking a rose one
needs to override the fear of being pricked by the thorn and, as
a consequence, suffering an unpleasant sensation. Indeed, the
potential power of THURS might be likened to a rose hedge

that not only marks a boundary between two properties – between ordinary and non-ordinary reality – but guards the access or 'gateway', which needs to be approached with care and knowledge. The Rune may thus be used as a defence against unwanted or harmful influences. Surrounding property with a ring of Th-Runes pointing outwards was a means of warding off undesirable intrusions.

What we need to understand is that Runic powers all operate beneath the surface of physical appearances – at subconscious, unconscious and superconscious levels. They are part of the 'forgotten' language of our 'inner selves' – the subconscious self, the unconscious Body Self, and the superconscious Higher Self. We are now trying to relearn that language, to bring it into conscious use so that our four 'selves' – the four 'spirits' or intelligences which are aspects of our total multidimensional being – may function as co-workers in a partnership that will help us to fulfil our Soul's purpose and advance us along our evolutionary path. These four 'selves' and their separate function as part of our totality are described in detail in my books *Where Eagles Fly*, *The Medicine Way*, and *Shamanic Experience*.

POTENCY: The clap of power that heralds new beginnings, protection that comes from taking the initiative
KEY QUALITIES: Awakening power, initiative, sharpness, aimed might, protective force
PRACTICAL USES: Helpful when it is necessary to break down barriers or clear a way through a confusing situation; incorporates the power of both attack and defence.
CHALLENGE: Cut away what hinders you, but take care to retain what is of permanent value. Don't make hasty decisions or you may create more problems than you solve.

The Th-Rune can help you to:

- fight against detrimental influences
- clear away lethargy and arouse enthusiasm
- stimulate the subconscious self into action
- break down barriers
- prepare the ground for new initiatives

ᚠ

3 ASS, the A-Rune – The Creative 'Mouth-piece'

ASS (pronounced 'ace') means 'god' or 'mouth-piece' – the one who speaks and brings into existence. It was the divine Word that brought everything into existence out of the nothingness of the Void. ASS is thus the power of opening and of releasing so the Breath of Life may come forth and the creative Spirit be expressed. ASS, therefore, embodies the power of thought and inspiration and functions at the deepest levels of the Mind from the 'inside' out, for it is that which 'opens' the subconscious to enable the innermost Spirit to find tangible expression. The hat worn by Runic shamans was worn inside out as a representation of the principle behind the A-Rune. The power of this Rune releases blockages of energy to allow the passage of movement that can bring about required changes. So it opens up channels of self-expression and allows the creativity of the Spirit to come forth.

ASS is an expression of the ability of the Great Spirit to be both inside and outside Creation and to disguise itself in manifestations of the changing faces of material reality – the 'thoughts' of the Great Spirit expressed in tangible form and given awareness by the same Breath of Life.

ASS is *expressed* energy – an ability to *communicate*. It is a power that is also carried along by the Element of Air, as with the breath, and finds expression in sound, music and speech as well as in form. It is Air that enables us to hear the voices of Nature. Listen to the wind and you will hear the sound of ASS. ASS is the thoughtful expression of intelligent consciousness, and the entire Universe is an expression of the Consciousness of the Great Spirit.

ASS was regarded by Runic shamans as the Rune of Sacred Knowledge. It acted as a link with ancestral wisdom, enabling knowledge that had been 'lost' to be regained. It unlocks inspired knowledge – that is, knowledge that is not acquired by learning but is just 'there'. It does this by serving as a 'bridge' between the conscious and the unconscious, and by integrating the right and left hemispheres of the brain makes inspired thought possible. It is the power that enables the vital Mana-Chi bio-energy to be both conveyed and consumed.

ASS is thus closely associated with the Element of Air, which is necessary to all life forms and provides the medium through which sound becomes audible. The Element of Air integrates both masculine and feminine qualities – the Yang and the Yin – and out of this duality emerges a triplicity which, in Northern mythology, was represented by Odin, Vili and Ve (a much older concept of three 'gods' as co-workers in a single unity than the Trinity of Christian theology). According to the myths, the Three shaped the Cosmos from the body of Ymir – the primal substance of the Universe when it existed in a chaotic state – and this work was performed by bringing into being Runic powers which enabled the Cosmos to take form. Odin supplied the *breath* of Life, Vili supplied the waters of emotion and *feeling*, and Ve supplied the *Will*.

The stave is shaped like a Pine tree – an evergreen symbolic of immortality and divine power. The Pine tree is also both male and female and thus indicates that the Great Spirit has a male and a female aspect, as does our own Higher Self, which can appear in a shamanic experience in either male or female form.

ASS is the Rune of awareness and of a power that is both received and expressed *mentally*.

POTENCY: Creative and mental expression of the Spirit

KEY QUALITIES: Communication skills, creative thought, artistic inspiration, perceptive ability, application of knowledge

PRACTICAL USES: Useful for seeing beyond what is apparent and obtaining the help of the innermost Self. This adds a new dimension to any situation and brings in a coincidental quality which some people call 'luck'.

CHALLENGE: Learn to communicate with Nature in order to widen your horizons.

The A-Rune can help you to:

- find inspiration and new ideas
- tap into hidden creative abilities and discover new talents
- strengthen your mental resolve
- improve personal relationships and communicative skills
- increase your intake of vital energy
- release energy blockages of the body and mind

4 REID, the R-Rune – Direction and Movement

REID (pronounced 'ride') is the potency of movement and direction. It is the power in the movement that propels the Sun across the skies. It is the *ordered* movement through Space and Time which enabled the Four Directions to become established and provide orientation and proportion. It is what brought in the Four Seasons and measured the passage of time. It is the power that directed the Four Elements and made possible the fashioning of matter and thus allowed the first phase of Creation to be completed.

The power of REID can be felt in the measured rhythm and monotonous beat of the shaman's drum, which 'moves' the awareness on its visionary journey through 'inner' space. This is why REID is associated with the horse, for the drum was often referred to as 'the shaman's horse', conveying him or her to an awareness of other realities.

REID is movement and direction, without which you would not know where you were. It is a power that generates motion, creates rhythmic action, and controls cyclic and spirallic development. It is the power behind the cyclic movement of the Earth round the Sun and the Moon round the Earth, which institutes the order of Time – of day and night and the seasons of the year. Recognition of this brings to mind the concept of a wheel with eight spokes – each being connected to a direction of the wind, each making a division of the year into equal proportions, and each indicating a path to enlightenment and self-realization.

REID is also concerned with repetitive movement and therefore with ritual, which is a method of making impressions on the subconscious Hidden Self, the servant of the conscious Ego-self. However, it is a power that creates not only movement but also rightly ordered action. Because of this characteristic it was sometimes referred to as 'the Rune of right result'.

One of REID's most powerful attributes is the power to keep energies under proper control and for a specific intention – by the harmonization of forces under intelligent control. This might be likened to a rider who is in control of his horse and its speed and direction, rather than a passenger being taken for a ride. So REID is also the Rune of right balance.

The word *Reid* means 'counsel' or 'advise', which implies that this Rune is concerned with making right decisions and the courage required to carry them through.

Some writers have associated REID with travel, but it is essentially the Soul's journey that the Runic power is truly concerned with. It is the Rune of your own Inner Quest – your search for meaning, purpose and spiritual fulfilment that moves you to seek answers to life's most perplexing mysteries and to make sense of your own existence.

REID is also a protective Rune which enables you to be safe on any plane of existence. For this reason Runic shamans often held an R-Rune stave or wore it in some form so that it accompanied them on shamanic journeys.

POTENCY: Ordered movement like the passage of the Sun
KEY QUALITIES: Measurement, control and direction, balance and rhythm, cyclic development, balanced judgment
PRACTICAL USES: As it is a Rune that changes perspective, it is helpful when you need to find direction and see an overview of things.

CHALLENGE: Take control of your own life so that you govern its direction.

The R-Rune can help you to:

- extend your awareness
- gain access to 'hidden' knowledge
- come into attunement with natural and personal rhythms
- attain balanced judgment
- improve your sense of timing
- protect yourself from harm whilst travelling

5 KEN, the K-Rune – Inner Light

The K-Rune is a light within that turns 'raw' substance into a crafted result. Like the fire of a blacksmith's forge, it makes raw material pliable so it can be reshaped. The power, however, is an ability to reshape itself and its environment, for it is the inner fire of self-transformation.

The stave shape suggests a cleaving or splitting power, and it is interesting to note that in former times when flame torches were used as lights, they were often fashioned from clusters of the needle-shaped leaves of the evergreen Pine tree, so the flame literally consumed and merged what was previously divided and separate.

Ken is a word that means 'to know' and also 'to be able to'. The Runic potency is not only the power of knowing but it is combined with an ability to perform what is intrinsically known. When we want to 'shed light' on a subject we are exercising the power of the K-Rune. It is the 'light' in en-*light*-enment, it is the Rune of inner guidance, the power of seeking and also of recognition – of knowing what has been sought out through the very application of it. It is the bringing forth of knowledge, rather than the knowledge itself, and the very power that fires enthusiasm and sheds light.

KEN is the fire power that breaks down and creates new shapes under intelligent control. It is the power of analysis, of determined progression, of reasoned growth and development. The light of the K-Rune provides the clarity of thought that is required to visualize essential detail and to arouse the fire of enthusiasm that is needed to bring an idea into physical existence. In other words, KEN embraces the ability to create. It was through the activity of primal Fire that manifest and unmanifest existence came into being, and thus the creativity associated with the K-Rune may be physical or mental – craft or art.

KEN was used by Runic shamans to gain inner guidance; they took the Rune with them on shamanic journeys when it was necessary to make clear what was obscure, to obtain further insight into a specific matter, or to expose hidden aspects of the self. As a Rune of Fire, KEN has a protective influence in any hazardous enterprise.

POTENCY: The fire that comes from within to provide illumination

KEY QUALITIES: Clarity of thought, analytical ability, constructive expression, enthusiasm, intensity

PRACTICAL USES: Can help to banish the darkness that surrounds what you may not understand so that whatever troubles you may be brought to light.

CHALLENGE: Make sure that what you endeavour to do is rightly challenged at the outset so that you do not get 'burned'.

The K-Rune can help you to:

- express yourself more clearly
- attain clarity of thought
- bring to light what changes need to be made in your life
- generate the fire of enthusiasm
- turn knowledge into understanding

6 GIFU, the G-Rune – The Gift of Time

GIFU (pronounced 'gee-foo') is usually associated with the giving or receiving of a gift or sacrifice in the sense of an exchange of energy – of giving something of value in return for a blessing that has either been received or is anticipated. However, such interpretation barely scratches the surface of GIFU's inherent power. The gift that was given in the Cosmic scheme of things was the gift of Life itself – that awareness of existence which is experienced at all levels, whether human, animal, plant, mineral – or celestial. So the 'gift' this Rune is associated with is not material at all, and neither is the gift it refers to that is within the capacity of us all to impart whether we are rich, poor, or of modest means – the gift of TIME!

When we give of our time we are giving of our life, because our Earth life is conditioned and confined by Time. Like everything in physical existence, Earth life has duration. It lasts for only a number of years. There is a time constraint on our physical existence. Time is our life. So when we devote time to someone, when we work at something, when we concentrate the mind on a particular enterprise, we are putting our life into it. That time – that portion of our life that is being given or 'sacrificed' – is far more valuable than any physical object that can be purchased, because it is part of us. It is a part of our life. Time is a gift. Your time – your life – on this Earth is a gift that has been given to *you* to make use of in furtherance of your *own* individual evolvement.

In shamanic understanding Time is more than a measurement of space. It has an 'alive-ness'. It is an interwoven unity – an ever-changing Now flowing from that which has been to that which is and to that which may be. Time has reality of existence and it has power. The power of GIFU is not the power *of* Time but the power *in* Time!

And Time is not necessarily constant, as we have been led to suppose. Although it can be measured – 60 seconds in a minute, 60 minutes in an hour, 24 hours in a day, 365 days in a year, and so on – it is not necessarily constant in the way it is used. Indeed, we say 'time flies' when it appears to go quickly, or 'time drags' when it seems to go slowly. GIFU is the power to *extend* Time in order to get more things done, or to 'slow it down' so things can be observed and experienced in more detail. *You* do not have the power yourself to control Time, but GIFU has!

GIFU is also a quality that contains both the 'essence' of the giver and the 'substance' of what is given. So when the Manifest appeared out of the Unmanifest, and Life with it, Time conditioned its existence in physical reality. Each and all contained the essence of the Giver – the Great Spirit – and each and all was made from the very substance of the Great Giver. This the Runic shamans understood. Furthermore, the same power of GIFU encapsulates balance, for its stave X is a representation of the great Wheel of the Universe, revolving around its spindle in the middle. With it was established the concept of the Six Directions, which cannot be shown in a two-dimensional image for where the lines cross in the centre there is a perpendicular central column or spindle. Everything is thus held together in perfect balance so that energy moving from one place to another is compensated. The shamanic understanding of sacrifice is really related to this concept. Everything has its 'price'. Every act requires payment of some kind. You cannot gain without also experiencing a loss of some kind – again, an exchange of energy. In order to attain greater wisdom there needs to be willingness to sacrifice some current ideas.

The stave shape itself represents the process of an equal exchange of energies through which all comes into being. This is why it was a romantic symbol for a kiss, an expression of the balanced nature of love between two people.

GIFU also has to do with bonding – the reconciliation or integration of opposing or complementary forces – and with the marking of boundaries. So it is a power that both binds and guides to attain harmonious balance and to establish the extent of that arrangement.

GIFU, then, is the gift of consciousness, the balance of flowing forces within the boundaries of Time, and the potential for communion with the Source. It marks the sixth stage in the Creation process, when the vital Life-force was breathed into forms and consciousness entered in.

POTENCY: Giving and receiving
KEY QUALITIES: Bonding and binding, compensation, fair exchange, respect of boundaries, generosity and compassion
PRACTICAL USES: Helps you to make the most effective use of time so that what is expended is returned in suitable reward.
CHALLENGE: Everything you receive requires something offered in return to preserve the balance of the Universe. Be prepared to accept the consequences of your actions.

The G-Rune can help you to:

- make more effective use of your time
- receive more by giving more
- bond personal relationships
- come into active partnership with your Higher Self

7 WYNJA, the W-Rune – The Culminater

WYNJA (pronounced 'win-yah') is a potency of the all-encompassing Love Force that exists throughout the Universe and whose effect on a human being is a sense of joyfulness and a feeling of well-being. WYNJA is a totally personal power that brings delight to the senses and provides impetus to strive for perfection. It is what enables you to experience delight because it is the power of harmonious existence received through the senses.

The Nordic word *wynja* means 'the glory of perfection' – the culmination of perfect love, because it is an unconditional love that makes no demands and gives entirely of itself without expectation of return. WYNJA implies all that is lovable and beautiful, and an attitude of child-like innocence. It indicates the ideal towards which we should strive.

WYNJA arouses an awareness of self-worth and a recognition of the divinity within all creatures, and as such might be regarded also as the Rune of self-esteem. It is, therefore, the power that builds self-confidence – not the vanity of egotism and puffed-up self-importance, but the humility of self-worth in the totality of things.

WYNJA was regarded by Runic shamans as 'the fulfiller of wishes' because it is the potent force of realization. It is that thrill of joy we experience when a heart's desire is attained or when we realize a much desired objective. It is also the ability to recognize hidden affinities and to draw them together to establish a harmonious relationship. It is the balm that heals rifts and misunderstandings.

Runic shamans likened the stave shape to a shaman's crystal wand, which itself was a tool of realization or materialization of desire and thus a bringer of joy. It is a symbol of affirmation – of sending forth with purpose.

It is significant that WYNJA is the seventh rune in the Uthark arrangement, for seven is the number of perfection and affirmation, and in the Cosmic scheme of things was the stage where the Divine Will was confirmed and that which was to 'be' was assuredly coming into be-ing as a manifestation of the Idea.

WYNJA follows GIFU for it is the pleasure of possession that follows the act of giving and the joy that comes out of sacrifice.

POTENCY: Right timing for the release of energy
KEY QUALITIES: Unconditional love, culmination, orgasm, happiness in fulfilment
PRACTICAL USES: Can help in ascertaining the best time to take appropriate action and thus reach a satisfactory conclusion.

CHALLENGE: Everything in life is a lesson for your ultimate perfection. Look beyond the obvious.

The W-Rune can help you to:

- find happiness and well-being
- build self-esteem
- heel rifts
- bring an enterprise to a satisfactory conclusion
- strive for perfection

Rune-work: Assignment 4 Collecting Your Rune-stones

Although Rune-sets can be bought from New Age shops it is preferable to prepare your own. An effective Rune-set can be easily prepared with small stones or pebbles collected from a walk in a natural location.

Choose a time when you can go out into a natural environment – woodland, open countryside or seashore – in a search for your stone helpers. Shamans of all cultures and traditions who have a deep affinity with the Earth regarded the Mineral Kingdom as the most ancient since it appeared on the Earth before there were trees and plants, or animals, birds and humans. Rocks were perceived as the 'bones' of the Earth and, like a skeleton, provided the structure that supported and held everything in place. Rocks and stones are of great age so were considered to be 'wise' helpers for the human being who sought to commune with Nature and seek its support. Rocks and stones, including gems and crystals, were perceived as the 'holders' of energy since their vibratory pattern is very slow and they are in a state of inertia. This is why stones are very suitable for a Rune-set for they will hold firmly and constantly the vibration of each Rune pattern.

The search for 25 pebble-size stones for your set – one for each Rune plus a 25th which will serve as your stone of destiny – needs to be performed in an unhurried way, for it is not a question of simply picking up whatever stones may be seen during a gentle stroll through natural surroundings. You must allow the stones to choose *you*! How? Simply, by having that *intention* clearly in your mind as you set out on your quest. Just tell yourself – that is, instruct your *subconscious* self: 'I am taking this shamanic walk to enable the stones required for my Rune-set to identify themselves.' In some way your attention will be drawn to a particular place or places on your walk, to a stone or stones that will be lying there. What you are seeking are small, flat stones about 2 centimetres in diameter. The full set of 25 stones should all be approximately the same size.

When your attention is drawn to a stone, pick it up or gently prize it from the earth or sand using a pen-knife or small metal tool. If it looks the right size and shape, hold it in your right hand, close your eyes, and ask for an indication that it is a stone you need. Then wait for a response. You will have a clear 'feeling' or impression if the stone is right for you – an inner assurance which is intuitive. If no response comes, return it to the place where you found it. Treat it with respect.

You may receive a positive connection with only two or three stones in your quest, so you may need to make several such journeys before your set is complete. On each occasion take the stones home, wash them thoroughly and keep them in a safe place, preferably near a window where they can be in the light. When your collection is complete you will be ready for the next stage of preparation.

6 The Bridge Between the Worlds

THE EIGHTH RUNE, HAGAL, is at the completion of one phase of the creative process and heralds the beginning of another. It is associated with the rainbow – a bridge between the visible and the invisible. A rainbow is an arc of light composed of all the colours of the spectrum; and indicates the splitting up of the components of light, the distribution of light frequencies and the emission and absorption of energy by atoms and molecules in a transitional process. The word *hagal* means 'hail-stone' – a stone of ice that comes from above or beyond. A stone is a holder of energy in a state of inertia, and here is implied a process that comes from the invisible realm, within which is 'crystalized' the seed-pattern of what is to become – of what is to become visible in physical reality.

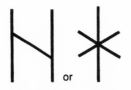

8 HAGAL, the H-Rune – Bringing into Being

The word *hagal* (pronounced 'har-gool') means 'hailstone', a substance that consists of frozen water and air, which might be likened to an icy egg. So Runic shamans associated a hailstone with the 'egg of manifestation' of Northern mythology, which came forth from the merging of Cosmic Fire and Cosmic Ice and was filled with crystalized power. HAGAL, therefore, might be regarded as an expression of the principle of ongoing evolution contained within a fixed structure. It is the power of the pattern of completion which is contained within the seed of every living and evolving thing.

HAGAL is sometimes referred to by Runic shamans as the 'mother Rune', because it has within it all 24 stave forms when it is contained within a 'solid' hexagram. It is the Rune of the primal crystal – a word which itself means 'ice'. Shamans of all cultures regard the quartz crystal as solidified Cosmic 'ice' or 'hail' – the holder and guider of force.

Figure 10 The 'solid' hexagram – a symbol of the primal 'crystal' (a word meaning 'ice') – is the 'holder' of all 24 Rune staves

HAGAL is sometimes represented as the glyph of the crystalline snowflake ✳ indicating that it is the power of a set pattern rather than a patterning force. Like a crystal, it is the controller and focuser of energies. It is, therefore, a Rune of structure held firm or constant for the purpose of constructing. It is the power of a pattern from which things come into being and are built. It is the power behind the DNA code itself as a pattern of becoming – of coming into being – and which determines the shape of the physical body. So HAGAL might be described as 'the Rune of bringing into being'.

The stave shape indicates a connecting beam between forces moving in opposite directions – the expansive power of Fire moving upwards and outwards, and the contracting power of Water moving downwards and inwards – together creating a binding force which holds a pattern of change and strengthens also the shape of what is coming into manifestation.

Some writers on the Runes associate HAGAL with disruption, and even destruction, but the Runic power is not wrathful in that sense. It is a power of natural change which is necessary in order to correct any imbalance and to create conditions that are necessary for growth and development. For instance, hail is one of the most violent and disruptive forces of Nature – hail-stones can be as large as pebbles and destroy crops and even kill birds and small animals – but it is also one of the most miraculous. A hailstorm is usually preceded by a heavy and oppressive atmosphere, and then with the storm comes the rainbow linking Sky with Earth. Afterwards the air is clear, refreshing and invigorating. So HAGAL is the potency that carries within it the ability to transform – to clear the air for what is to follow. What therefore may seem a setback due to events beyond apparent control can turn out to be advantageous in the furtherance of growth.

POTENCY: The focusing and control of primal energies into a patterning code in order to provide a way for a coming into physical existence.

KEY QUALITIES: Dramatic liberation, birthing, bridging, correction of imbalance, advantageous adversity

PRACTICAL USES: Helpful for keeping your 'cool' when being harrassed; an aid for transforming hostile or adverse influences into beneficial results.

CHALLENGE: Accept the challenge of a seemingly adverse situation. Trust your innermost 'Self' to see you through and turn it to your ultimate advantage.

The H-Rune can help you to:

- banish unwanted influences
- develop intuitiveness within a structured framework so it does not get out of control
- focus your intentions
- find a way of bridging differing points of view

9 NAUD, the N-Rune – The Spinner of Time

It is with the N-Rune, NAUD (pronounced 'need'), that the Norns enter Creation, bringing in the *reality* of Time. The Norns are the powers that spin the thread of the Wyrd through the different levels of existence and shape the destiny of everyone. Time, as an interwoven unity, might be likened to a thread woven from various strands. Everything that has happened – what we call the Past – forms part of an ever-changing Present, and the patterns being formed in the Present, through our thoughts and actions, shape what is to be. The essence of what has been has not vanished forever but forms an active part of what we call the Present, out of whose patterns the Future is shaped.

This shamanic concept of Time was expressed in the symbolic imagery of the Tree of Yggdrasil, whose three main roots were watered from a well. In Northern mythology this Cosmic Tree was likened to the 'body' of the mythical giant Ymir, from which form came into being and which defines Space. The waters which feed it were likened to the Cosmic cow, Audhumbla, whose nourishing 'milk' defined Time and conditioned it. In the myth, the well is attended by three goddesses – intelligences called Norns – each functioning at one of the three levels of the well.

Urd is the name of the oldest of these three influences and her name means 'origin of existence'. She was often depicted as an aged grandmother. The second of the Norns was called Verdandi, a name which means 'that which is becoming', and was often depicted as a mother. The youngest was called Skuld, whose name means 'that which should be', and was usually depicted as a maiden. The Norns were perceived as not only being *in* the Universe but also *within ourselves*. In other words, we each have our own Norns weaving our own individual destiny through the choices and actions we make and are making.

Wyrd is an Anglo-Saxon word which means 'to turn' and has a different meaning from the concept Western traditions have applied to it by calling it 'Fate'. A Wyrd comprises patterns from past actions which have shaped what is happening now and are conditioning also what is yet to be. We can consciously change our own future (the consequences of our own choices and decisions) by applying the lessons we have learned from past actions.

So the Past of our individual lives is not something that has been and gone and is lost forever, as we have been educated into believing. Even Time itself is an energy. It is active in the Present for it has served to fashion what is here now, and it is also involved in determining the Future. In other words, we are what we are now as a result of the collective experiences in the life we have lived in the past, and we shall be in the future what is being determined now in the Present. Similarly, our past lives are not completely over. They, too, are energies – each life a facet of our total being, each existing in another 'portion' of Time. But their essence is still within us, although in another dimension, affecting the way we are, for they, too – individually and collectively – have brought us to our present state of development. Because these energies are within us, though in another dimension, it is possible for their 'data' to be accessed shamanically and so help us to fulfil the Soul's purpose in this present lifetime.

So everything in physical existence – including ourselves – has a position in Time and Space. Development is in accordance with the condition and situation of each of us, for we are not all at the same stage. In other words, everything develops at its own proper time and when the situation and circumstances are right for that development to take place.

It needs to be recognized, however, that there is a random factor at work in the Universe which results in conditions that are not under control. These results are mistakenly called 'acts of God' but they are, in fact, no such thing. Indeed, they are the very opposite of an action by a harmonious Creative Intelligence. It would be more appropriate to call them 'acts of Chaos' for that is what they are – chaotic activities. It is essentially this random, chaotic factor working in our lives that causes us stress.

NAUD is thus the power of coming into being under stress and constraint. Time is the constraint because it puts a limit on the duration of what is coming into being. So NAUD may be regarded as an unleashing of self-generated life put under constraint. Its stave shape has been likened to the bow-drill used by native peoples to kindle fire. So the stave itself is indicative of self-generated fire – a bringing forth of the flame within. Once in the dimension of Time, it can continue to grow and develop for a duration. The Rune emphasizes the necessity for friction or resistance before manifestation can occur. It is a friction which kindles an inner fire in order to serve the need. This same power can be a strength within ourselves that can be called upon when facing trials and difficulties and when we need to gain advantage from what may appear as an adversity.

NAUD is an ability to turn weakness into strength and to develop self-sufficiency. It is that which is inherent in those life experiences that contain the lessons that need to be learned in order that the purpose of the individual Higher Self, or Soul-self, may be fulfilled. It is a recognition, too, that it is sometimes essential to face the resistance and upheaval that necessitate change in order that something better may replace what has gone before.

NAUD is the power behind the instinct for self-survival – the necessity to endure. It is the strength behind fortitude and defiance. So it is the Rune that can help you to cope with stress and provide you with the strength to face trials and difficulties with confident hope.

POTENCY: The power of coming into being under pressure and constraint. It is in the sudden rush of adrenalin that makes achievement possible under challenge.

KEY QUALITIES: Necessary resistance, self-generated power, enduring strength, self-sufficiency

PRACTICAL USES: NAUD is a great help in meditation for it can help you to recognize what is truly needed rather than what seems to be desirable.

CHALLENGE: You cannot effectively meet the needs of others

until you first recognize your own needs and take action to satisfy them.

The N-Rune can help you to:

- cope with stress
- succeed in a crisis
- achieve the seemingly impossible
- break through your limitations
- develop perseverance
- value endurance

10 ISS, the E-Rune – The Formation

The E-Rune is a formative force that slows movement and causes density. Its name, ISS (pronounced 'ees'), means 'ice', implying contraction, solidity and immobility. ISS is a power that binds together and shields. It is the power that holds the atom together. It suspends development as ice freezes the fluidity of water. It may also be likened to stopping a motion picture so that a static frame may capture the dynamics of motion at a precise moment. It crystallizes the spiritual into the material so that its influence may be preserved, much as the icy coldness of a refrigerator preserves the nature of food that is placed within it. ISS is a stabilizing factor that acts to preserve what comes under its influence so that it stays as it is.

ISS is thus the inner strength of self-control. In human beings it shows expression in our ability to take charge of our life and to accept responsibility for our choices and actions. For this reason it was likened to the blackthorn staff of the shaman, which was a symbol of authority, and to the spear, which was a symbol of courage.

ISS is associated with stillness. Stillness, though passive, is not a state in which nothing is happening. Whatever change is taking place is unseen and beneath the surface. It is suspension of movement in order that development can be assured. The crust of ice that covers a lake in winter is but a covering for what is taking place unseen at deeper levels. The power of this Rune is a concentrating effect that attracts, brings together and holds in place. An icicle is water that has been frozen 'solid' whilst still in flow. A snapshot is a moment of Time suspended. So ISS is the power to retain what needs to be kept in being. It is the slowing of an energy process that causes density and prevents dissolution. So it is a Rune of control – a stabilizing force that shields what is taking place at deeper levels.

ISS is the power that upholds the Spirit as it passes through the turbulent waters of Earth life, providing it with opportunities to be cultivated. But that process of cultivation is hampered if the Ego becomes so self-important that the power of cultivation is broken, like brittle ice.

ISS is the power of self-containment, and so can help us to recognize the powers that we need to hold fast within us. Just as ice is a preserving agent, so ISS is the power to keep things as they are and to conserve that which has been attained.

Whilst ISS can concentrate the mind and steel the heart, it must be approached with caution for, as on an icy surface, it is possible to lose one's balance.

The first ten Runes represent primal creation and the forces that make up the inner, spiritual structures of the Universe and ourselves. They are related to the fluctuations of invisible signals that precede the formation of matter into atoms and molecules. These ten Runes might be compared to the gestation period from conception to birth, when the various structures of the physical being that is coming into existence are established. Within these structures are contained the powers of potential which, once released, find expression and ensure growth and development on other levels. These potencies are contained within Nature – whose purpose is fruitfulness – and within human beings whose purpose is similar – to thrive, endure and fulfil. These same essences mould and shape all life forms in accordance with the laws of each being's existence.

Before manifestation can take place, the vibrational rate must be stepped down. Characteristics – which are non-material influences that enable purpose to be worked out – precipitate into matter as potentials which can only become actualities when activated. The first ten Runes are thus concerned with the Life-force as it is moving towards physical manifestation. They indicate life in the abstract.

The coming together of all the potencies necessary in order to manifest in physical reality and to provide the full pattern of the future form, is the focal point – the precipitation from the Unmanifest of all the characteristics and qualities that are inherent within the form itself. With regard to a human being, that focal point is the moment of conception. Conception is when the first 'cell' is created and intelligent motion in physical reality beings. As development continues from inward movement to outward expansion during pregnancy, there is preparation for external action. Emergence into the realm of physical reality takes place at birth. Creation of matter follows a similar route.

Each of the Runes I have so far described characterizes an influence of the Life-force itself and is a potential for movement and change once it is activated and those qualities are brought forth into manifestation. What manifests in physical reality comes into the dimension of Time from a state of timelessness. It is then conditioned by the Mind. It is not a question of life beginning at birth – as something that is somehow acquired or possessed. We *are* Life. And every life form is itself an expression of that Life.

BACK TO THE ICE AGE

Pia, a Runic shaman I befriended in Sweden, lives the Runes. She had shown me how to meditate with them, how to experience them in an altered state of awareness, and how to recognize a Rune's influence at any hour of the day. Now I will let her convey to you in her own words how the dedication of a period of time – be it an hour, a day, a whole month or even an entire year – can be of benefit in the process of personal development and the cultivation of the Spirit. Here is Pia's account of how, for a complete year, she worked with ISS.

The first understanding I had of the power of ISS was that it contains a great portion of beauty. I naturally connected with my experience of winter, for winter for me in the heart of Sweden is clarity, quiet nights, moonshine on the white shining snow, and air that is easy to breathe. Altogether a kind of razorblade light, for its light is sunlight multiplied by the glittering snow and moonlight that makes the nights as light as day.

About three years ago I had a vision of ISS that pointed out two aspects of its power. First, the power of beauty and structure, as in a snow crystal – a kind of power that makes it possible to see things that have been hidden in disorder. Or a kind of 'frozen' moment – a snapshot of Time like stopping a river from flowing so you can see the fishes in the water and the stones on the bottom clearly. Second, I saw in that vision how a person dominated by ISS is someone who has a strong need to experience things for him- or herself, someone who can't accept any kind of borrowed know- ledge or second-hand experience. As a winter-wisher I knew the weakness of old, grey, mud-like spring ice – so dangerous and resistant, keeping a grip on its existence as long as possible yet unable to bear me over the lake. I also knew that ice is not melted by Sun alone. There is no spring until there is heavy rain and the last ice on the lakes sinks in the water and melts. The wind is also part of it, breaking the ice into smaller pieces so Water and Sun can do their work. But altogether I had a strong, positive feeling for the beauty and clarity of ISS.

So with this understanding I found it quite natural when I real- ized that ISS should be my road between my 39th and 40th birth- days. The situation was that I had an essential part of my Soul life-energy retrieved around my 39th birthday, and I knew that by re-integrating that part of my life I needed to go through whatever experience in order to bring me clarity and a more structured life-style. On a shamanic journey I learned that this should be the year when I become the person I really am *inside*. And I was glad to go on that journey because my life had been involved in confusion and I was reaching a point where I could not stand any more chaos. ISS seemed to be the right power to teach the structure of 'I' – of me. I figured that ISS would force me to do just that. And I figured right.

Just as you cannot stop winter from coming, it came, and I soon realized that one part of ISS power I hadn't been in contact with was the aspect of Arctic glacial ice – the ice of the Ice Age. The only way to get away from that is to move away from it. If you don't it will press you down or in towards yourself, and as I see it the only way to survive ISS in its most powerful form is to be willing to be transformed by its weight and power, just like the landscape was transformed during the Ice Age. As I had invited ISS I could not escape by moving away from the situation my life was in. However tempted I might have felt to simply opt out of the circumstances of my life at that time, I recognized that now I had put myself in a situation where there was no way out! As ISS has a tendency to cut you off from communication, it was impossible for me to express to anyone what was going on in my life. Every time I tried to reach out, I was forced back into myself again. Trust, and a willingness to transform, were the only things I had to hang on to. And as we all know, these things are not easy at all. They are easy to talk *about* and believe in, but to *do*? – that is something else. With ISS's clear eye watching me, every attempt to pretend I was able to trust and transform was an expensive mistake. ISS wouldn't let me pretend anything of the kind. My experience is that if you let ISS loose in its full potential you must transform, otherwise you will break. And I had to do it alone.

Then the climax came. Something broke in me and the ice started to melt. And with that amount of ice to be melted the result, of course, was a lot of water – emotions, tears, anger. Memories that had been frozen in the ice like big stones, came to me, and with them all these feelings. There was water all over the place. It seemed for a while that all of me was hidden under an ocean of emotions. But then I became able to reach out to friends and helpers in all levels of Reality. New land was starting to rise.

For a time I was so 'new' I could not go to shops or make contact with people I had not met before. My own inner landscape was so new I couldn't figure out how I might react to outer stimuli. Anything could happen. I could not put my finger on what had changed. 'New' is the only word to describe how I felt: I had new eyes to perceive things differently, new ears to hear what I had not understood before, a new brain to reason conclusions I had not arrived at before, and a new mind that no longer wanted to judge and make comparisons. ISS has instilled a positive attitude that seeks to support, put in order, make beautiful structures of seemingly confusing information.

In my experience, ISS has not only the power to bring structure out of chaos, but the power to teach you to act and experience for yourself. It also helps to bring about transformation. I did not really understand this before, because I had not realized that ISS acts as a transformer. It changes the way things appear. It changes the way you function. It changes the strength of the energy you apply. It changes the mode of exertion from one which was alternating and sporadic to one which is continuous and persistent.

So I now feel a great respect for ISS's power, though I have applied this power in the form that some who understand the Runes might call its negative aspect. But just as dear Mama allows herself to be renewed by ice and winter, so we two-leggeds need to do that, too. Sometimes we do need to undergo an Ice Age in our lives. Then we need to bear in mind that the more we resist, the heavier the pain. But I wouldn't have changed it for anything. There really is something beautiful about such clear moonlit nights and the cold Northern winds that make it easier for us to breathe and to have a cool head to face difficult decisions.

POTENCY: The power to maintain and preserve. Stability and the stillness of inertia. The concentration of single-minded purpose.

KEY QUALITIES: Contraction, cohesion, preservation, stability, inner strength, stillness, suspension, self-containment.

PRACTICAL USES: When the pace of modern life causes concern, ISS can slow things down and enable you to focus on the real issues. It is an aid also to bringing your dreams into 'solid' reality.

CHALLENGE: Just as winter does not last forever, neither does any situation in which you may find yourself. Have the courage to move forward. You need to *do* in order to *know*.

The E-Rune can help you to:

- still your mind and meditate
- focus attention
- immobilize unprovoked attack or harmful intent
- strengthen your Will
- calm hyper-activeness
- overcome restlessness

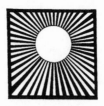

7 Transition into Physical Reality

WITH JARA, THE Y-RUNE (the letter J is pronounced as a Y in Nordic and some other languages), the Runes move into physical reality and the division of Time. This Rune is the very power behind the cyclic growth and seasonal change that keep material existence in its state of constant motion and activity.

11 JARA, the Y-Rune – Cycles of Change

The stave shape of JARA (pronounced 'yah-rah') indicates two halves of the year – the 'ice' of winter and the 'fire' of summer – circling after one another, interacting and complementing each other: summer's harvest providing winter's food.

JARA is the process of organic development through orderly movement which cannot be hurried or forced because what is taking place on the 'inside' must be in harmony with what is happening in the outside environment. If this natural order is forced in order to obtain quicker results, the ultimate consequences will be adverse. In other words, seeds grow into plants in accordance with the seasons and when they are ripe and ready.

This Runic power does not force change but brings it about gradually through the subtle flow of a spirallic motion that enables things to come into physical existence at the proper 'turn' of the cycle. This is another Rune to indicate that our linear concept of Time is a false one and that in Nature everything moves in cycles and not in straight lines. Everything that happens arises out of what has gone before, and what is to transpire is shaped by what is currently taking place. There is no returning to a 'beginning' – only a process of endless development.

JARA indicates cyclic movement – a constant change, nothing remains the same. Everything is in a constant state of movement and the completion of one cycle is but the beginning of another. It can be compared to the Taoist Yin/Yang concept.

Whereas ISS indicates a descent into matter, JARA is the progression *through* matter and the ascent into the spiritual. Spiritual understanding cannot be forced, however. It, too, is a natural process. Not until we perceive that what is happening in the external environment around us is related to the inner environment and what is happening within us, can such an understanding take place.

Applied personally, JARA enables the seeds of potential that are inherent within to develop through careful nurturing so they can manifest effectively when they are truly ready. It emphasizes that actions that are in harmony with Nature will culminate in right results because that is the natural order of things. Your inner vision cannot be hurried, either, any more than you can hasten a harvest.

POTENCY: Natural change

KEY QUALITIES: Gradual development, sequential timing, cultivation

PRACTICAL USES: Helpful for gathering the benefits of past actions.

CHALLENGE: Be patient. You cannot harvest before everything is ready. Make the most of what you have now.

The Y-Rune can help you to:

- see that patience brings its own rewards
- nurture your creativity
- bring your schemes and ideas to fruition
- come into attunement with the cycles of Nature
- harmonize with your body clock

12 PERTRA, the P-Rune – Birthing

The stave shape of PERTRA (pronounced 'pert-rah') is similar
to that of a draw-stringed pouch in which Runes are contained
and from which they can be cast. The casting of Runes is not a
question of discerning one's 'luck' like gambling on the toss
of dice, nor is a Rune cast a random arrangement, and the
relationship of one Rune to another purely coincidental. A
Rune-cast by a Runic shaman was perceived as a capturing of
the Web that was being woven by the one for whom the cast
was being made, so bringing into awareness the many streams
of energy that are flowing at unseen levels and, though invisible, are in the process of coming into manifestation.

The Rune-bag, fashioned by hand, is symbolic of the womb.
In the womb the unborn child holds within it an imprint of its
ancestral past and potential for the future. Indeed, PERTRA is
the power of the Inner Child – the child that is still within you
and *is* you, and needs to be loved and cherished still, whatever
your age now in Earth years.

PERTRA is the process of holding together what needs to be
preserved and recovered so that it can be 'birthed' and pro-

gressed further. This is the very nature of the Mineral Kingdom, whose mountains, rocks and stones were regarded by the
'Wise-Ones' as the great 'holders' of energy and associated
with strength and durability. PERTRA is a transformational
process that preserves the potentials inherited from your ancestors – from your own past lives – that are hidden deep
within the level of the Unconscious yet waiting to be released,
brought to the surface and developed so they can be manifested. It is a process of containing the 'raw material' from
which the threads of your life can be spun and new patterns
created in Time and Space.

This is the Rune of self-identity – the power that assures that
everything is after its own kind. It is the power that makes
certain every human being retains his or her own individuality.
It is the power which guarantees that however may lives you
live you will always be 'You'! The P-Rune many be likened to
iron in the Mineral Kingdom. Iron can be turned into a myriad
of forms and its appearance can be changed, but its original
'substance' is maintained.

Another facet of PERTRA is that its association with the
Mineral Kingdom and its action of giving birth or formation in
objective reality, is through a process of layers, or levels, of
activity. Slices of onyx or agate express something of the
wonder of this layered structure or process of what comes into
being.

PERTRA is the ability to think 'Runically' – that is, to perceive the layered structure of Reality, to take it into account,
and to reclaim the knowledge of the Runes themselves that can
only be revealed. Reality is not confined to a single level of
existence, though we may have mistakenly assumed that to be
so. It is structured in layers, one upon another. Even the 'ordinary' reality of our mundane, everyday living is so structured.
For instance, there is the objective reality of 'appearances',
which we share with other human beings in going about out
everyday life. It is how the immediate environment seems to
be. Then there is a subjective or 'conditioned' reality, which is
an interpretation we put upon what we experience and results
in beliefs, opinions, judgments and comparisons we form
within ourselves. There is also another 'layer' – an aspect which
we might call 'creative reality'. This is a reality we actively
fashion for ourselves from our ideas, desires and aspirations,

and which we project into objective reality where they become manifest.

POTENCY: The process of cause and effect which manifests that which is hidden
KEY QUALITIES: Containment, vitality, durability, self-identity
PRACTICAL USES: Helps you to get to know yourself for what you *are* rather than what you are expected to be.
CHALLENGE: Don't be afraid of change, but ensure that you are fully in contact with your physical body during any transformational experience.

The P-Rune can help you to:

- give birth to your plans, ideas, and hopes
- hold on to what is essential
- experience pleasure in abundance
- bring your hidden potentials into conscious awareness

13 EOH, the Ei-Rune – Continuity of Life

EOH (pronounced 'yo'), the Ei-Rune, as in h*ei*ght, is the power of perpetuality – a continuity that enables life to be hidden in death and birth and death to be inherent in the natural cycle. It is associated with the Plant Kingdom and particularly the Yew tree, which characterizes longevity and symbolizes that which is eternal.

The stave is shaped like a spine or a trunk of a tree, with its 'tail' like the main root feeding from the depths of the Unconscious, whilst at the crown power is being drawn in from the eternal realm of the Spirit. Darkness and Light are combined into a single power of connectedness, indicating also that Life and Death are not separated opposites or 'enemies' but complementary, each being 'hidden' in the other. The stave shape, too, indicates that Spirit and Matter are one and that we are each a personified expression of a Life that continues after Death and leads to further expression through rebirth. Death, thus perceived as a process of Life, loses much of its fear.

EOH is the power that supports the different layers of reality and levels of multidimensional existence – the so-called Middle, Upper, Lower and Under 'worlds' of shamanic cosmology – drawing up from the source that which survives death, bringing it forth into a new expression of life. The Rune might be likened to the trunk of a tree, rooted to the earth but extending to the sky, or to the spine which enables messages to be conveyed between the feet 'on the ground' and the head which is sometimes 'in the clouds'. Significantly, the human spine has 24 vertebrae and each resonates to a specific Runic energy.

EOH is the power that connects the mortality of our physical existence with the immortality of our spiritual reality, and is the power in Nature that conquers Death! It is through this Runic power that we can transform our lives by perceiving the spiritual in the physical and by finding true spirituality in the mundane activities of our everyday living.

POTENCY: Perpetuality that is inherent in transformation and development

KEY QUALITIES: Supportive energy, endurance, longevity, perseverance

PRACTICAL USES: Helpful when you need enlightenment – perceiving how your ideals can be transformed into practical reality – and hope, which sees not an end but a continuity of existence.

CHALLENGE: Whatever it is you want to achieve, hesitate no longer. Get started and stay with it. This Rune can help you to reach for the stars!

The Ei-Rune can help you to:

- feel liberated from the fear of death
- develop qualities of endurance

- connect with other layers of reality
- avoid confusion
- find enlightenment
- release your inner strengths

14 ALGIZ, the Z-Rune – Instinctive Protection

ALGIZ (pronounced 'all-giz') is an attracting power that links the individual Spirit with the human entity that is coming into physical existence on the Earth plane and which shields and protects the four aspects that are embraced in this supreme act of creativity – Body, Mind, Soul and Spirit.

The stave shape may be likened to the Cosmic Tree with its branches reaching for the Upper World of superconscious existence, and its inverted form ⅄ as roots delving deep into the Lower World of Unconscious reality. It may be likened also to a swan in flight. The swan was regarded by Northern shamans as a 'messenger' between Heaven and Earth, bringing divine wisdom. The stave has similarities also with the defensive antlers of the elk – for ancient Northern peoples the equivalent of the buffalo of North American Indians. The elk was associated with survival for it provided tribal peoples with all their needs – food, clothing, shelter, implements and weapons.

So ALGIZ, the Z-Rune, has to do with both connectedness and protection. It is essential that in being 'connected' directly to our 'higher' (spiritual) Source we have our feet firmly planted on the ground, for unless we are grounded in the practical world in which we are living out our lives we are in danger of becoming unbalanced. We can be very religious about our spirituality but if it has no expression in practical, everyday reality it is of little real value. We would just be deluding ourselves. Our potential immortality must be expressed through our mortality. That is part of the purpose of our Earth life. It is protection from the delusion of spiritual egotism that the Z-Rune offers. It is concerned very much with the process of what goes on in the time span between 'life' and 'death'.

The religious moralists with repressive sexual attitudes who campaigned to undermine the Runes, considered the Rune-stave shape was a portrayal of the vagina and, when upturned, a symbol of the penis. They therefore associated it with sex magick, Satanic orgies, and all manner of sexual perversions which derived from their own troubled minds. Actually the Rune-stave had no such connections. It was often engraved on tombstombs to precede the date of birth and, in its upturned form, to indicate the date of death. This was in accordance with the universal law that all things are given birth through the female and that death, in many cases in a hunter/warrior society, often came through the hand of man!

The Runic power of ALGIZ is closely related to the instinct of survival, and self-survival is its principal defence mechanism. We human beings are supplied with this instinctive protective power and it resides in all of us. We also have another protective influence which comes from the Source and is 'inspirational'. This means that our survival is not entirely dependent on a fight-or-flee instinct but relies also on the intelligence of creative thought that seemingly comes 'out of nowhere'. Again, this is the power of the Z-Rune.

This 'instinctiveness' is what relates ALGIZ to the Animal Kingdom and with what shamans and shamanists call 'power animals'. A power animal is an energy-pattern of an ability to perform a specific task or function in a particular way. In non-ordinary reality such energy-patterns appear in animal form. In other words, the animal form characterizes the specific ability or abilities of the energy pattern. My book *Shamanic Experience* explains this.

The powerful protective influence of ALGIZ can be used to put an egg-shaped shield around you and anchor you more firmly to the Earth. Imagine the Rune like a rod or staff in your hand and on which you can rest and feel safe, secure and well grounded. Its force-field around you will act like a shield against any form of attack, and as a defence in warding off any danger. It will protect you at all levels – physical, emotional, mental and spiritual.

POTENCY: Grounding power
KEY QUALITIES: Instinctive and inspirational protection, ability to defend the aura and strengthen resolve, connectedness
PRACTICAL USES: Can draw power from the spiritual Source and bring it into ordinary reality where it can be grounded into practicality. Defends us where we are vulnerable
CHALLENGE: Be aware of your own vulnerability and the tendencies that allow you to become diverted from your chosen Path.

The Z-Rune can help you to:

- obtain inspirational and creative ideas
- find hidden powers to meet any challenge
- ward off negative influences
- connect with an inner drive to achieve more
- centre and balance yourself when stressed
- keep your ideas and aspirations well grounded in practical reality

15 SOL, the S-Rune – The Impossible Possibility

SOL (pronounced 'sole') is a source of power like that of the Sun, which is the bringer of Light and the sustainer of Life.

The Rune-stave is shaped like one side of a Figure of Eight

8, which is a symbol of infinity. Or, put another way, a Figure of Eight is composed of two S-Runes ζ ζ . S indicates energy in a spiral motion, moving in seemingly opposite directions. The movement is both horizontal and perpendicular for the power is multidimensional. Shamanically, the symbol is seen as a Figure of Eight on the horizontal plane and a Figure of Eight on the vertical plane – the two crossing at the centre. As a two-dimensional image this might be presented as a symbol like a four-petalled flower.

SOL is a spinning energy like a humming top. The child's toy revolves on a point, whereas the S-Rune revolves from a vortex. The energy is pushed outwards and upwards, then contracts back to a point in a repetitive process.

This power moves the 'space' around it and causes unusual things to happen – things that might normally not seem possible. This movement can sometimes cause destruction, but mostly it causes beneficent things to happen for it can spin the impossible dream into reality by drawing desirable change into its energy-vortex.

SOL is a power that enlightens and enables things and situations to be perceived as they really are. It provides an inner illumination that can enable you to see your way ahead more clearly, serving as a guiding light. Like the Sun, it has radiance, and so is a power that activates, vitalizes, energizes and gets you going.

SOL also indicates the light of the Soul – the substance of which the Soul Body itself is composed – so it relates to the 'higher' being, the Higher Self or Soul Self, rather than the Ego-self which projects its own self-image. It is, therefore, the Rune of *purpose* – the Soul's purpose – and of hope and ultimate success. So it is the power also of self-realization – of realizing your own self-worth, of releasing the potentials that are at the very core of your being and essential elements of your own unique individuality. SOL is the activating power of your own Life-force and the releasing power of your own essence so that it can be expressed in creative ways. As a vitalizing force it not only rejuvenates but regenerates. At cellular level it slows the ageing process, and for older people – like myself – provides them with the zest of youth.

POTENCY: Illumination and Hope – Illumination to see things as they are and Hope to perceive them as they can be

KEY QUALITIES: Radiance, activation, zest, enlightenment, rejuvenation

PRACTICAL USES: Brings things into the light so they can be seen for what they are. Provides knowledge and strength in times of trouble.

CHALLENGE: Be as generous as the Sun!

The S-Rune can help you to:

- attain the enlightenment and need to see things as they are
- seek inner guidance to discern the way ahead more clearly
- boost your energy levels and gain extra vitality in order to attain what you want
- realize that 'impossible' dream
- connect with your Soul's purpose
- feels years younger

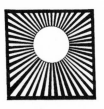

8 Enter Humanity

HUMANITY ENTERS INTO THE scheme of things with TYR (pronounced 'tire'), the T-Rune – man – and BJARKA (pronounced 'be-yarkah') the B-Rune – woman. They also indicate Heaven and Earth, Sky Father and Earth Mother.

16 TYR, the T-Rune – The Spiritual Warrior

The stave shape of TYR ('tire') is that of a spear – a symbol of male power, and of courage, honour and victory. The power of the T-Rune provides a sense of direction, the courage to follow it in an honourable way, and victory over whatever is confronted along the way. It is the power of the masculine principle in Nature, directed along creative paths. It is a power that can cut away what may be hampering or obstructing so that a way is clear to live in harmony with Nature, with oneself, and with others.

Another aspect of this Runic power is that of penetration, for the Rune-stave can be perceived as an upright penis between outspread legs. Conception must take place in order to procreate offspring. The purpose is not only to continue the human race but *to reproduce oneself* – to provide, in due course, another physical vehicle through which the Spirit may continue its journey through matter and further its own cultivation. In order for procreation to be achieved a vital force must be activated – the seed must impregnate the blood of the egg for generation of new life to become possible (a seed is sacrificed in order that the 'greater' Self may perpetuate another 'self' in the future!). Sacrifice is thus very much a characteristic of this Rune. Another facet of this self-sacrifice is a willingness to dethrone the Ego in order that the spiritual self – the True Self – may have predominance. This is why the T-Rune is sometimes associated with the concept of the Spiritual Warrior. A soldier takes orders from another and is thus not fully responsible for the outcome of his actions. A warrior, on the other hand, makes his own decisions and takes full responsibility for his actions. A Spiritual Warrior is not a person who is at war with others; his/her battles are with the 'self' – with the Adversary within, with the Ego! So the TYR is the power to strive for a higher purpose. It is the ability to give up something of value for the greater good of others, and to achieve a long-term improvement in one's own life.

TYR is a supportive power that discerns and separates in order to protect from chaotic forces, so Runic shamans associated it with law and order. It was perceived as a symbol of a column which supports a structure, just as a pillar in a church, temple or meeting hall supports the roof and provides orderly space for assembly. TYR, then, is the power that holds everything up! It is uplifting. It is that which upholds natural and Cosmic Law. It is the power that prevents the Universe from reverting to Chaos!

TYR is the power of singleness of purpose – of clear direction. Traditionally it has been associated with courage, honour, and victory in conflict. However, its true nature is not warlike; it is one of determination, of reaching the mark whatever difficulties may be encountered, but by means that are just. The means are what determine the end and shape its eventual character. So TYR is also a Rune of moral force.

POTENCY: Penetration and precision with consideration
KEY QUALITIES: Determination, single-mindedness, fortitude, tenacity, fair play
PRACTICAL USES: Provides courage in adversity or when facing a difficult situation. Helps to evaluate the price that must be paid to achieve and attain.
CHALLENGE: Have the courage to take responsibility for the consequences of your own choices.

The T-Rune can help you to:

- become more vigilant
- strengthen your reliability and determination
- work more methodically
- face hardships and difficulties with fortitude
- develop greater trust in yourself
- perform your deeds in an honourable way
- have the courage to take responsibility for your own actions

17 BJARKA, the B-Rune – Female Power

BJARKA (pronounced 'be-yarkah') is the feminine power that brings things into existence. It is the power behind the cyclical process of creation, manifestation, growth and disillusionment. It is a power that encloses and contains what is being brought forth; concealing, protecting and nourishing it until it is ready to come into being. It then influences the way it develops. It is this caring and nurturing influence that associates it with fertility. So BJARKA is regarded as the 'mothering' Rune.

The stave shape may be perceived as the firm and inviting breasts of the maiden and the full nourishing breasts of the mother.

BJARKA is the Rune of Rites of Passage – that is, of transition from one state of being to another. It is the power that conveys development through its most critical stages – birth, adolescence, marriage, parenthood, maturity and death. The power of BJARKA is to enable development to take place in accordance with the way it is required to be. Its action is gentle but generous.

BJARKA is related to the concept of the Earth Mother who brings into being, feeds, nurtures and protects. Its power has to do with newness of life and also with new life – that is, a life experience on the Earth as another stage in an individual's Earth Quest. The fullness of the breasts-like stave is an indication that this is a Rune of fertile power and of fruitfulness. But it is not solely a mothering quality; rather, one that is like the relationship between mother and child. It is that nurturing power that is applied to a cherished project in its early stages of development when it is in need of constant attention. It is a quality of 'belonging' and of being cared about, like the protectiveness inherent in a close family relationship.

With this Rune you can alter your life and also your perception of things. It is both a conserver and a renewer of energy, and restores to a state of wholeness and belonging. It thus has inherent within it powerful healing attributes.

POTENCY: Nurturing, maternal energy
KEY QUALITIES: Care and compassion, conservation, protectiveness, ability to form close relationships, blossoming, fruitfulness
PRACTICAL USES: Helpful for focusing on partnerships and close personal relationships, calming the mind when troubled, and nurturing new ideas.
CHALLENGE: Get close to Nature and the natural way of things.

The B-Rune can help you to:

- effect closer relationships
- conserve your energies

- come through a crisis safely
- let go of whatever may be blocking your progress

18 EH, the Eh-Rune – Communication

EH (pronounced 'e' as in 'help') is often associated with Odin's mythical eight-legged horse, Sleipner, which carried him to other dimensions of existence. Among ancient Northern peoples, the horse was an honoured and trusted animal because it was a means of travel and transport. Although many writers on the Runes have associated EH with the horse's rider – man – and with the virtues of trust and loyalty, these attributes are not its essential qualities.

The essential power of this Rune is the ability to communicate at different levels of existence. That was the great *gift* that was imparted to human beings in the next sequence in the Creative Scheme. This is partly what the ancient myth was intended to convey – that wisdom is acquired through the ability to communicate at different levels of existence, not just with other human beings, but with animals, plants, rocks and stones and with beings that exist in non-ordinary realities, and with Cosmic intelligences.

Some Runologists have rightly interpreted the horse association as a *pair* of horses – a stallion and a mare – being ridden in harness. This explains the eight legs attributed to Sleipner.

The stave shape can be perceived as two L-Runes, with one reversed upon the other. The stave shape thus suggests an equal partnership – man and a woman 'joined' together in mutual endeavour but without loss of individuality; man not having 'ownership' of the woman, but each as equal partners. Indeed, man is 'incomplete' without woman. Without women the human race would become extinct. Without man, woman could still perpetuate the human race by artificial insemination from sperm banks! The Eh-Rune emphasizes that equal partnership between male and female is the 'natural' order of things. The idea that man is in some way 'superior' is a concept introduced as a means of gaining control and manipulation. The whole of Nature denies the validity of a belief that the Creator is wholly male. 'Everything is Born of Woman' is a Cosmic Law that operates at all levels and in all dimensions. Nothing can come into existence through the male principle alone. That is not a matter of belief but a matter of fact. EH actually emphasizes the need for an equal partnership between male and female that operates not just on a physical level, but on mental and spiritual levels also. It is for each of us to bring the masculine and feminine aspects of our total being into harmony so that we can communicate more fully our spiritual nature. Male dominance actually cuts us off from our true spiritual nature!

The L-Rune, as we shall see, has to do with the flow of Life. The Eh-Rune, through its stave shape, indicates a co-operative and caring partnership between male and female – horse and rider – enabling an equal exchange of energy to take place in a balanced way. A harmonious union of complementary opposites enhances the flow of Life. This is how the Universe 'works' and communicates with itself!

Before our technological age, the horse was a means of communication between individuals, groups of people, and whole communities, and this is what its association with the Eh-Rune implies. EH is the power that makes communication possible at any and all levels. It is thus a carrier of knowledge and a bringer of 'togetherness'.

POTENCY: Dynamic harmony

KEY QUALITIES: Balance and control, communicative skill, adjustment

PRACTICAL USES: Attains harmony and balance, and strengthens bonds of friendship.

CHALLENGE: Keep your balance at all times.

The Eh-Rune can help you to:

- become a more effective communicator
- find more fruitful ways to achieve what you set out to do
- attain a more harmonious relationship with a partner
- find the right balance in any situation
- respect the opposite sex

19 MADR, the M-Rune – Integration

MADR (pronounced 'marder') is an Old Norse word for human and the name of a pagan god who was 'made flesh' – not as a historical event but as a universal fact, because within an individual human being there is that which is divine.

The power of this Rune enables human beings to become 'perfected' – that is, to become more fully integrated within the totality of their own existence. It is a power that can enable you to know about *yourself* – what you are, who you are, and why you are as you are. The M-Rune is thus the power that puts meaning and purpose into your life.

Traditionally, MADR is regarded as the Rune of the family of mankind, but its power is actually that of motivation. It is that which pushes us towards perfection. It is what pulls us towards divinity, whilst at the same time we remain fully human. It might be regarded as the 'seed' of divinity within us seeking external expression, seeking manifestation, seeking to be shared and consumed in a family relationship. It is the power of the divine inherent in the Self, striving to live an ordinary life in a non-ordinary way.

Some writers on the Runes associate the M-Rune with the intellect and with human reason, but actually its Runic power is that which welds the intellect and intuition together. It is a power that brings left- and right-brain activity in harmony with one another in order to serve and guide the Spirit. This is what was symbolized by the two ravens that accompanied Odin and served as his guides – Huginn (representing thought or the activity of the reasoning mind and left-brain activity) and Muninn (representing the intuition and right-brain activity). So MADR is the power that *sharpens* the intellect and *awakens* intuitive abilities and enables them to function in unison.

The stave shape is like two W-Runes joined together ᛗ and suggests co-operative effort as a means of acquiring perfection and fulfilment. It is humankind co-operating with Nature in order to bring the environment into total fulfilment. This is achieved by tending it with loving care so that it can reach its peak of beauty and harmony, rather than exploiting it and polluting it for short-term gain. It is co-operating with others for the benefit of one another. It is co-operating with other life forms – with animals, plants, trees, rocks and mountains – because we are mutually dependent on one another for the maintenance of the environment which we all share.

MADR is the power that strengthens your awareness as a co-creator with Nature and enables you to take control of your own life, through self-knowledge. It is also the cohesive power of family relationships. In other words, it is what bonds members of a family together in kinship.

POTENCY: A striving for perfection

KEY QUALITIES: Motivation, cohesiveness, co-operative endeavour, kinship

PRACTICAL USES: Awakens potential and identifies your special gifts.

CHALLENGE: Get to know *yourself* – the good, the bad and the indifferent – so you can become what you have the potential to be.

The M-Rune can help you to:

- know yourself
- become more fully integrated within yourself

- get your 'act' together
- sharpen your intellect
- awaken your intuitive senses
- strengthen family relationships
- attain a more co-operative attitude toward others

20 LAGU, the L-Rune – Energy Streams

LAGU ('largoo') is the Rune of the Element of Water – that is, primal water, a fluidic power that rises from the Well of the Unconscious and cleanses and refreshes as it flows through all layers of existence, for it is a carrier of the Life-force. It is the power of a potential brought forth into manifestation and actualized. Its emblem is the leek.

LAGU is the power that comes from immersion in an experience. It is like water flowing around you whilst swimming – you are in water and feeling it acutely, yet at the same time are separate from it. You are *in* it but not *of* it.

The traditional meaning of the Nordic word *lagu* is 'lake', meaning body of living water which serves as a 'carrier'. Runic shamans emphasized LAGU's transitional quality, for water was often used anciently to symbolize the transition from life to death, and also from death to rebirth. This was a 'hidden' meaning behind the demonstration of Jesus walking on the waters, as recorded in Christian sacred writings.

POTENCY: The priming of sensitivity
KEY QUALITIES: Fluidic power, cyclic and rhythmic flow, sensitivity of experience

PRACTICAL USES: Helps you to understand your feelings and emotions.
CHALLENGE: 'Listen' to your feelings and learn from the message they have to convey.

The L-Rune can help you to:

- become more adaptable
- increase your sensitivity
- actualize your potentials
- come into harmony with the ebb and flow of the energy-streams of life
- flow with the tide of events

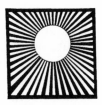

9 Reach for the Stars

THE IMPULSE NOW MOVES from the process of Earthly existence and reaches out towards the eternity and infinity of Spiritual reality.

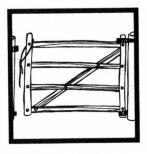

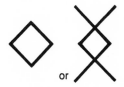

21 ING, the Ing-Rune – Continuity of Life

ING is the power that stores for the future, and is associated with the Soul Body. It is a power that holds on to the essence of what has been fashioned through Earth experience so that it can be brought forth in due course. Its function is similar to that of a seed which is produced by a plant in order to regenerate itself. In the case of a human being it is the storage of information for future life. This is what is implied in the Amerindian saying that you are your own grandfather and grandmother!

So this Rune is associated with descendance and genealogy –

but it is *your* descendants and *your* genealogy that is being fashioned. The continuity of *your* life. *Your* reincarnation!

The Rune-stave indicates an opening in which the seed is stored. The semen contains the seed of life which is contributed by the masculine principle, and the blood of the female principle is that which holds it through gestation so that it can come forth into physical being. So ING is the power that stores potential and holds it until the time is right for it to be released as active energy. Everything in existence undergoes a gestation period before it can be manifested. Similarly, that which seemingly 'dies' and passes out of Earth life, goes not into oblivion but in due course rebirths through a process of re-entry into a source of origin before it can manifest again as a new form.

The alternative stave shape has the appearance of two X-shaped G-Runes, one on top of the other, suggesting a union that results in procreation. The stave shape can also be discerned as the entwining symbol of the DNA molecule which contains within it all the information necessary for the creation of a physical being.

So ING is the power that carries genetic information and confers inherited characteristics to the individual. Physical likenesses and physical attributes are conferred by the parents, whose merging together in the sex act makes it possible for a physical body to be provided as a vehicle for the incoming Spirit. They do not, however, produce the 'person' or individual qualities of the personality. Non-physical qualities are inherited and infused from the individual's past life and previous lives. We – each of us – are quite literally our *own* ancestors. And the essence of the life we are living now will be passed on – through the power of ING – to our next life!

ING also indicates a withdrawal so that progression to another stage of development – to another state of conscious awareness – can take place. The stave shape suggests an opening – an entrance – to another state of being. It indicates, too, an emergence – a coming into a new realization of the enormity of one's own multidimensional being-ness and another stage in evolutionary development.

POTENCY: Access to another reality.
KEY QUALITIES: Gestation, regeneration, continuity, renewal.

PRACTICAL USES: Helpful for exerting influence and strengthening persuasion.

CHALLENGE: Accept your power – your own 'medicine'. Do those things you were 'made' for.

The Ing-Rune can help you to:

- improve your memory
- strengthen faith in yourself
- have hope for the future
- extend your conscious awareness
- open up new areas of self-realization

22 ODAL, the O-Rune – Accomplishment

ODAL (pronounced 'owed-all') establishes boundaries. It is an enclosure that encompasses whatever comes into form and encloses the inherent qualities which determinate nature. It is a power that establishes law in order that liberty can be established in a secure environment. The Nordic word *odal* implies 'right of possession' and the Rune-stave – a combination of the G-Rune ✕ and the Ing-Rune ◇ – indicate the power of acquisition. What is acquired and possessed are the inborn qualities that have been inherited from a *spiritual ancestry* – that is, from past lives that have been lived. It contains within it talents and abilities that are imprinted on the Soul and integrated within the True Self that are rightfully yours!

ODAL is the Rune of accomplishment – of what has been

performed after a persistent process of activity, and safe-guarded so it can be passed on and integrated into the totality of the whole. It is what has been established materially as well as spiritually, and for this reason ODAL has been sometimes related to the home. Indeed the Nazis made use of the O-Rune as a symbol for the home front. In the Northern tradition the homestead was the 'enclosure' in which life and identity sprang!

POTENCY: The power of accomplishment
KEY QUALITIES: Inborn talent, acquisition, accomplishment, security, law and order
PRACTICAL USES: Useful for acquiring property or material goods; encourages practical organization.
CHALLENGE: Don't be afraid to look back, for what has been earned in the past is the seed of future abundance.

The O-Rune can help you to:

- develop the talents you have
- recognize your limitations
- maintain a sense of order
- acquire prosperity
- honour the home environment

23 DAGAZ, the D-Rune – Transformation into the Light

DAGAZ ('dargaz') is the Rune of awakening. It is the power that is in the Dawn and brings new light. It is the Rune of new beginnings based upon past achievement. It is the power that is in the moment of orgasm. It is the power of triumphant victory, the power of ecstatic enlightenment, the realization after long and hard endeavour of 'seeing the Light'. It is the power of what some have called 'cosmic consciousness'. It is seeing reality through the eyes of the Soul!

The word *dagaz* means 'day', but it is 'day' in its entirety of 24 hours, so includes the period of darkness also. Indeed, the stave shape itself suggests that the period of light and the period of darkness are of equal length, with the 'dawn' in the centre. The stave shape may also be perceived as an angular figure of eight on its side – a symbol of infinity and continuity, and also of infinite possibilities. It can also be seen as a bridge and understood as a link between the realm of matter and the realm of Spirit. The D-Rune is the power of coming into aware-ness of the true nature of the Universe, in which light and darkness, matter and Spirit, male and female, and all such 'opposites', are transcended and recognized as complementary aspects of the same Reality.

The stave shape may also be likened to a butterfly to symbol-ize the transformation that occurs when we can crawl out of the cocoon of conditioning that has imprisoned us and held us in 'darkness' so that we cannot perceive what life is about, and gain the freedom to soar into an existence that is full of light and charged with Love and which transcends all that we have experienced so far. It is the power of experiencing the One-ness of existence. It is the power of becoming one with the Spirit – with *your* Spirit. That is the true power of the D-Rune.

DAGAZ is thus the Rune of self-transformation. It is the 'wake-up' Rune. It is the power of completion and also, as in a day, a period of existence. It is the end of a process the moment of triumph, a finishing of what has been incomplete, a success-ful conclusion so that reward can be received.

POTENCY: Ecstatic conclusion
KEY QUALITIES: Transformation, self-fulfilment, completion, one-ness
PRACTICAL USES: Brings about spiritual advancement, and recognition of new beginnings.
CHALLENGE: Don't be afraid to bring things into the light.

The D-Rune can help you to:

- awaken you to a realization of your own true reality
- get in touch with your own Spirit – the essence that is you
- realize the connectedness of all things
- become a good finisher as well as a keen starter

24 FEH, the F-Rune – Fulfilment

With FEH (pronounced 'fe') we reach the fulfilment of Creation – the accomplishment of what was intended to be accomplished. It is the Rune of eternal *becoming*, because although it is at the end of the Rune series, it is *not* the end but a new beginning, for in the circular arrangement of the Runes, FEH comes next to UR. And both have a cow as their emblem!

The power of FEH is the ability to transfer energies. It is the power of exchange. It is the fulfilment of what has gone before so that out of it can be projected the power of a fresh new beginning. It is for this reason that FEH was associated with *movable* wealth – with cattle, which was a means of measuring wealth in a primitive society, and with money, which is circulated wealth in a modern society.

FEH is the power of generated wealth – like sap is to a tree – flowing from its source to be distributed in order to bring the well-being of fruitfulness. Or it might be likened to oil being pumped up from subterranean depths in a rhythmic push-pause motion, and to the milk of a cow which feeds and nourishes others as well as its own kind.

The 'wealth' indicated by FEH is not that of static possession, like money in a bank or owned property. It is wealth put to use and which multiplies through activity and motion. It is power put to use for enrichment and nourishment and which benefits all.

FEH synthesizes the process of birth, life, death and rebirth – a mobile force which flows through it all and which, when it reaches its culmination, is redistributed in another cycle of activity. This Runic power is a conserving of what has been gained and learned through life experience, which is then distributed for use in the next life.

POTENCY: Fulfilment
KEY QUALITIES: Culmination, exchange and distribution, generated wealth
PRACTICAL USES: Useful for ascertaining the true cost of any endeavour.
CHALLENGE: Be sure what it is you want out of life.

The F-Rune can help you to:

- recognize your true wealth
- evaluate the true value of things
- find fulfilment in your endeavours
- bring things to completion satisfactorily
- draw down the power of the Sun, the Moon and the stars into your own personal universe

25 the 'Destiny' Rune – Trust

The blank 'Rune' represents a power that exists outside the organic process of orderly arrangement. This power is some-times referred to as 'destiny', but its meaning is more that of the creativity of the unknown rather than what is 'pre-determined'. The important thing is how one responds to the situation it 'announces'. That is what largely determines the out-come, rather than a decision or choice. Perhaps for this reason it is sometimes referred to as the Odin Rune, because it initiates trust and the courage of faith.

Selecting this Rune is an indication to expect the unexpected, and a confirmation that self-change is working in your life.

The 'traditional' meanings of Runes should not be regarded as absolute. They are helpful *indications* to layers of meaning – nothing more. Applying traditional key words like 'wealth' to FEH, 'travel' to REID, or 'joy' to WYNJA, limits the Runes to interpretations of the analytical mind and subjects them to mental manipulation. This is not the way Runic communication was carried out by the Runester who functioned at deeper levels and brought information through from the inner planes of existence. You have to come to a practical understanding yourself, and that can come only by working with the Runes – as this book is encouraging you to do – and experiencing their potencies for yourself. That is the purpose of the Rune-work Assignments, which are not ends in themselves but a means of *priming* yourself so the Runic powers will flow for you.

Rune-work: Assignment 5 Runic Meditation

Runic meditation is a method of accessing a subconscious aspect of the mind in order to obtain inner knowledge of the Runic powers that exist within both the Universe and our individual selves. It does not entail self-hypnosis, neither is it mediumistic or supernatural. It is simply a way of relaxing the physical body and the mind and slowing down brainwave activity so that an altered state of awareness can be achieved whilst remaining fully awake and alert.

Runic meditation should be performed in a quiet place and at a time when you will be undisturbed. It is advisable to do this form of meditation in a sitting position, with the back firmly supported. A high-back chair is ideal. It is also helpful to sit beside a table or other firm surface where a lighted candle can burn safely in a holder, and where there is room for a note-

book and pen and any other items which in due course may aid
your meditation, such as your Rune-stones. For this early work,
have with you the Rune-stave of a Rune you want to work
with. Follow a sequence if you wish, beginning with UR the
U-Rune and working through to FEH the F-Rune, but work
with only one at a time. It will take perhaps a month or more of
regular meditation to complete the entire 24.

A lighted candle serves as a 'messenger' to your subconscious, indicating that you have made a change from normal
mundane activity and are now 'switched on' to shamanic work.

Close your eyes and in your mind take yourself to a place in
Nature where you have been happy and at ease. It may be a
place you visit regularly or it may be somewhere you went
long ago but has happy memories for you. Just recall it to
mind, remembering the atmosphere which surrounded that
delightful location where you felt happy and content. This
method will calm your mind, release any mental stress, and
help you to attain a tranquil state quickly and effortlessly.

Should you have an itch or feel discomfort in any part of
your body during your meditation period, deal with it by a
gentle scratch or movement of a limb. This is less distracting
than putting up with a demand for attention by the physical
body in a mistaken belief that in some way enduring discomfort is an aid to spirituality. The important thing is to be
comfortable and at ease with your body, your mind and
yourself.

Now, with your eyes still closed, call to mind the Rune. See it
as a glowing blue pattern in front of you like a neon sign.
Examine the lighted shape as if it were a solid object. Whisper
its name several times. Then ask the Rune to reveal to you
something of its nature which will be helpful for you to know
now. Ask for a deep personal insight but don't inject thoughts
of your own into it. Be passive and wait for a response to come
from your inner 'Self' through your subconscious mind. It may
come as words springing up in your mind. If this is your experience, simply let them flow. It may come in the form of a
visionary experience. The Runic shape may disappear to be
replaced by something else. It may be a change of scene. Your
attention may be drawn to an object. An event may unfold
before you. Again, just observe. Watch and listen. Don't
attempt to analyse or interpret what is happening. Just allow

the experience to run its course. You will know intuitively when it is over. Then, open your eyes, take one or two deep breaths, stretch your arms and legs and become fully oriented to the room in which you are sitting. Then make notes of your experience.

Do not be concerned if you found difficulty in visualizing the Rune-stave or disappointed if you had no visionary experience. Your inner senses may need to develop before that happens. At the outset it might be likened to going into a cinema on a bright, sunny day when the programme has already started. At first it may be difficult to find your way to a seat because your eyes are not accustomed to the dimness of the auditorium. In a little while, however, by looking around you from your cinema seat you are able to discern your surroundings quite clearly, even the features of other people watching the movie. Your eyes have become adjusted to the light. It is the same with your inner vision. It, too, may need time to function effectively, so be patient.

In writing notes of your experience have in mind that an important part of this form of Runic meditation is *feeling*. How did you *feel* at each stage of the experience. What kind of feeling was engendered by the words that may have come into your mind or the visual experience you may have encountered. If you inwardly 'saw' and 'heard' nothing, what kind of *feeling* was there?

Compare your experience with indications given in my commentary on that particular Rune. What further understanding has been brought about through this Runic meditation?

When you have completed your session, extinguish the candle flame as an indication that you are switching off from shamanic work and resuming mundane activity.

Later in this book we will examine another form of Runic meditation which can help us to further our experience of working with Runes. Meanwhile, try to find a few minutes each day, or at least a few times each week to devote to this particular Rune-work.

10 Crafting Your Own Runes

HAVING LEARNED SOMETHING OF the nature of the potencies of the Runes, we need now to come to an understanding of how to write them, carve them, colour them and activate them for practical benefit. When Rune-staves are written or carved, physical representations are made of unseen potencies, that is all. In spite of all the mystique attributed to their angular shapes, Runic writing has no power in itself. As with a foreign language that has not been learned, identifying individual letters is of little practical value. Only when their context is comprehended are they activated into a word or words. Similarly, for Runic images to be effective they need to be comprehended and activated, though in a dimension which is outside the range of normal human senses.

So far in this book the Runes have helped us to recognize that the fundamental fabric of Nature is not in manifestation at all. Indeed, it lies beyond even the smallest atoms and molecules, in a state where matter and energy are interchangeable. At that level, before anything begins to become a particle of matter or an impulse of energy, there are invisible fluctuations. It is not even correct to call them vibrations. They are fluctuating processes that at most might be described as 'ghosts' of energy. It is at that subatomic level that the Runes have their origins. This is why I have called the Runes a 'language' of the Universe. The Universe is not in a state of Chaos. Contrary to what some evolutionists have assumed, the powers inherent in Nature are not random forces which, by great coincidences over enormous aeons of Time, have produced an infinite number of species of plants and creatures and, ultimately, the human 'animal'. Intelligence is there. Nature is inherently intelligent. The Universe itself constantly and consistently displays incredible intelligence! Intelligence is defined in dictionaries as 'an ability to think, reason, and to profit from experience'. It is further described as 'the capacity to acquire and apply knowledge'. In other words, inherent in Nature is the presence of Mind. Shamanic understanding of the Runes enables us to comprehend that Nature and the Universe function in accordance with intelligent principles which are the Laws of its own being.

This is another reason why the Runes must be treated with respect and not misused – not because they have occult and 'magickal' properties but because they embrace the very organic nature of the Universe. To misuse them is to tamper with the Laws of the Universe. This is why our motive for working with the Runic process is of paramount importance. I have already indicated in earlier chapters the consequences of using Rune potencies in order to manipulate, subjugate and exert power selfishly out of self-interest, greed or vanity. Our motive should be Love and Harmony – that is, whatever the specific intention and outcome, it should harm no one, bring well-being to all who are touched by it, and create beauty in some way.

So far our purpose has been to familiarize ourselves with the Runic patterns – with each Rune-stave – and to understand something of the nature and character of the Runes collectively and individually. Now we need to come to understand them more deeply as we learn to craft them and thus work with them in a more intimate way.

Rune-staves comprise only two components – a vertical and a diagonal line. The reason for this is not simply so that they can be carved more easily on wood and stone. It is primarily because the Runic fluctuations flow in directional streams – upwards and downwards and outwards and inwards – through the different layers or planes of existence!

Runework: Assignment 6   Drawing the Rune-staves

For practice, draw each Rune-stave outline first in pencil on a piece of graph paper, using the character heading each commentary in Chapters 5–9 as a guide. Then thicken each stroke by drawing over it with a medium felt-tip pen. Use a *blue* felt tip pen. 'Traditionally' Runes have been written in red because that is a colour of Rune magick. For magickal use the Rune-staves were written with the blood of the one who formed them, in the belief that blood contained the Life-force to empower the Runic forms with the supernatural powers that were invoked. It was this practice of using shed blood to activate the Runes that injected fear into the Runes and unleashed unpleasant phenomena. The lifeblood thus offered – usually from a cut on the palm or under the heart area in the chest with a consecrated knife – was in exchange for the power of the Runes in accordance with a statement in the Eddas that 'a gift demands a gift'. However, when the motivation is to cause harm, further 'sacrifice' is engendered, bringing loss of some kind, and even pain and suffering to the instigator.

The colour that was sacred to Odin was not red but *blue*. This was because in ancient symbolism the Life-force itself was not represented as blood but as water! This was to make it clear that life belonged to the Spirit and not to the body. Water – representing the life of the Spirit – was associated with the colour blue. Blue is the colour of the 'Deep' and also of the Sky – in other words, of the 'Space' which contains everything in existence. And blue is a colour associated with truth, wisdom and virtue.

Once you have formed each stave to your satisfaction, write each one again, this time speaking its name as you do so. (The phonetic sound of the name is give at the beginning of each Commentary). To Runic shamans, the sound was important because in the Creative process of the Universe there was movement and sound before there was Life. This is indicated in the sacred writings of the Hebrew people (Genesis 1.1–3) and in the Christian gospels (John 1.1). According to some oral traditions, the Five Elements – which include Aether, the 'hidden' Element, as well as Air, Fire, Water and Earth – were also five primary *sounds*. Sound is dynamic power which has an ability to create and harmonize or to induce chaos and confusion. Sound is defined as a sensation produced in the ear by vibrations of movement in the air. But it is more than that. Everything vibrates, so everything is in movement and therefore has a sound that underlies its essential beingness and distinguishes it from all others.

At one time, among some North American Indian tribes, Polynesian peoples, ancient Chinese, Egyptians, and others, the power of a word was in its *sound*, for its sound was a release of the energy that was the essence of the word as a thought-form. Vowel sounds were regarded as the most powerful components because they were understood to resonate with the primary energies of the Universe and with the creative intelligences that maintain and sustain the Earth and all life forms on it. For example, the ancient Hawaiian language, which contained layers of meaning behind each word, was composed of only 12 characters, five of which were vowels. The ancient Hebrew language, on the other hand, was composed *only* of consonants because vowels were considered at one time to be so sacred, with such 'activating' power, that they were too 'holy' to be written! They could only be 'indicated'. Resonance may be defined as the ability of energy to trigger a response. So a word – a power sound – generates a response from the intelligent forces of the Universe.

The Runic shaman used his or her voice to release creative power in accordance with the thought and intention. By this means the potency of the Rune, once activated, could be transferred from a non-physical realm into material existence. The Runic sounds were so powerful that they released energy-patterns that influenced and changed external conditions; they could also banish negativities that conditioned energies had on a person and thus physical ailments. As far as I am aware at the time of writing, this knowledge has been mostly lost. Today few, if any, know the original sounds of all the Runes. They have yet to be reclaimed. Nevertheless, simply speaking the phonetic sound of a Rune can have a positive effect.

You are now ready to begin crafting your set of Rune-stones which you collected in Assignment 4 of this book. This crafting is important because the Runes you make for yourself, if shaped in love, will serve you as your friends and allies for the rest of your life and be far more effective than any you may buy. This is because they will be imbued with your Life-force and your energy and will have been crafted for you personally. We will deal first with Rune-stones and then I shall go on to describe how you can craft a set using wood or other materials.

Rune-work: Assignment 7 Crafting Your Rune-stones

You will need the following materials to complete your set of Rune-stones.

- a soft pencil
- a watercolour painting brush
- blue enamel paint (miniature tin)
- clear varnish (a miniature tin from a craft shop)
- white spirit for cleaning brush
- cocktail sticks
- tissues

Choose a place to work where your stones and the materials can be left safely for a few days as this work cannot be completed in a single session. On each occasion light a candle before you begin. The candle flame serves as an on-off switch when shamanic work is undertaken. It is also a powerful symbol of the living Light that is within you – the inner light of your Spirit and the illumination which you seek. It also serves as a reminder of the Greater Light that is at the Source of the Universe. Again, make sure the candle is secure in a holder and is safely located where it will not be a fire hazard.

Lay out a sheet or two from an old newspaper to protect your working surface and have handy all 25 stones you have collected. They should have been thoroughly washed to remove any dirt, grease or grime.

Cover each stone with a coat of clear varnish, using the watercolour painting brush. This task will need to be completed in two stages to allow the upper surface to dry thoroughly before turning each stone over to varnish the other side. Apply just a little varnish at a time so it covers the surface evenly. If you overload the brush the varnish will run and spoil the finish. You will need to exercise patience by ensuring that the varnish has thoroughly dried on both sides before attempting to apply the paint for the Rune-staves.

The kind of paint best suited for Rune-sets is one that has a strong pigment, is quick drying and permanent. Matt enamel as used for plastic models and sold in miniature tins is both convenient and inexpensive. Do not apply the paint with a painting brush. Use a cocktail stick instead. The sharp end of the stick is simply dipped into the paint and spread gently along the lines of the Rune-stave, which is best outlined first with a pencil. Just a globule of paint is required for each application. Continue carefully in this way until each line of the Rune shape is complete. Remove any excess paint with a tissue. Replace the cocktail stick frequently so you maintain a sharp point for the painting. This task should be carried out with great care and concentration. As you apply each portion of paint, whisper the Rune's name and sense the flow of Runic potency into the stave as the pattern takes shape. Remember, vertical strokes should be made downwards and diagonal lines generally from left to right, but do what feels natural to you.

The 25th stone is the 'destiny' stone and is left blank after varnishing.

Once thoroughly dry, the stones are ready for consecration and I will explain this shortly.

A Rune-set can also be crafted using any natural material such as wood, clay or leather. The most suitable material, however, is wood. Because historically Runes have been associated with trees, wood has always been a preferred material by Runic shamans.

Ash is much favoured because it is said to be the Cosmic Tree or Northern mythology. However, Oak, Hazel and Pine, or any tree that has a special relevance to you personally, is suitable for the wood from which a Rune-set can be fashioned.

If carving your Rune-staves, uniform circular shapes are preferable, and it is best to collect the wood for them from the wild. Take a walk in your garden or woodland with the intention in mind of obtaining a small branch of a tree for the basic material. When crafted, a set of Runes should be containable in your cupped hands, so each needs to be only 3 or 4 centimetres in diameter (little more than an inch) and half a centimetre thick. Bear in mind that by removing a small branch from a tree you are amputating the equivalent of, say, a finger of a human being, so seek the tree's permission before undertaking such a venture. This task must be done with consideration and respect. You will, of course, need the permission also of the owner of the land on which the tree is located.

Before performing the task, tell the tree why you want the wood. That's right, talk to the tree! You are seeking its co-operation and help. It, too, is a living being which has a Spirit – in the case of a tree it is a group Spirit – and it has an awareness of its own existence as you do of yours, though it is a different kind of awareness because a tree is not organized in the same way. A tree has no larynx and no ears, but it has intelligence because it has a Spirit, and your words are attempts to express the intention of your Spirit. When you 'talk' to a tree, it is an attempt to enable your Spirit to communicate with the Spirit intelligence of the tree. To achieve this it is necessary to speak from the 'heart' rather than the intellect. Once communication is established the tree will indicate in some way the most suit-able branch – and even where to make the cut! What is more, the tree will not withdraw its life-energy from the branch as you cut it, so you will have a piece of 'live' wood from which to fashion your Runes and the ever-active support of the tree intelligence whenever you use them.

Take with you a sharp knife or small saw to cut the branch where appropriate or indicated. Heal the wound by rubbing into it a little of your spittle, and thank the tree for its gene-rosity. Also take with you a portion of dried herbs or cornmeal to sprinkle around the base of the tree as a token of your grati-tude and as an offering to the tree. You may also leave a 'token' of yourself with the tree – a lock of hair attached to an appendage in the bark is suitable. Do bear in mind that in Shamanics you never 'take' from Nature. You should always seek permission so that you will receive what you need. And always give something in return so there is a fair exchange of energies. Cut away any twigs that may be growing from the branch so that you carry away only the length of wood you need to slice up later.

An alternative, if you live in a big city, is to purchase a piece of dowelling from a hardware store.

You will need to cut 25 pieces of equal thickness from your branch or dowel. It is best to do this work with a fine-toothed tenon saw or a modelling saw, so the grain of the wood is not scored or damaged. Place the branch firmly in a vice before attempting to saw it. Afterwards, sand the surfaces smooth with fine glasspaper. Each piece should then be carefully varnished before you start to paint. You may need to apply two or more coats of clear varnish to seal each surface so, again, this is work that requires patience for it should not be hurried.

Carving can be done with a craft knife or a Stanley knife, which should be purchased specially for your Rune-crafting work. You will need a firm, clean surface on which to work. A small cutting board is ideal, or a piece of hardboard will do. If you are working on a table or desk, make sure you cover the surface to protect it. The knife itself will need to be consecrated before use. Although the act of consecration is generally associated with religious ritual, it is not necessarily so. Consecration is simply a wilful act of setting apart for special purpose – in this case working with Runes – and is a very ancient tradition that is older than all religions. It incorporates the principle of cleansing, not just for material purity, but also for purity of *intent*.

Let us now consider the act of consecration, not only for the preparation of your knife for Runic carving, but for your entire Rune-set, a talisman, and any object you prepare for yourself or for someone else. It should only be done at a time when you can be undisturbed for a while. You will need to have your candle alight.

Rune-work: Assignment 8 Consecrating Your Runes

Consecration is in four stages. The first is to consecrate through the power of AIR (Mind) and SMOKE (Spirit), and we can do this through a process called *smudging*. Smudging is exposure to the smoke from smouldering herbs or from incense. Smoke from a smudge-stick of sage and sweetgrass is preferable to that of incense for it has a pleasant aroma with none of the supernatural or religious overtones sometimes associated with incense. Smudge-sticks fashioned by native peoples are obtainable from some New Age shops. Use sandlewood incense cones or sticks if you find difficulty in obtaining a smudge-stick.

Use a small earthenware pot in which to rest your smouldering smudge-stick. Sprinkle a little sand in the bottom so when you have completed the smudging the lighted end can be extinguished by pushing it into the sand. The smudge-stick can then be used for future occasions. If you are using an incense cone or stick, ensure that you have a proper container to hold it so that it can burn safely. If you are using a smudge-stick you will need also a feather or piece of card to serve as a fan to keep it smouldering.

Before consecrating the knife, draw some of the smoke towards yourself with your hands as a gesture of your own need for consecration and purification. Gently breathe in some of the smoke so that you have a sense of being immersed in its cleansing qualities.

Then pick up the knife and pass the blade through the smoke several times, turning it over slowly so it becomes thoroughly immersed in the smoke. As you do so, concentrate on your intention of setting the knife apart for the special task of carving Runes.

Having cleansed with smoke, wipe the blade with a tissue and put it down. The second stage is to consecrate through the Element of EARTH. Salt is often used in ritual to represent the essence of Earth because it is used to preserve and to conserve and therefore emphasize these qualities inherent in the Element of Earth when used in consecration. The salt used should be rock salt, which comes from the Earth, and not sea salt. Pour a little into a shallow dish or bowl. Then, in an act of consecration and with your mind focused on the intent, hold the knife just above the dish and sprinkle salt over the blade. Then immerse the blade into the salt in the dish. Wipe the blade on a clean tissue immediately afterwards.

The third stage is consecration through the Element of WATER. Use another shallow bowl or dish to contain a small quantity of water. Preferably use spring water, but if this is not readily available use ordinary tap water. This should be boiled beforehand to purify it, and allowed to cool. Dip the blade into the dish of water so that it is fully immersed and again state your intention silently. Wipe the blade on a piece of clean tissue before the fourth and final stage, which is consecration through the Element of FIRE. You may here use the candle flame as a symbol of the Element of Fire and its great transmuting powers. To consecrate the knife through the Element of Fire, simply pass the blade through the flame several times, rotating it in a clockwise circle as you do so, and again repeating your intention. Afterwards wipe the blade with a clean tissue. You are now ready to begin the carving work.

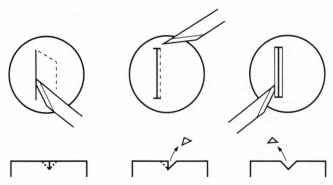

Figure 11 Draw an outline of the Rune-stave with a pencil as a guide for the carving. First cut a centre line down or along each stroke. A horizontal nick at the ends of each line establishes its extent. Then cut an angled slither on each side of the centre line. In this way a v-shaped channel can be fashioned in the wood for the paint

Each Rune should be carved, painted and completed separately, and since this task cannot be hurried, completing your Rune-set may span a number of sessions.

Before you begin to carve, pencil the stave shape onto the piece so you have a clear guide. As you carve each stave, whisper its name and seek to connect with its essential potency. Sense the power that is flowing into the shape and taking tangible form as your knife cuts the channel or channels along which it may flow from the unseen into that which appears. Vertical strokes should be made downwards in three distinct cuts. The *first* cut establishes a centre line. Before cutting the second line, make a horizontal nick at the top and bottom of the centre line to establish its boundary. The *second* line should then be cut slightly to the right of the centre line and at an angle so that a triangular slither of wood can be removed. The *third* line is then cut slightly to the left of the centre line and angled into it so a complementary slither of wood can be removed from that side. In this way a shallow v-shaped channel is cut into the wood. Diagonal lines should be cut in a similar way, mostly from left to right.

Colouring is done by applying paint into the channel with a cocktail stick. As with Rune-stones, the paint should be applied sparingly – a globule at a time, until the channels are filled. Should paint overflow onto the surface, just wipe it off with a tissue. As you apply the paint, whisper the Rune's name. Once each piece is painted, put it aside to dry.

Once all 24 Runes have been carved and painted make sure that the paint has thoroughly dried before applying a final coat of varnish. This will protect the pieces from grease or stains whilst being handled as well as providing them with a smooth and pleasant finish. As with Rune-stones, varnish one side at a time, turning each piece over when the varnish on one side is thoroughly dry.

A third method of crafting is to fashion a set of ceramic Rune-tiles by using Das – a mouldable, putty-like material which is obtainable from most craft shops. This material can be cut into small thin tablets about 3 centimetres long, 2 centimetres wide and half a centimetre thick. The stave shape can easily be engraved on each tablet simply by using the point of a cocktail stick. It can then be coloured, glazed and baked in an oven to produce a hard, porcelain-like product. Consecration can then be performed in accordance with the principles I have just described.

Once crafted, your Rune-set is then ready to be activated. I shall explain this in the next chapter.

Rune-work: Assignment 9 Making a Rune-bag

Now that you have your own set of Runes, you will need something to keep them in and to protect them as they are carried about. Traditionally, Runic shamans kept their Runes in a pouch made from natural material such as linen or leather. Choose a material that is soft and pliable, or chamois leather which is readily obtainable and easily worked. The pouch can be plain and simple or elaborately decorated with embroidered or painted symbols, tassels, or whatever is significant to you. It can be sewn together by machine or by hand.

It should have a drawstring to enable it to be closed and opened. A simple way with chamois leather is to cut a series of slits near the top to allow a thong or cord to be passed through. With a cotton, linen or velvet material, the top edge will need to be turned down to make a hem through which the drawstring can be pulled.

The stitching should be done on the reverse side and as near

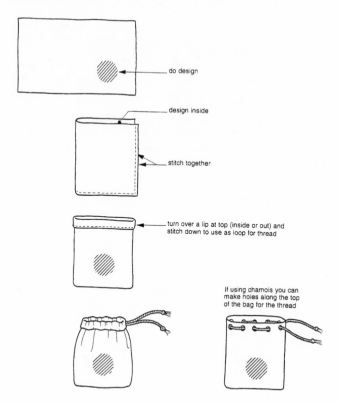

Figure 12 Making your own Rune-bag is quite simple. If you wish you can work in a personal design, a relevant symbol, or even your own monogram, to really personalize your pouch

to the edge as possible. When the sewing of the sides is completed the bag is simply turned inside out. (See *Figure 12*)

Have the Runes in their bag with you as often as possible to begin with. When relaxing, keep the bag and its contents on your lap so it is near your navel region, the centre of your physical being. When you go to bed, put them under your pillow. In this way the Runes will quickly become attuned to your energy-system.

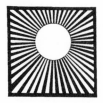

11 Activating the Runes

THERE IS AN ESSENCE INHERENT in the Universe which enables every living thing to experience its own aliveness. An essence may be defined as a vital reality that enables all phenomena to have existence and to *be*. This essence generates activity in every living creature, from elementary amoeba to sophisticated human being, and gives it *life*. Although that essence has defied scientific analysis, different cultures have recognized its existence and, indeed, have different names for it. A Norse name for it was *Megin* ('may-gin') which means 'inner power'. Polynesians and some Native Americans called it *Mana* ('mah-nah') meaning 'miraculous power'. In India it was known by the Sanskrit word *Prana* ('prah-na') meaning 'absolute energy'. In China it was called *Chi* ('chee') meaning 'Life-force', and in Japan *Ki* ('kee') 'vital essence'. Each of these words describes an *aspect* of the same vital essence that activates all living forms yet is itself *not* matter.

The Hawaiian word *Mana* was also understood by kahuna shamans as simply 'the Life-force' – a source of power that enabled them to perform apparently 'miraculous' deeds. The word *kahuna* means 'Keeper of Secrets', and kahuna shamans were guardians of an ancient but hidden knowledge. The title 'Keeper' did not necessarily mean 'to keep out of reach' but rather 'to preserve'. The kahunas preserved the integrity of the ancient wisdom with which they had been entrusted. Similarly, Runic shamans preserved the knowledge they had, sharing it only with specially chosen initiates who had demonstrated that they could be trusted with such awesome knowledge. Knowledge was passed on orally because few could write other than symbols. A peculiarity of the Hawaiian language is that a word may be broken down into component units – or root words – which extend its meaning. The word *Mana*, though comprising only two syllables, contains within it several other words: *Ma, Na, Ana, Maa.* Each of these beneath-the-surface words adds detail to the original meaning of Mana. *Ma* can be understood as 'to entwine' and make 'solid' and also 'by means of,' and *Na* as 'belonging to'. So Mana has the ability to make things *appear*. In other words, *to make the invisible visible. Na* also means 'particle'. A particle of what? A particle of its original source! *Ana* means 'a pattern' and also 'balls of substance that satiate'. So Mana is a cluster of particles of a spiritual essence that satiates what it brings life to. *Maa* means 'breeze' or 'breath' and this carries our comprehension still further.

Mana is a spiritual substance that may be likened to breath, for its primary function is ***movement***.

Although Mana is taken in with the breath, it is not atmospheric substance, the gases contained in the air, or the breath itself. The air and the breath are merely *charged* with it. Charged with the breath of Life! Charged with an energizing force that gives life to every creative thought, and the power that enables such thoughts to manifest in physical reality. Not only the *breath* of **life**, but the *power* of **thought** also! Not a physical *energy* but a spiritual *essence* that has fluidity.

Taoist shamans of China and Tibet knew this same fundamental essence as *Chi*. The word *Chi* not only names the essence but expresses its nature, for Chi is a sound. The sound of Chi reaches beyond audible frequencies for it is the sound of the harmonious vibration of the Universe that reverberates *within*. It is the life-energy of harmony, which is a quality that creates beauty and originates in Love, for it is Love that creates harmony. So Chi is a power of Love.

The motivating essence of Chi is what breathes life into *all* things, linking Spirit with substance, and generating awareness from within because Life itself is manifested *outwards* from within.

Everything has its own Chi, which is the Life-force that is absorbed *into* it. So there is Chi of the Earth, and Chi of the Sun, Chi of the Moon, and Chi of the stars and planets. Trees and plants have their own Chi, as do all creatures that walk, run, crawl, fly or swim, and even the rocks and mountains that stand still. And there is Chi of the Runes. Chi is the connection between all things and all dimensions when your honour the Life-force – the Chi – that is in all things.

That is why motive is of paramount importance. Motive is coupled with desire and generates activity. From a shamanic perspective there are different kinds of desire. There is desire of the *senses*, which is a deep-seated urge for physical gratification. There is desire of the *mind*, which exercises the Will (this is the desire activated by those who work 'magickally'). And there is desire of the *spirit* (the desire activated in a shamanic approach). In Shamanics – a word I have coined to describe the essence of ancient shamanic wisdom adapted for modern times – whatever is done is performed out of loving service in order to restore to wholeness or to retain harmony through co-operation with the powers of Nature. Manipulation and exploitation of natural processes motivated by the self-interest of the Will, by greed, or by egotism, create stress, cause pain, and can even hurt the Soul. It is the cause of division, confusion, unhappiness and misery. An intention is a positive affirmation that prepares a channel through substance along which energy may flow. It specifies not only the *aim* but the *outcome*. An affirmation is a positive statement that reprogrammes the subconscious and frees it from the encumbrance of a previously held belief-pattern. An affirmation pulls energy from an inexhaustible source that is accessible within you.

Shamanic techniques for connecting with the life-energies of Nature remained largely hidden within the oral traditions of tribal peoples. In ancient China exercises to generate Chi developed out of the earlier shamanic knowledge and became known as *Chi Kung* ('Chee Gung'), which means 'life-energy exercises', but these were taught only to dedicated students and supervised by a Chi Kung Master. Chi Kung systems were developed for health, personal development and the martial arts, and today all these systems are openly available.

Humankind has now reached not only the threshold of a new millennium but a critical phase in evolutionary development – an opportunity for human consciousness to expand and bring about an awareness of multidimensional reality. However, the human race in general has lost its way. We have reached a stage where we have never been more powerful at designing our energies in an adverse way. Our technology and science is brilliant – but fatally flawed for the continuation of life on this planet, because it has little or no respect for forms of life other than human, and a declining respect in many ways for human life itself. The Earth is regarded as an inanimate object that has been 'given' to mankind to use in whatever way seems fit or appropriate, rather than as another living being. Humankind has now become a parasite and we must either change our ways by co-operating and seeking harmony with our environment, or bring about the ultimate destruction of the Earth and ourselves. It is not intellectual agreement that is needed, but a change of *heart* and a way of life that will restore harmony. The Runes have an important part to play in this endeavour.

As I have already implied, there are two distinct ways of working with the Runes. One is that of the sorcerer, who uses them for his or her own benefit and empowerment, and sometimes at the expense of others. The other is that of the Runic shamanist who approaches the Runes as a means of coming into harmony and balance with the forces of the Universe and as an aid to personal development and the cultivation of the Spirit that will bring benefit to others also.

The method by which Runes are activated not only determines *what* they do but *why* they do what they do, for the Runic powers are in their totality a law-abiding process with moral and ethical neutrality. It is a process that functions in accordance with what *initiates* it. It 'works' in accordance with the attitude with which it is invoked. In other words, you either generate powers of self-interest or of Love and Harmony. Freya Aswynn, in her book *Leaves of Yggdrasil*, makes it clear that from a magickal viewpoint the Runes are imbued with the power to work in whatever manner is required. The sad fact is that Runic powers have been largely evoked primarily to serve the Ego in satisfaction of the desires of those wishing to employ them. Now, at last, they can be employed to inject the powers of Love and Harmony into the world.

How is this activating attained? By breathing life into the Runes. By 'awakening' potential powers which would otherwise remain dormant. With Chi or Mana. With *your* Chi. Your Mana.

It has long been magickal practice that in order to impart the vital Life-force into the Rune-staves, they should be coloured

red – traditionally from a vegetable dye mixed with blood. With a male Runic magician the blood was usually obtained from a self-inflicted wound – in modern times from just a prick of the thumb, perhaps. With women it was probably menstrual blood. What lies behind this ritualistic practice is a belief that Life is in the blood. It is a mistaken belief because the reality is that Life is in the *spirit*! When a baby is born, its blood is already circulating within its body and taking nourishment and sustenance to each and every cell; but life as a human being does not begin until the baby draws its first breath, and by so doing the Spirit enters the body!

Anciently, it is not blood that has been symbolic of the Life-force but *water*! Whilst blood may be regarded as a vital fluid of the body and *maintains* physical life, it is the Spirit that actually *gives* life. When the Spirit is withdrawn, physical life ceases and the individual is pronounced dead – but there is still blood in that 'dead' body. The Life-force – vital essence – *flows* like water, which is why water perhaps represented as just a wavy line has been symbolic of it. But it *carries* like air! In the natural environment we do not know where air comes from. We cannot determine its source. We can only be aware that it is *there*. We are aware of its *presence*. The Life-force is similar. It is the Life-force that enlivens or 'awakens' Runic powers, not blood. Mistaking blood for the Life-force – the shedding of blood in order to release spiritual powers – is what has released fear and sinister forces into the world. The colour blue should be used, not red. Blue is the colour associated with water and with the sky (air). It is also the colour associated with the Spirit. The blue inner flame of candle light is indicative of the Spirit that 'resides' in the Inner Light of the Soul. Red as a colour is at the lower end of the spectrum and although associated with vitality, it is also related to the grosser passions of physical existence. Blue is a colour at the higher vibratory scale of the spectrum and is associated with the nobler aspects of the Mind and aspirations of the Spirit.

Let me stress again: a set of Runes has no power in itself. Nor will buying a Rune-set and learning certain key words from an instruction book make you a Runester. The Runes need to be activated. Activating the Runes is essentially an act of direct personal involvement, because we are each participants in the 'Dance' of Life and the way the Universe *is*. In so doing we create and experience our own reality. Runic powers have their origin in a dimension that is beyond our Space and Time continuum – in what myths and legends describe as 'the realm of the gods', and their activation fertilizes our own individual consciousness and awakens latent powers of sensory perception that are within us at that level because they are encapsulated in the collective unconscious of the human race.

Rune-work: Assignment 10 'Activating' Your Rune-set

Each Rune-stave you have crafted is activated by holding the piece in the palm of the left hand and curling up the right hand into a cylinder through which the breath can be blown forcefully into the Rune-stave. Each time you breathe in you should have the deliberate intention of taking in the life-energy of Chi. Hold that breath briefly as you place your mouth over the top of the curled hand and concentrate on the name of the Rune, and then blow the breath of life into it. Repeat this action *three* times.

This procedure is repeated for all 24 Runes and for the blank Rune which may be called 'destiny'.

Your Rune-set is now ready for use. By crafting your own set of Runes, consecrating them, and activating them through your own Life-force, they have now become entirely personal to you. So treat them with the care they deserve. To ensure that they can be protected and carried about safely, keep them in a special Rune-bag. A suitable drawstring bag may be obtained from traders who sell native products, but it is preferable to make your own. It requires no special skills.

Rune-work: Assignment 11 Rune-thinking

The first essential in working with the Runes is to get the *feel* of your Rune-set. Take the stones out of their pouch. Hold them in the palms of your hands and focus on the intention of obtaining understanding about their individual qualities. Essentially the Runes have to be *experienced* rather than intellectualized. Then put them down and select each of the 24 Runes in their natural sequence, beginning with UR ᚢ and concluding with FEH ᚠ.

The Runes themselves are not just symbolic patterns but the carriers of information through different layers of existence. Knowledge about the Runes is not just a matter of recognizing a shape, knowing its name, relating to an alphabetical character, and remembering appropriate key words. It is understanding their dynamics.

Examine the pattern of the stave. Familiarize yourself with it. Close your eyes and get the 'feel' of it. As you hold it in your hand, be aware of what thoughts and impressions flow into the mind. Make a note of them, together with any physical sensations and feelings you have.

Do not allow others to handle your Rune-set; the stones will become tainted with their vibrations. Treat them as something 'special' and personal to *you* – which, of course, they are.

12 The Craft of Runic Writing

NOW THAT WE HAVE LEARNED how to form Rune-staves and to awaken dormant potencies, let us now consider the craft of writing Runic texts and inscriptions. Perhaps the simplest form of Runic writing is the use of Runic characters as a code. By simply substituting letters of the common alphabet with a Runic character, a name, message or text can be 'hidden' from all but those who have access to a Runic 'alphabet'. In this way secret messages can be conveyed, and personal jewellery like rings, bracelets and pendants, and shamanic tools like rattles and drums, can be inscribed with the owner's name or with words of particular significance to the user.

Some people have been led to believe that converting letters of the alphabet into Runic characters imparts magickal, mystical or supernatural power to the item. But this is not so. Indeed in Sweden – which has more historical examples of Runic writing than any other country – the vast majority of the 3,500 monuments containing Runic inscriptions have nothing to do with the supernatural or the occult, and no magickal intent initiated them. The stones – some of them quite large and taller than a human being – are simply memorials to perpetuate the memory of a person or persons, or a particular event or achievement. Some are quite plainly boundary markers. Others perpetuate poems or sagas. In his book *The Runes of Sweden*, Professor Sven B F Jansson of the Royal Academy of Letters, History and Antiques, and one of Sweden's leading Runologists, makes this perfectly clear. Indeed, even Runic inscriptions on personal jewellery and ornamental and personal weapons were a means of identifying the owner or, perhaps, to indicate the object's special purpose. No magickal purpose is apparent or implied. One of the oldest pieces of personal jewellery – some 1,700 years old – contains in Runic characters the name 'Unwood'. This is believed to be the name of its owner, for the word apparently means 'calm one' or 'the unfrenzied' and is thus describing something of the nature of the person the piece belonged to. Many of the Runic stones and personal items make use of the 24-character Rune series which was in being before a 16-character series was introduced around 800AD.

So Runic characters can be used to personify appropriate objects and even form a Runic text – by substituting Runic characters for letters of the common alphabet. However, the point I am leading to is that whilst this coded writing was a common practice for many hundreds of years, it is a rather simplistic way of applying a Runic code, and one that drew attention to the Runes. A more sophisticated method did not reveal the Runes but actually hid them from view.

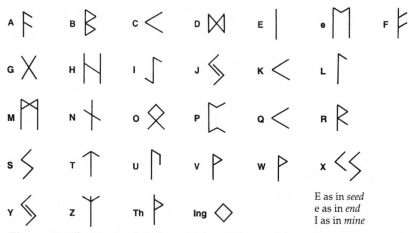

Figure 13 The Runic alphabet which can be used by substituting a runic character for the letter of the alphabet. It should be borne in mind that in some 'traditional' representations ISS is used to indicate the letter 'I' MADR for the letter E, and EOH for 'Ei'

It was partly because of the need or the intention to 'hide' the Runes that the Futhark arrangement was devised (Futhark indicates the first six Runes in the sequence – F ᚠ, U ᚢ, TH ᚦ, A ᚨ, R ᚱ, K ᚲ.

The 24 Runes were arranged in three rows of eight. The first row began with FEH and was named after Freyja, the Norse goddess of love and beauty. The second group was named HAGAL's Eight after the Rune which began it, and the third group was called TYR's Eight after its leading Rune. This division enabled a Runic cypher to be devised, indicating on which of the three rows the intended Runic character appears and its place in that row. A simple binary system was applied by writing a long or a short stave | ı, much as the Taoist shamans of China indicated Yang and Yin by using a solid line and a broken line. In this way no Runic character was actually written, but was simply a series of notches. The long stave indicated the row and the short stave its place in that series.

Another reason for hiding the Runes in this way was not for the purpose of sorcery or to avoid religious persecution, but in recognition that the Runes function at subjective layers of existence beneath the surface of objective reality, and it is there that their work in bringing about changes in the external environment is actually performed. The change from a circular to a linear arrangement, and a switch of places between certain Runes, was sufficient to hide the natural order, even from those who could break the code!

A coded system of writing using Runic characters as a cypher should not, however, be confused with Rune-script. Rune-script is entirely different because it cannot be comprehended merely by substituting Runic characters for letters of the common alphabet. A Rune-script is a group of Rune-staves which indicates the *flow* of Runic energies in order to attain a desired result. It can be written on paper or parchment, or carved in wood. The group is usually limited to no more than five Runes, because longer stave groupings are unwieldy.

A Rune-script is designed to fulfil a particular purpose, and when that purpose is achieved it should then be burned or buried so that any excess power that is retained in the Rune-script can be released back into the Universal 'source' from which it was drawn forth.

The first Rune in a Rune-script should indicate the intention or purpose, and the last Rune should provide an indication of the desired outcome or conclusion. A Rune-script you create for yourself for specific *needs* will be far more effective that copying pre-created Rune-scripts from a book. So I am going to provide only one or two examples, in order that the fundamental principles of how the flow of Runic forces can best be applied can be properly understood. You must take responsibility for devising your own Rune-script to bring about whatever desired changes you want in your life or to help you to resolve certain problems or difficulties.

In the first example, let us say you want to bring about more opportune circumstances in your life so that your abilities may be more readily recognized and your efforts properly rewarded, resulting in greater prosperity. We could begin with DAGAZ ᛞ which is a Rune of gradual change, since we are not seeking a sudden and dramatic influx – which could cause us to lose our balance and bring with it more problems than it might solve – but the kind of change that maintains a steady growth. So we will follow it with EOH ᛇ which is the Rune of growth, and then FEH ᚠ which indicates prosperity. So here, the first three Runes are powers that bring about a prosperous fulfilment through gradual growth and development. In order to sustain that we will add ODAL ᛟ which indicates reward for past efforts and, finally, JARA ᛃ which is the power of continuity. The Rune-script will, therefore, look like this:

ᛞ ᛇ ᚠ ᛟ ᛃ

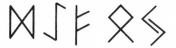

Let us say that you want to improve your vitality so that you can achieve more. In this second example, I am not referring to any health problem for which medical advice should be sought, but rather a lack of the zest for life that goes with achievement. We can begin with SOL ᛊ which is a Rune of vitality, and follow it with TYR ᛏ which is a Rune of success. The third stave could be ALGIZ ᛦ which is a power that 'grounds' energy and protects physically. ING ◇ is the Rune of balance and equilibrium at all levels – mental, emotional and spiritual as well as physical – so we will put that next in order than all our energies find their outlet in practical reality. Finally, we could complete this Rune-script with WYNJA ᚹ which is the Rune of joy – the happiness that springs from achievement. So this is how that Rune-script looks:

ᛊ ᛏ ᛦ ◇ ᚹ

Since the motive for all shamanic work should be one of Love and Harmony, my third example is a Rune-script that will generate these qualities. The obvious Rune for Love and Harmony is GIFU ᚷ because it expresses both these qualities. However, we will precede it with KEN ᚲ which brings out our 'inner' light, for only when our own inner light is enabled to shine forth can the Love that is within us find true expression. We could then bring in ISS ᛁ the Rune that holds things firm and solid, and follow it with FEH ᚠ which is the Rune of fulfilment. The Rune-script could then be completed with WYNJA ᚹ which is the Rune of joy and happiness. This is how that Rune-script looks:

ᚲ ᚷ ᛁ ᚠ ᚹ

These examples provide you with a basis on which to prepare your own Rune-scripts. Once you have clarified an intention, an outcome, and have determined which Runes should constitute your Rune-script, it can be painted on paper, card or parchment, or carved in wood. It should then be consecrated and activated along the lines given in the previous chapter. Then carry it with you or keep it in a special place. Once the desired result is attained, burn or bury it. The Rune-script has done its work. Now we give it back to the Universe.

BIND-RUNES

A Bind-rune is an amalgamation of two or more Rune-staves to form a single, harmonious pattern that incorporates the Runic powers. A Bind-rune can be used as a personal *sigel* – a 'signature' of your own essential energy-expression – which is a distinctive mark that will function on all levels of existence. Like your signature on a cheque or document, it is not only a means of identification but one of authorizing action. Your signature on a cheque authorizes the bank to release from your account whatever sum of money is indicated and give it to the payee. Your signature on a certain kind of document can authorize a bank to release a specific amount of money which it has and to pay it to you. A signature establishes the authenticity of its owner and has the power to authorize action – that is, to release energy. The purpose of a Bind-rune is similar. It authorizes the release of Runic energies in accordance with what is stated on it.

Although a Bind-rune is a blending of Runic characters, each Rune-stave should retain its own individuality. For practical reasons a Bind-rune should be limited to no more than five characters and appear balanced and harmonious. A Bind-rune is devised for a specific purpose. It can be used to generate a particular kind of activity: to protect personal property, to preserve a relationship, and so on. Let us examine some examples.

Say you want to direct Runic energies to protect your personal property – your home, your car, a camera, a briefcase, a purse or wallet, perhaps? Look for a Rune of protection. ALGIZ Ⓨ , for instance, is not only a Rune of protection but it has strong connections with the Earth and what is physical, material and practical. We also require a Rune that indicates a relationship with possessions. ODAL ◇ is not only related to what the inner nature has inherited from the past, but with ownership – with right of possession. So these two Runes combined should make a powerful Bind-rune for the protection of personal property. By merging them together we come up with a Bind-rune that looks like this:

Let us say that you wish to preserve a special relationship that is currently mutually beneficent to both parties. Here I am not referring solely to a marital or sexual relationship. ISS | is a Rune that not only holds or solidifies; its qualities include that of keeping things as they are – of preserving things, like the ice box in a refrigerator. Now we need a Rune that indicates partnerships. GIFU X does that, as it is concerned with bonding and an equal exchange of energies. Combine the two and we have a Bind-rune that looks like this:

My last example is again concerned with down-to-earth practicality. I am involved in writing and teaching and, as with any other occupation, I feel the effort and energies involved are deserving of a just reward. Both REID ᚱ and ASS ᚠ are connected with communication, but ASS is especially related to writing and speaking and with inspiration – creativity with words. Indeed it was sometimes referred to as 'the Rune of poets'. So we will choose ASS ᚠ and bind it with FEH ᚠ which has to do with fulfilment, wealth and well-being. Merging these two Runes together, however, present a shape that does not appear balanced and harmonious.

But by inverting the F-Rune so that it faces in the other direction we are presented with an interesting and balanced Bind-rune that looks like this:

As this example indicates, in a Bind-rune, a Rune-stave can be written facing in either direction or inverted, in order that a balanced design may be attained. This is possible because the energies are not flowing in a particular direction, as with Rune-script, but are 'contained' in one place, as it were, to become a vortex of energy emanating both outwards and inwards.

We will now consider a third method of Rune-writing.

MONOGRAMS

A monogram is a character form composed of the interwoven initials of a person's names. A Runic monogram is made up of equivalents of the initial alphabetical letters of the forenames and surname *or* the Runic characters of the person's first name or its abbreviation if the individual is known by the shorter version: Pat for Patrick, for instance, Ken for Kenneth, Jo for Josephine, and Tony for Anthony. A Runic monogram is composed like a Bind-rune and similar principles apply.

A monogram, however, has the effect of drawing Runic powers *into* yourself—including those of any 'hidden' Runes that are perceived in the completed Bind-rune. It is not that these Runic powers are *outside* yourself and you have to be connected with somewhere 'out there'. They are *inside*, but dormant at unconscious levels. By devising a monogram in the form of a Bind-rune and consecrating and activating it, you connect with the Runic powers and draw them out, enabling them to find outward expression. Those potential powers are 'there' all the time. They are an expression of what you are. They merely need to be 'awakened' to find fuller expression through your thoughts, deeds and actions.

As with Rune-script and Bind-runes, it is the actual *construction* **of the monogram, followed by its consecration and activation, that 'awakens' those latent energies so they can find positive expression in your life.**

Like your name, they are personal to *you*. They 'belong' to you. They are an essential part of who and what you *are*. Fashioning a Runic monogram in this way unlocks that power. Let us examine some examples.

ANNE: The A-Rune ᚠ combined with the N-Rune ᚾ = ᚠ

JOHN: The J-Rune ᛋ combined with the O-Rune ᛜ and the N-Rune ᚾ = |

PAT: The P-Rune ᚲ combined with the A-Rune ᚠ and the T-Rune ↑ = ᚲ

Rune-work: Assignment 12   Designing Your Monogram

Close examination of the Bind-runes given as examples on pages 127 and 128 reveals the presence of Runes other than the ones with which the Bind-runes were fashioned. These 'hidden' Runes apply additional power to the Runic pattern. For instance, the Bind-rune for preserving a personal relationship ᛉ was fashioned on GIFU ✕ and ISS |, but if we look at the Runic pattern carefully we can see in it three additional Runes – KEN <, indicating insight and understanding, ALGIZ ᛉ which provides not only protection but the quality of practicability, and NAUD ᚾ indicating, perhaps, the partners in a balance relationship, observant of each other's needs.

If you look closely at the Bind-rune for protecting personal valuables you will observe as many as seven 'hidden' Runes in addition to the two 'primary' Runes with which it was fashioned: ALGIZ ᛉ and ODAL ᛜ. There is GIFU ✕, ISS |, NAUD ᚾ, TYR ↑, THURS ᚦ, ASS ᚠ, KEN < and ING◇. Seven 'hidden' Runes load this pattern with power.

So, first, exercise the knowledge you have acquired of the qualities of each Rune and apply it to your understanding of this Bind-rune, and do the same with the other two examples I gave.

Then design your own monogram, first as a Bind-rune of the name by which you are known, or, if it has more than one version (Pat and Patrick or Patricia, Tony and Anthony, Ken and Kenneth, Tom and Thomas, Linda and Belinda, for instance) choose the version you prefer.

When you have established a design that looks pleasing, see if there are any 'hidden' Runes contained in it. Now recognize the qualities that are inherent in each of the Runes that constitute your name. What do they tell you about yourself?

Now form another monogram, this time by converting the initial letters of your forename and surname into Runic characters. When you are satisfied with your design, examine it for any 'hidden' Rune or Runes and, again, consider the qualities and characteristics inherent in them.

13 The Runic Circle

THE RUNES HAVE BEEN presented traditionally as a linear arrangement – in rows of eights – but this has been primarily for purposes of manipulation and control. They have also been interpreted in accordance with the hierarchical and separatist structures of Western mystical and theological concepts. Originally the Runes were a circular and cyclical process, as in Nature and the Universe, and more akin to the holistic spiritual principles of the Medicine Wheel of Native Americans.

The Medicine Wheel is an ancient shamanic device which recognizes that there is no division between the natural order of things and the unseen intelligences which some regard as 'God', 'gods', or 'goddesses'. The Creative Intelligence was perceived as being *inside* Nature, not *outside* it; not apart from Creation like an inventor and his invention, but actually *in* it with us and evolving with us. This was the relationship that ancient Northern peoples had with their 'gods' before the Christian era. (We will be examining the nature of these 'gods' in Chapter 14.) Through the contact that had been made with North American Indians by Viking and Celtic mariners before the end of the first millennium, travelling shamans were aware of basic Medicine Wheel principles and that the Medicine Wheel itself was a catalyst. The word *medicine* – or, rather, its equivalent in Native American tongues – did not mean a substance taken in sickness to make one well again, but implied *power* or *empowerment*. The word *wheel* had no equivalent in any Native American tongue. The word they used might more accurately be translated as *hoop* – meaning 'a circular container'. In Native American understanding the 'hoop' was a

131

ring or a boundary that put a limit on the unlimited. The 'Sacred Hoop' was a circle of power or empowerment – a Medicine Wheel.

The great mariners of the Northern peoples were the Vikings and the Celts, who crossed the seas and established settlements on the North American continent long before Columbus 'discovered' the land he mistakenly believed was India! Stone structures unearthed by archaeologists in eastern North America indicate that these ancient settlers lived peacefully alongside native tribes. Professor Barry Fell of Yale University, a distinguished historian and linguistic, in his book *America BC*, advanced the view that this might have been because of a similarity in their understanding of life.

Like their Native American counterparts in the West, shamans of the indigenous peoples of the North perceived what was seen around them as a circle. A circle may be considered as an energy-field which holds together all that is contained within it. It is a structure whose occupants are part of a cohesive whole whilst still retaining individual identity. It is a vortex of energy whose power is available to each and all.

A shamanic circle is charged with Love to become a healing – that is, a *whole-making* – power, because fundamentally healing is a restoral to wholeness. All work done in and through a shamanic circle is focused through Love so that – as with Creation itself – all work has its beginning *in* Love and is fulfilled *through* Love. A shamanic circle, does not disintegrate but stays in existence to be drawn upon at any time and in any place because it is established in Sacred Space – in a spiritual dimension where the Here and Now exists perpetually. So it is always 'here' whatever the time, and it is always 'there' wherever the place, and exists on the *inside* and not just on the outside.

The 'directions' of a Medicine Wheel mark the apparent daily motion of the Sun, which rises in the East, is at its strongest in the South at noon, and sets in the West at dusk. In the Northern tradition a day began and ended at sunset, not at midnight, and this is why some ancient festivals which celebrated different aspects of the cycle of the year were prefaced with an 'eve' – Christmas *Eve'*, 'New Year's *Eve'* 'May *Eve'*, Halloween (All Hallows *Eve*). Their observance began at sunset and was a prelude to the daylight festivities which began the next morning.

It needs to be recognized that Christianity, which supplanted the Nature religions of the Northern peoples a thousand years ago, introduced a mythology based upon concepts of supernaturalism and an obsession with so-called miracles. Northern customs were merged by Christian missionaries into the new faith, creating festivals such as Yule (Christmas) and Easter, both of which were foreign to the Jewish tradition out of which Christianity arose. The historical Jesus, for instance, was not born in the midst of winter on Christmas Day but in the autumn at the time of the Jewish New Year, which was an occasion for family celebration and an appropriate time for the Roman authorities to conduct a census of the population. Ancient Northern festivals were embraced into Christian customs not only to win adherents of the 'old religion' but also to confuse heathen beliefs.

The Runes were associated with the hours of the day by Runic shamans because, according to an oral tradition, this is how they were revealed to Odin – one at a time over a 24-hour period. The Runic hours were not clock hours of 60 minutes' duration, for Runic hours divided the day and the night into 12 periods, from sunrise to sunset and from sunset to sunrise. Runic hours thus differ in length according to the time of the year. In winter, for instance, when the period of darkness is longer than the daytime, the 12 Runes of the night will each be longer than the 12 Runes of the day, and in the summer the reverse is so. Only at the period around the Spring and Autumn Equinoxes will the Runic hours be of equal length. The myths do not reveal at what time of the year Odin underwent his experience, but what *is* clear is that the first Rune that appeared was UR ᚢ, which indicated not the beginning of the day but of the night, and is a reason why the Runes acquired a superstitious association with darkness. The 'darkness' was misapplied and linked with evil, whereas it was in fact the 'night-side' of Creation – the *unmanifest* side.

It needs to be recognized that the Runes embrace both light and darkness. Now that does not imply a moral dimension of good and evil, for the light and darkness I am referring to transcends the moral dualism of religious belief and philosophical conjecture. It might better be understood as the manifest and the unmanifest. The Runes are a means of enabling us to 'see' in the dark – that is, to perceive that which is hidden from view

Figure 14 The Runic hours – the 24 Runes associated with the 24 hours of the day and night, in their natural sequence

because it has not yet 'appeared', and to receive the enlightenment of understanding about that which has appeared. The darkness of night has its rightful place in the natural cycle. It is a time for refreshment and the renewal that sleep brings. Consider how difficult life would be if there was perpetual daylight and no twilight, night-time or dawn – no period to wind down and switch off! It is interesting to note that the word 'evil' in Hawaiian is *ino*, which means 'doing intentional harm to someone' – causing deliberate harm with a full understanding of the consequences of such action.

PERTRA, the P-Rune ⊏, appeared to Odin at the period when the Sun was rising from behind the Earth. So the progression of Runic hours was from the west through the north to the east – the 12 hours of the night – and involved the first 12 Runes of the Uthark order. The 12 Runes from EOH, the

Ei-Rune $\int$, to FEH the F-Rune $\not\vdash$, were revealed during the daylight hours because they were related to the manifest side of Creation.

Runic hours wax and wane according to the time of year – night hours are longer in winter and days hours longest in summer. The longer the Runic hour the greater its influence on that portion of the day or night and the stronger the quality of the Rune associated with that period of Time.

In the Northern tradition there were four periods of the day and four of the night. The first period from sunrise was called *Morntide* – the arousing and awakening time which heralded the beginning of a new day. *Daytime* was the period to mid-morning and a time for gentle activity. *Mid-day* was the period from mid-morning until early afternoon and its quality was of increasing strength and sustaining power. The afternoon period was called *Undorne* and was associated with the power of transformation and completion. Early evening was called *Eventide* – a time of group activity and the joyfulness of sharing. *Night-tide* was late evening when the lessons of the day were considered and absorbed. *Midnight* was the period that extended from perhaps 10.30pm to 1.30am and was associated with regeneration. *Uht* was the name given to the early hours whose qualities were stillness and transition – a time for sleep and recuperation.

The circular mandala could also be related to the natural cycle of the year, with the equinoxes – when the length of day and night is the same – forming one axis and the summer and winter solstices of the longest and shortest days forming another. The indigenous peoples of the North and the Native Americans thus shared an identical symbol with which to perceive Time, Space and Direction. The natural divisions of the Sun Wheel, or Medicine Wheel, were commemorated in Northern traditions by eight annual festivals that provided opportunities for the mysteries of birth, life, death and rebirth to be understood in relation to the physical and spiritual cycles of Nature – for human beings were regarded not as *creatures* of Nature but creations through which Nature was ceaselessly working and by which it could be understood. The eightfold division of the circle was, therefore, no mere exercise of the intellect, nor was it arbitrary. It was recognition of natural law – of how Life 'works' – and an essential key to unlocking the mystery of what Life itself is about.

Religious mythology and materialistic science have one thing in common: they have each elevated humankind above other life forms and separated us from them. The Mineral, Plant and Animal Kingdoms do serve humanity but it is in order to teach us things of value and to further the cultivation of our own individuated Spirit. We should honour and respect rather than exploit them, for we have a responsibility in advancing their evolution, too. All the Kingdoms are interrelated and reflect a one-ness with all life. That is why a shamanic perspective regards all members of the Animal, Plant and Mineral Kingdoms as teachers and helpers, each providing ways of honouring our own spiritual nature and understanding our own individual place in physical reality, unravelling the complexities of our own mortality and keeping us connected with the spiritual Source at the centre of our own Circle of Being.

In a circular arrangement, DAGAZ ᛞ and FEH ᚠ are seen to be at the conclusion of the daytime cycle, and JARA ᛃ and PERTRA ᛈ mark the period when night-time is turning into a new dawn. Similarly, in the seasonal cycle, they mark the ending of one phase and herald another. A fuller understanding of the Runes is thus arrived at when they are perceived not in a linear way but as part of a Great Circle in which each and all are potencies which function in an organic and cyclical process along with Nature itself.

The Circle is thus an essential component of Runic work. It defines sacred space – an area set apart for non-ordinary work and from mundane activity. It establishes a boundary so that unwanted, disruptive and chaotic influences can be excluded. It serves as a means of focusing the energies that are being worked with towards a singular purpose. The Circle, however, should be perceived not as a flat, two-dimensional image, but as a shining sphere of light – itself an energy-field. A Circle helps us to establish a sense of direction and to align ourselves in a balanced way because it enables us to establish a position in Time and Space. There is that which is before us and that which is behind. There is that which is to our left and that which is to our right. And there is also that which is above and below.

In ordinary reality the rising Sun helps us to establish the **East** and the principle of new beginnings, like the dawn of a new day. It is the direction from which light first comes so that we can perceive more clearly what is around us. So it is the direction of enlightenment which comes through an extension of the vision. The Sun is at its strongest in the **South** when the day blossoms into its period of greatest activity. The **West** is the direction in which the Sun sets and is thus an indication of the need for us to withdraw into the deeper recesses of our being in order to draw strength from within so we might renew ourselves. The **North** is where the Sun is hidden from view and appears to 'rest'. It is associated with calmness and the absorption of knowledge gained through the experience of the day in order to become recharged for the morrow. **Above** is associated with the fathering and generating power which 'seeds' potential so that it can be brought into manifestation. **Below** is the mothering power that provides substance and feeds, nurtures and protects that which is coming into form. The **Centre** is the point of balance where all powers and qualities are harmonized and held in existence. The Centre is also the place of access to non-ordinary realms that lie beyond the limitation of boundaries and which can be discovered only by going **Within**.

In a Circle one works *inwards* to contain energy and *outwards* to transmit energy. Clockwise movements *concentrate* energy and anti-clockwise movements *banish* and release energy. Solar (Yang) energy spirals *downwards* in a clockwise movement. Earth (Yin) energy spirals *upwards* in an anti-clockwise movement.

When setting up a shamanic Circle with others the first step is to join hands. This is not only a physical expression of individual desire for unity and a sense of being a vital component in an integral Whole (though still retaining one's own individual identity), but it also imprints the relevance of the Circle on the subconscious 'hidden' self of each person. Singing a song of empowerment whilst holding hands helps to bond the Circle. The following power song expresses the caring quality of a Circle and the interdependence and interconnection of all who comprise it.

> I am a Circle
> I am healing you.
> You are a Circle
> You are healing me.
> Unite us. Be one.
> Unite us. Be as One.

There is much spiritual truth in those simple words, which contain 'beneath the surface' a depth of meaning.

We have examined how, before matter comes into being, energy is generated which can be transformed into substance – what is essentially 'spirit' substance becomes physical substance. Runic shamans shared an ancient concept that everything physical was affected by spiritual influences. These influences were called 'Elements' and were understood as intangible Cosmic intelligences which themselves required no body of any kind through which to express their being-ness – and which 'conditioned' substance as it was being formed. These invisible, intelligent powers were, and are, involved in the process of Nature – of natural development.

Let us understand a little more about Nature. As I indicated earlier, Nature is not an object or a characteristic. Nature is the inner character and creative and regulatory process of physical existence. It is a process through which Force is enabled to come into Form, and Form is enabled to revert back to Force. It is a process which allows every living thing to develop in accordance with laws that regulate its own being. When we come into harmony with Nature we align ourselves with the natural flow and movement of the Universe – with the process of continual and perpetual transformation. Transformation itself is also a process – one of construction and destruction. It is a coming and going, a waxing and waning, for the Universe itself is composed of pairs of complementary opposites – active and passive, objective and subjective, positive and negative, masculine and feminine – which correlate and involve each other in the unceasing movement of the spontaneous stream of Life.

Everything in Nature consists of energy. On a physical level this energy manifests as *matter* in a reality of 'appearances'. On a spiritual level it is experienced as *awareness*, which is an expression of divine consciousness. Motivated by Love and towards Harmony, Nature 'supports' us by serving as a catalyst, enabling our consciousness and sensitivity to become elevated to a frequency level where it is possible to receive information previously inaccessible and enabling us to comprehend what was formerly incomprehensible.

There are invisible yet intelligent powers involved in this process of Nature – this natural development. In ancient times they were referred to as Air, Fire, Water and Earth, because their qualities and attributes were similar to physical air, fire, water and earth. But these powers are intangibles. Like Spirit and Mind they cannot be seen or measured, although their existence can be known and their presence can be experienced. These Four Elements condition and maintain everything in physical existence and they achieve this from *within*. So they are *internal*, not external powers. These Four Intelligences were perceived as coming out of the 'Nothing' – which Native Americans called 'Great Mystery', Taoist shamans of China called 'Tao', and Norse shamans called 'Ginnunagap' – and served a Supreme Intelligence called 'Great Spirit'. These Four were the providers of the basic components of the Universe and of Nature itself.

In the symbolism of Northern mythology, the fashioning of the basic components of Nature was likened to the making of a law-abiding new order out of the substance of the body of a primal 'giant' called Ymir. On an infinitely smaller scale, our own human body is fashioned and shaped by unseen intelligent forces within us acting under the direction of a 'spirit' which is the body's 'self' – the intelligence of the physical body. This body 'self' has itself come into existence seemingly out of nothing. Since these intelligences – these spirits of Air, Fire, Water and Earth – seemingly expressed their actions in much the same way as humans, it was possible to relate to them.

These same powers that are in the Universe and the environment that surrounds us were perceived also as being *within ourselves* and an influence on our behaviour. A person in whom the Element of Air predominates is seen to express its elusive qualities and freedom of movement by being constantly busy and active – here, there and everywhere – thoughtful and full of ideas. A person who expresses most the Element of Fire has a fiery temperament and an enthusiastic nature. A person whose life is an expression of his or her feelings is emotional and impulsive is demonstrating the fluidic qualities of the Element of Water. And a person who is practical and down-to-earth is expressing the pragmatic characteristics of the Element of Earth. The Elements thus indicate the qualities that are seeking expression through a human being. The disposition and proportion of all Four Elements within an individual are an indication of *temperament*.

The Runes were regarded as a Cosmic 'language' through which communication at all levels of existence became possible. A linear arrangement of the 24 Runes – which switched FEH ᚠ, the omega, to the beginning of the series, to precede UR ᚢ, the alpha – served also to hide knowledge of the natural sequence and to keep it guarded until a time in human history when it was appropriate for it to be revealed.

Rune-work: Assignment 13   The Tides of Time

The Runic hours of the night begin at sunset, and those of the day start at sunrise. Since the Sun's movement is in an East to West direction and the tides of Time are affected by the tilt of the Earth and the seasons, these hours are not constant and vary depending upon the latitude of the place where you live. To have direct personal and conscious experience of the Runic hours and their effect on the quality of Time, you need therefore to compile your own Time Chart, which will need to be amended on, say, a weekly basis. You can begin this by checking the current sunset and sunrise times in a daily newspaper, or in an almanac or diary which gives these daily times in the country or region in which you live. The period of night-time and day-time varies during the year. Only around the time of the Spring Equinox in late March or the Autumn Equinox in late September is the period of night and day of equal length. Only then are the periods affected by the 12 Runes of the Day of a 60-minute duration. As the period of darkness lengthens during autumn and winter, so does the period covered by each of the 12 'night' Runes, whilst that of the 12 'day' Runes shortens, until they equalize at the Spring Equinox. In spring and summer the 12 Runic periods of the night will shorten and the daytime periods will lengthen until they are of equal length around the time of the Autumn Equinox.

Figure 15 shows how to devise your own Runic Hours Chart. From this you can experience for yourself the changing qualities of Time. The example given was drawn up in England for a week in early October when sunset was at approximately 4.30pm and sunrise at about 7am. So the period of night-time was from 4.30pm to 7am – a total of 14 hours and 30 minutes. As there are 12 Runes of the Night, a Runic hour is arrived at by dividing 14½ hours (870 minutes) by 12. There are thus 12 periods of 72½ minutes duration. The daytime is from 7am to 4.30pm – a total of 9 hours and 30 minutes (570 minutes). Divide this by 12 and a Runic 'hour' works out at just 47½ minutes.

Runes of the Night		*Rules of the Day*	
4.30pm–5.42pm	ᚢ	7am–7.47am	ᛇ
5.42pm–6.55pm	ᚦ	7.47am–8.35am	ᛏ
6.55pm–8.07pm	ᚨ	8.35am–9.23am	ᛊ
8.07pm–9.20pm	ᚱ	9.23am–10.10am	ᛏ
9.20pm–10.32	ᚲ	10.10am–10.58am	ᛒ
10.32pm–11.45pm	ᚷ	10.58am–11.45am	ᛗ
11.45pm–12.57am	ᚹ	11.45am–12.33pm	ᛗ
12.57am–2.10am	ᚺ	12.33pm–1.20pm	ᛚ
2.10am–3.22am	ᚾ	1.20pm–2.08pm	◇
3.22am–4.53am	ᛁ	2.08pm–2.55pm	ᛉ
4.35am–5.47am	ᛃ	2.55pm–3.43pm	ᛗ
5.47am–7am	ᛈ	3.43pm–4.30pm	ᚠ

Figure 15 A Runic Hours Chart. In preparing this example I dispensed with half-minutes and simply rounded up alternately. The appropriate Runes, in their natural sequence are then applied, starting with UR, the U-Rune ᚢ at sunset and EOH, the Ei-Rune ᛇ at sunrise, concluding with FEH, the F-Rune ᚠ at the final period of the day

This chart should be modified on, say, a weekly basis as the times of sunset and sunrise wax and wane.

The qualities of the appropriate Rune is present in that period of Time. In other words, the Runes are the natural qualities of Time as it unfolds and in its waxing and waning.

Once you have set up a chart you can draw on the power of the appropriate Rune for whatever activity you have in hand or are engaged in. You can also make a point of observing how a Runic potency is affecting a specific duration of Time. Make notes and comparisons of what you conclude and this will help you to further experience the Runic potencies and the qualities of Time for yourself. Indeed, your Tides of Time Chart can have many exciting applications.

Figure 16 The 'directional' arrangement of the Runes in their circular sequence

In the circular arrangement presented in *figure 16*, the Runes are also associated with a Direction, and each Rune influences that Direction with its specific qualities.

In addition to their effect on the hours of the day and night and the seasons of the year, the Runes are also involved in the movements of the Moon – the lunar months, which are the moon-ths of Time as they affect Earth life.

A combination of all these influences has a bearing on the Time period in which we are born. In other words, the qualities inherent in that 'segment' of Time are impressed also on each individual and contribute to his or her inherent personality. The Runes that influence the month of our birth we could call 'Birth' Runes. A Birth Runes Chart is given in *figure 21* on page

204. A detailed analysis of personality traits for each month can be found in my book *Earth Medicine*.

Runework: Assignment 14 A Rune for the Day

An effective way of learning to 'read' the Runes is to study how a Runic power underlies the events of the day.

When you get up in the morning and before the day's activities begin, choose a Rune at random from your Rune-bag. The intention is to discern the character of the day ahead and to obtain guidance in approaching the day's events.

When you have selected a Rune make a note of its characteristics – with the help of this book if necessary. Then close your eyes and ask for words of guidance to come into your mind. Make a note of them in your notebook. Return the Rune to the Rune-bag.

In the evening, again select a Rune at random from the Rune-bag. In choosing an evening Rune the intention is to obtain help in learning what has been gathered from the day's events in furtherance of your well-being. Again, examine the qualities of the Rune selected and apply them to the principal activities of the day. Make notes of what teaching you receive, and return the Rune to its bag.

14 Who and What Are the 'Gods'?

The 'gods' of ancient traditions have been much maligned and misunderstood through religious intolerance and historical ignorance. They were honoured and respected rather than worshipped because they were treated as emanations of a Greater Spirit, not competing adversaries to it. They were perceived as intelligences who, although more powerful than the human intellect, behaved in human-like ways. They were not, therefore, regarded as elusive deities who could only be approached through an intermediary – they were approachable on a direct personal level as a friend, companion or respected one.

It has been suggested that the 'gods' were originally extraterrestrial beings who came to Earth from another galaxy, inhabiting it with physical creatures who were impregnated with the seed of their immortality – part mortal, part immortal – Hu-mans or 'gods'-mans. Children of Star-beings! From such a premise one could conjecture that the 'gods' were simply 'godforms' – dynamic mental images based upon racial memories of space travellers who frequented the Earth in prehistory and impressed upon humankind's Collective Unconscious.

'God-forms' are fashioned in another reality by the collective mind of a group, tribe or culture which ascribes to them superhuman powers and attributes, and gives them expression. Their survival depends upon the worship and sacrifice of their adherents, because the 'god-forms' reflect the nature of the Egos of those who have collectively shaped them and kept them in existence by their beliefs. Without such adoration these forms fashioned from mental substance would simply fade into oblivion.

Whether 'god-forms' or extraterrestrial beings, the 'gods' of the Northern tradition were powerful energy-fields and power centres. To invoke a 'god' was a *practical* act of summoning help from a source of superhuman power in empathy with the human condition. The word *invoke* means 'to call upon' or 'to summon assistance'. Invocation was thus a way of drawing upon specific qualities and abilities for the purpose of personal transformation. For instance, if a Runester required inspiration for a new project, he or she might have invoked Odin, because inspiration is among his principal attributes. If strength and courage were required to face an ordeal, then the 'god' Tyr might have been appropriate. A woman concerned about a relationship might have invoked Freyja, a goddess of sexual love. Such invocations were a means of drawing power from another source and strengthening a quality which was already within the invoker. In other words, an invocation was a method of boosting a power that is within, albeit at an unconscious level. Sorcerers and others went beyond this understanding, seeking through ritual methods to become *possessed* by the 'spirit' they invoked so they could not only be *like* the 'god' but actually assume its personality. To all intents and purposes they *became* the 'god'. But that is *not* what is being advocated here, nor is it to be recommended. We should be wary of any teaching or method, however high-sounding or persuasive, which entices us to abandon our own individual identity, thus allowing another spirit to take possession of our physical being. Not every spirit is benevolent, whatever its guise. Should you ever be troubled in this regard, ask for your heart to be filled with Light and Love. Malevolent spirits do not like the penetrating and illuminating power of Light or the melting radiance of Love.

'God-forms' are endowed with an ability that can be attributed to the mind, because they are a product of the mind.

According to myths, the Northern 'gods' occupy a dimension called *Asgard* – a word which means 'god-realm' or 'enclosure of the gods'. Asgard might be described as a realm of timeless existence – of a continuity uninterrupted by death and rebirth and similar to the *Nagual* of Native American understanding. In the Northern tradition there were classifications of 'gods': some were concerned with the powers of expression – with the mind and the Soul, others were involved in the organic process of growth and development – with physical *form*. Together they co-operated in the cultivation of the Spirit.

The 'gods' might be regarded not as 'god-forms' or celestial beings but as centres of higher energies. This does not deprive them of their influential power but reserves the prospect of greater understanding that may come through an expansion of our own conscious awareness.

Let us consider briefly some of these ancient 'gods' and the qualities which associated them with the Runes.

Principal among them was ODIN, also known as Woden in English and Woten in German. Wednesday – Woden's-day – at the very centre of the week, was named after him. Each of these names was linked to the concept of a 'hidden' source of supreme power and wisdom – an All-Father who seeded, and therefore caused, all that came into manifestation. This is similar to the concept of Great Mystery in Native American cosmology – giving of its own substance in order to bring manifest reality into being – rather than one of belief in a Supreme Being who is outside of Creation and apart from it.

The experience of the shaman Odin on the tree was both a historical event and an allegory. It demonstrated a willingness of the 'self' to give of itself in order to bring about a greater realization. It not only indicated that the giving of the 'self' makes a Greater Self the object of its own self-sacrifice, but illustrated also that the Lesser Self may expand its own aware-ness to comprehend the totality of its own 'greater' being. It is both the inside looking out and the outside looking in to perceive the reality of its own being. The intention of this act was to serve as a model for the evolution – the transformation – that is a possibility for humankind, for it portrays not only a power to reshape the individual in a dynamic process of inte-gration into a Greater Whole, but also a separation of the Greater Whole in order that individuation might be cultivated to enhance the Whole! It is a description of the evolutionary process of transformation in which the Runes play a vital role because they are the very patterns which enable the internal to externalize and extend its own comprehension. The 'gift' to humankind was the expansion of consciousness and self-aware-ness – the gulf that distinguishes human life from other life forms on the Earth – which itself has a capacity to extend to the higher levels or descend to the depths in a transformational process.

In order to transcend death, Odin is said to have sacrificed an eye. According to some writers it was the left eye, but all such accounts were influenced by Christian fundamentalists who attempted to imply something sinister because of a religious superstition that the left betokened evil (in the Middle Ages, left-handed people were considered to be influenced by the Devil!). The left hemisphere of the brain controls the analytical process whilst the right side is concerned with intuitive ability. However, as modern medical science has determined, there is a cross-over point behind the eyes at the forefront of the brain, so the left eye is concerned with the right hemisphere and the right eye with the left brain (see *figure 17*). Odin had to choose between sacrificing analytical or intuitive ability. He chose to sacrifice the *right* eye, which led to increased development of the left eye and intuitive ability. Odin was thus willing to give up something of great value for a higher purpose. The depths of the Unmanifest which the shaman Odin looked down into as he hung on the Tree were the depths of his own being, and in an instant he saw the knowledge that he had sought and made sacrifices for, illuminated by the light of the Spirit.

LEFT LOBE
(Masculine)

Analytical
Logical
Linear
Specific
Time oriented
Verbal language
Judgemental
Beliefs
Logical thinking

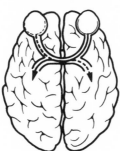

RIGHT LOBE
(Feminine)

Creative
Intuitive
Spatial
Holistic
Timeless
Symbolic language
Non-judgemental
Knowingness
Holistic thinking

Figure 17 The visual fields cross over in the brain. The right visual field goes to the left side, and the left visual field goes to the right side. Comparisons reveal the different qualities and functions of the two sides of the brain

Odin was also portrayed as the wounded healer – a wandering shaman and teacher concerned with the survival of others, guiding them through shifts in conscious awareness. In other words, he was seen as a guide towards the next stage of evolutionary development, who has undergone the experience for himself and knows practical reality at first hand. This, per-haps, is one reason why Odin was sometimes referred to as 'the god of Inspiration' – inspiring through example. Odin himself was clearly on a quest for wisdom, a path which itself is endless.

Inspiration is a quality personified by Odin, so let us examine its relevance to our own personal development. According to dictionary definitions, inspiration is 'an inhaling or drawing in,' and to be inspired is 'to be animated toward creative activity'. To the 'Wise Ones' it was being infused with the Life-giving breath of the Great Spirit, with the Mind illuminated by the Light of the Soul. To be inspired is to be 'fired up'. To be inspired is to be illuminated so that one is enabled to see what previously was not perceived. To be inspired is to become innovative and creative. To be inspired is to become invigorated and energized, because it is a sudden and brilliant influx of energy from the dimension of the Soul, which transcends that of the Mind and the Intellect.

Odin was presented as a master of disguise – a suggestion that spiritual realities are not readily recognized in the mundane world of our everyday experiences. They are about us, but disguised in ordinary things that we often take for granted.

Odin as a 'god' is the power of inspiration, creativity and inner wisdom that works with us through the Soul.

A Rune that is characteristic of Odin is the A-Rune ASS, ᚠ.

In the same way that Odin might be perceived as a power that enables us to see what previously could not be perceived, HEIMDAL ('hame-dall') is the power of hearing what is not spoken and of listening to the 'silent' things that cannot be heard ordinarily. According to the myths, Heimdal committed a sacrificial act which lost him an ear but imbued him with acute hearing, much as Odin lost an eye but became all-seeing. Heimdal was regarded as a mediator between Asgard and Midgard – 'Heaven' and Earth – and a teacher of 'hidden' knowledge. MADR, the M-Rune ᛘ is associated with Heimdal.

TYR is a mythic figure who was the embodiment of justice and the well-being of the community. The day Tuesday was named after him. Tyr is personified as the eternal planner who is able to observe the structure of things and to establish and maintain orderly arrangement through all the realms of existence. He complemented the creative activity of the All-Father with the shaping of forms. Tyr is the power of the rational mind and the ability to reason and make sound judgments.

A Rune associated with this 'god' is TYR, the T-Rune ↑.

THOR – Thursday is named after him – was regarded as the god of War who wielded a mighty hammer. But the strength he actually personified was the power that keeps the forces of Chaos at bay. Thor was said to be the ruler of thunder and lightning – themselves functions of Nature that protect the Earth by clearing away what has gone before and by revitalizing the atmosphere and bringing refreshment and renewal. The hammer was not so much a weapon of aggression as a symbol of masculine, generating power – of work force: the ability to achieve through physical effort and mental application.

Thor is the power of physical force, of steadfastness and loyalty, and the protector from hostile and destructive forces.

A Rune associated with Thor is THURS, the TH-Rune ▶.

FREY – the name means 'Lord' – personified peace, plenty, pleasure and sensual love. He was regarded as a god of this world because he was considered as an earthly provider who ruled the forces of Nature responsible for growth and vegetation. For this reason he was often worshipped as a god of fertility and abundance.

The Rune associated with FREY is ING ◇.

BALDUR – the name means 'Prince' – is the god of Light and enlightenment and was associated with eloquence and joy. Baldur characterizes reconciliation and the power of gentle persuasion. Sunday was dedicated to Baldur and to SOL – the 'shining goddess' – who was a personification of the Sun which, in pre-Christian times, was perceived as female. The Rune associated with Baldur is SOL, the S-Rune ⌇.

FREYJA ('Frey-ah') – the word means 'Lady' – is the name of a goddess to whom the day Friday (Freyja's day) was dedicated. She is the embodiment of feminine attraction and thus the goddess of beauty and sexual pleasure.

A Rune associated with Freyja is GIFU, the G-Rune ✕.

FRIGGA – the name means 'beloved' – is a goddess sometimes confused with Freyja. Frigga was associated with physical love, commitment, marriage, childbirth and children, and with reconciliation – a necessary attribute in domestic affairs.

A Rune associated with Frigga is PERTRA, the P-Rune ⌐.

MANI is a personification of the Moon, which in Norse

mythology is male, and associated with the measurement of Time and the regulation of natural processes. Monday (Moon's-day) was dedicated to Mani. A Rune associated with Mani is NAUD, the N-Rune ⴽ, indicating the necessity of change in the cycle of life.

The NORNS were the embodiment of the process of cause and effect and of evolutionary change, and were depicted in female form. They were regarded as the weavers of Fate rather than its creators, for each individual is largely responsible for the fashioning of his or her own destiny. Although there is a random factor at work, it is the individual's *response* to unexpected change that determines eventual outcome.

The oldest of the three Norns was named URD. The word *Urd* means 'origins' or 'that which has turned', implying that which has originated from past actions. The second was named VERDANDI, meaning 'that which is turning' and governing the present – what has *turned out* from what has gone before. The youngest of the three Norns was named SKULD, which means 'dispenser'. Dispenser of what? Dispenser of the Wyrd. The word *wyrd* (pronounced 'wierd') means 'destiny', or 'that which is destined' – that which is coming into formation out of ever-flowing Time. Skuld was perceived as the weaver of the future, from the threads of what has gone before and is now in being.

In Runic divination the three Norns are associated with the 25th Rune – the Rune of Destiny – which is blank.

Saturday was dedicated to the Norns.

The seven days of the week were dedicated to 'gods' because they indicated qualities of Time associated with their namesake deities. **Monday** was the first day of the Northern week, and its emphasis was on attraction and banishment for the purpose of wealth creation. **Tuesday** was a day for calling upon strength and courage in order to persevere. **Wednesday** emphasized knowledge and the wisdom to be gained from the experience of applying what has been learned. **Thursday** brought out the principle of speculation and of break-through to the culmination of one's efforts, which was embraced by **Friday. Saturday** was the day for reaping rewards of endeavour in refreshment and relaxation. **Sunday** completed the week's end and was a time of healing – of making whole.

A trinity of 'gods' – ODIN, and his two 'brothers' VILI and

VE – were believed to be intelligences that shaped the Universe along organic patterns, similar to that of trees, and who fashioned human beings from the substance of the Earth, impregnating them with the seed of their own divinity. So it was that the human being became a microcosm of the Universe. So it was that a human being has an inner recognition of the 'fatherhood' of divinity. So it is that the realms of the 'gods' and of humanity are inexorably linked. We share the same Wyrd, for by our choices and actions we shape the world in which we live, as they shaped the Universe.

Human beings are individuated spirits who are involved in the process of birth, death and rebirth, and who have taken on physical life on Earth in order to advance individual development and establish immortality through the cultivation of the spirit under the constraints of Time. The 'gods' were understood as spirits also, but ones who had no need to incarnate in physical form.

Whilst we may be wary of becoming the willing and subservient clones of a 'god' who demands obedience and the sacrifice of individual will, the establishment of a partnership with Higher energies, however we may perceive them personally, can further our own individual development.

The 'gods' and 'god-forms' are thus a means of forming relationships with qualities that are eternal. In this way we can raise the level of our awareness by emulating the qualities associated with a particular 'god' or 'god-form'.

The above listing is merely a selection of some of the key characters who figure in Northern mythology, with their principal attributes and Runic connections. It is not intended to be comprehensive.

Forming a relationship with Higher energies was not a matter of belief or an act of faith but, rather, an expression of a desire to come into attunement with a power centre that was able to 'charge' an individual with an input of energy, empowering him or her with qualities that could then be expressed more effectively. The 'gods' were, therefore, not only models of behaviour patterns but a means of enabling the attributes they exemplify to be enhanced in an individual.

A 'god' was invoked to make a connection with a quality that was timeless, and to magnify the power of an intention that was perceived as being in accordance with the characteristics of a particular deity. In other words, invocation was a way of boosting the flow of energy – like kicking the accelerator of a motor car into overdrive so that more fuel is injected into the engine to give the vehicle a boost of power so that it can move ahead more quickly. The action of putting the foot down to activate the overdrive is in accordance with the desire to go faster. In the context of a leading oil company's promotional advertisement it 'invokes' the 'tiger' in your tank!

Rune-work: Assignment 15 Obtaining Runic Help

A Rune-stave is a pattern which conveys that which transcends shapes and yet is an essence from which form is enabled to take shape. Each Rune-stave is a means of relating to a natural potency that is within *you* and the Universe, and is a means of obtaining an inner guidance which transcends the reasoning mind and emotional feelings.

In working with the Runes it is important to do so in a relaxed and harmonious atmosphere as well as in a respectful way. Light a candle, which can serve as your on-off switch and symbolize to your subconscious 'hidden' self that when the candle is alight you are 'switched on' to shamanic work with the Runes and when it is extinguished at the end of a working you revert back to the mundane activities of everyday life.

The commentaries on the Runes in Chapters 5–9 are intended to impart information about their inherent nature and principal qualities, but from a shamanic perspective information is not enough to acquire understanding. Understanding can come only through personal experience. You can come to *know* these potencies for yourself only through a process of *experiencing* them. So you need to strengthen the knowledge you have acquired so far by working *with* the Runes in a co-operative endeavour, for your own personal development and in order to *experience* them. Here's how.

At the end of each commentary I gave indications of how the Rune can help you in your *personal* life. These indications are brought together in the quick-reference chart given on pages 153–6. Cast your eyes over these objectives and choose one that has particular relevance to your life now. I will then describe how to work with the Rune indicated for your choice.

THE RUNES CAN HELP YOU TO:

1 UR
- begin a new project or endeavour
- find the courage to make a fresh start
- feel rejuvenated
- increase your resolve
- be more assertive

2 THURS
- fight against detrimental influences
- clear away lethargy
- strengthen your determination
- break down 'barriers'
- find both the unity and division within things

3 ASS
- obtain inspiration
- discover your 'hidden' potentials
- improve your communication skills
- increase your intake of Chi
- strengthen your mind

4 REID
- gain access to inner wisdom
- come into attunement with your personal rhythms
- extend your awareness
- see things in their proper perspective
- make balanced judgments

5 KEN
- express yourself creatively
- see what needs to be transformed in your life
- turn knowledge into wisdom
- attain clarity of thought
- generate enthusiasm

6 GIFU
- make more effective use of your time
- receive more by giving more
- bond personal relationships
- turn wisdom into understanding
- come into active partnership with your Higher Self

7 WYNJA
- attain a sense of well-being
- strengthen personal relationships
- encourage good fellowship
- build self-esteem
- heal rifts

8   HAGAL
- banish unwanted influences
- develop intuitiveness within a structured framework so it does not get out of control
- clear the air
- focus your intentions
- prepare the way for desired changes in your life

9 NAUD
- cope with stress
- succeed in a crisis
- achieve the seemingly impossible
- break through your limitations
- develop perseverance
- value endurance

10 ISS
- still your mind as an aid to meditation
- concentrate
- create a protective barrier to immobilize harmful intent from whatever quarter
- strengthen your Will
- overcome restlessness

11 JARA
- learn that patience brings rewards
- nurture your creativity
- know the secret of proper timing
- come into harmony with the cycles of Nature
- harmonize your body 'clock'

12 PERTRA
- give birth to your hopes and dreams
- hold on to what is essential to be retained
- experience pleasure
- be aware of your hidden potentials

13 EOH
- liberate yourself from unnecessary fear
- develop within you the quality of endurance
- connect with other levels of reality
- avoid confusion
- release your inner strengths
- receive flashes of enlightenment

14 ALGIZ
- find the powers within you to meet any situation
- ward off negative influences
- connect with an inner drive to achieve more
- keep your ideals and aspirations grounded

15 SOL
- see things as they are
- receive inner guidance to discern more clearly
- boost your energy levels
- attain that 'impossible' dream
- connect with your Soul's purpose

16 TYR
- become more vigilant
- strengthen your reliability
- work more methodically
- face difficulties with fortitude
- develop greater trust in yourself
- have courage to accept responsibility for your own choices and actions
- perform deeds in an honourable way
- allow your 'greater' Self to have more influence in your life

17 BJARKA
- effect closer relations
- nurture what it is you want to bring forth in your life
- conserve your energies
- come through a crisis safely
- let go of what may be blocking your progress

18 EH
- find more fruitful ways of achieving what you set out to do
- attain a more harmonious relationship with your partner
- impart trust and loyalty
- become more balanced in your ways

19 MADR
- become more fully integrated within yourself
- sharpen your intellect
- activate your intuitive senses
- adopt a more co-operative attitude towards Nature and others
- strengthen family relationships

20 LAGU
- become more adaptable
- actualize your potentials
- identify your true feelings
- come into harmony with the ebb and flow of energy-streams of life
- increase your healing powers

21 ING
◇

- strengthen your faith
- renew your hope for the future
- open up new areas of self-realization
- access 'higher' powers

22 ODAL
⬘

- develop the abilities you have
- connect with past lives
- feel more secure

23 DAGAZ
ᛞ

- realize your true Reality
- get in touch with your Spirit
- recognize your connectedness with all things
- become a good 'finisher' as well as a keen 'starter'

24 FEH
ᚠ

- recognize your true wealth
- evaluate the true value of things
- find fulfilment in your endeavours
- bring things to completion satisfactorily
- draw down the power of the Sun, Moon and stars into your own personal 'universe'

At each working, after you have lit your candle, copy the Rune-stave very carefully onto the white paper or card. Draw it about 5–10 centimetres high (2–4 inches). The stave should be formed with the vertical strokes being written downwards and the diagonal strokes usually from left to right, but essentially as feels natural. For instance, the Rune-stave THURS is formed with three strokes:

ASS is also formed with three strokes:

KEN is formed with just two strokes:

You may need to practise writing the stave several times until you are satisfied that its shape and proportions are right. Then place that image in front of you and dispose of whatever else you may have written whilst practising.

Now concentrate your attention on that Rune-stave and couple with it the intention you have chosen from the list. If, for instance, the Rune you are working with is UR ᚢ and you have chosen to seek help to enable you to become more assertive, by focusing your awareness on that stave you are seeking to awaken the Runic potency so that its power is activated and directed into that aspect of your life, enabling you to be more confident and sure of yourself. You don't need to *do* anything. Just be aware of the Rune and your intention. Then let the thought go. If you close your eyes, an image of the Rune-stave should stay with you for some time.

In this tranquil state allow any sensations, visual impressions or feelings to come to you, but don't do anything about them. Just allow them to come, and also to pass. You are merely being attentive and monitoring the result. You may experience a gentle physical sensation – a warm glow, a tingling, or perhaps a coolness. Visual images other than the stave shape may come into your mind, or words silently spoken from a still, small voice within you. You may even experience a 'waking' dream.

After a while you will know intuitively when it has come to a close. When it has, write an account of what you have experienced in your Journal.

Before extinguishing the candle flame, silently thank the Rune for its help. Retain the Rune-stave you have written and worked with. Put it away in a safe place. During the next few days observe if the area of your life that the Rune was working on has changed in any way.

Repeat this Assignment for each of the other Runes, with a different intent. Do not feel pressurized to work with all 24 Runes within a specified time. Shamanic work cannot be organized and performed in quite the same way as most other tasks in our lives, because essentially it is spiritual. Being determined and persistent allows this work to flow naturally and almost effortlessly. *Enjoy it*!

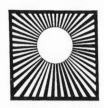

15 An Affinity With Trees

THE RUNIC SHAMANIST RECOGNIZES that human beings have a natural affinity with trees. We humans are structured similarly, with trunk, root and branches, though our 'root' is in the head and our arms and legs are like branches which enable us to stretch forth and to reach upwards. We, too, are shaped from similar organic material – the substance of the Earth who is our 'mother' also.

Within the Northern tradition trees were recognized as fulfilling a vital role in protecting the Earth's environment and maintaining a healthy atmospheric balance, but they were guardians, too, of the spiritual ecology that lies hidden behind the world of appearances. Trees, when respected and honoured, provide access to an inner reality which enables insight to be gained into the workings of Nature and the Universe.

Trees fulfil a vital role in Nature's mechanism for maintaining proper atmospheric balance. Their leaves take carbon dioxide from the surrounding atmosphere to make sugars and starches, and release oxygen into the air. Without trees the atmosphere would become polluted through an excess of carbon dioxide.

Before industrialization, large areas of Britain and northern Europe were covered in vast areas of forest and woodland. At the beginning of the Piscean Age, some 2,000 years ago, 90 per cent of the land surface of the Earth was covered with forest. At the turn of the 20th century only 20 per cent was forest. Today, destruction of the rain forests is affecting the delicate balance between oxygen and carbon dioxide in the atmosphere.

Continuing urbanization and the construction of motorways also have a disruptive effect and contribute to the so-called greenhouse effect.

It is estimated that it takes more than 30 metres of tree to produce the wood and paper products consumed by one individual annually in the most industrialized nations of the world today. Replanting of devastated areas by lumber companies does not restore the balance, because plants of a single species for purely commercial reasons do not provide a balanced ecological system. In Sweden, shamans took me to see vast areas of forest region which had been devastated by tree harvesting. Great swathes in the forest were left burning after the tree felling, with further loss to plant and animal life. The topsoil itself was thus depleted and exposed to erosion.

Chief Seattle, in his message to President of the United States Franklin Pearce in 1854, had this to say before turning tribal lands over to the government: 'All things are connected like the blood which unites one family. Whatever befalls the Earth befalls the sons of the Earth. Man does not weave the Web of Life. Whatever he does to the web he does to himself.'

A tree's growth is circular rather than linear. The culmination of its growth is the flower that produces seeds from which new trees may arise, indicating that an ending is but an opportunity for a new beginning. The roots provide a tree with its anchorage and are the means for it to absorb nutrients from the Earth. The bark protects it from the weather and from intrusion. The inner layer is the growth ring that enables the trunk to grow 'fatter' and to make new bark. Under that inner layer is the sapwood, which conveys the sap produced from the water taken in by the roots to the branches and leaves. At the centre of the trunk is the heartwood which provides the tree with its structural support. Thus trees provide valuable lessons – in how the diversity of life develops from a single seed, or an idea produces an expression of the continuity of change and the necessity of growth – and are thus a source of spiritual wisdom.

A young tree is vibrant and energizing because its strength is derived from its connectedness with the Earth. So it can teach the importance of being grounded in practical reality. A mature tree has grown more extensively for its roots reach down more deeply to provide it with resilience and flexibility. An old tree expresses more of its true essence and the value of its own presence, so it can teach us to esteem our own unique identity and the importance of cultivating the creativity inherent in each of us. In this way we can come to recognize that life's experiences enable us to express our own individual spiritual nature.

The tree as a source of wisdom is depicted in the legends of all cultures and traditions and in the sacred writings of religions. In the Northern tradition the Tree of Yggdrasil symbolized Life, Space, Time and Destiny. In the Bible there is a Tree of Life and a Tree of Knowledge around which mankind first came into a realization of being in control of its own destiny. In the mystical branches of Judaism, the Tree of Sephiroth represents an inner knowing. Buddha received his enlightenment whilst sitting under a bodhi tree. In ancient Britain Druids venerated trees and regarded oak grooves as particularly sacred. Indeed, the word *Druid* means 'men of oak trees'. Native Americans honoured the Spirit of each species of tree because of the special gift it conveyed.

In bygone times in Britain and other parts of northern Europe, outdoor gatherings were held at certain seasonal festivals in a cluster of trees usually situated near a spring or stream. This grove was considered a sacred place where all could be linked together in a common purpose and where people could meditate. The grove provided not only a gathering place but an opportunity to understand the lessons of life that were hidden to most others because, quite simply, 'they could not see the wood for the trees' and could not understand the underlying pattern behind what was seen on the surface of their lives. So a grove indicated hidden knowledge being made available and the sharing of it with others.

Today, humanity generally is largely unaware of such close affinity between trees and humans. Like a tree we each began physical life as a seed which contained within it the totality of our individual potential as a physical being. Like trees, we are nourished from the soil and by the Sun. Like a tree we grow and develop and blossom, and in adulthood we provide shelter and protection for others. And, like trees, we withstand the storms and traumas of life.

The section which follows provides an insight into the

special qualities of trees that are associated with the Runes, and their relationship to the human experience. Trees, and the Runic powers with which they are associated, respond to the motive of Love and Harmony by sharing their power and wisdom with us as we radiate that motive. They come into attunement with our specific intent, which provides the channel along which their qualities can be routed.

When our motive and intent is to come into harmony with Nature and with other life forms, our Soul 'frequency' comes into attunement with the subtle energy-frequencies within Nature. So when we make a connection with a tree we become sensitive to its frequency and 'dialogue' becomes possible. Communication and co-operation with a tree aligns us not only with the qualities inherent within it, but also with the Runic potency with which it is associated. These qualities and potencies resonate with the spiritual essence that is within us, thus enhancing our spiritual development and evolvement at all levels. 'Connecting' with a particular tree species and with its associated Rune also furthers our knowledge and experience of the spiritual ecology.

The human energy-system is surrounded by a force-field which is commonly referred to as the Aura. This Aura consists of several layers, like an onion, which is why some sensitive people and clairvoyants can sometimes perceive it as shimmering colours and tones.

The layer closest to the skin constitutes what I have described in my previous books as the Energic Body, which serves as a mould for the physical body which it interpenetrates.

The next layer, surrounding the Energic Body, is the Mental Body, which I have described in some detail in my book *Where Eagles Fly*. Its vibrations are even more subtle than those of the Energic Body and resonate in accordance with a person's thoughts and emotions.

The outer layer is that of the Soul Body, which is the most subtle of all and resonates to motive and intent, which function beyond physical awareness, and actually colours our actions and thoughts. This outer layer is actually more closely related to our innermost being – the essence that is the Spirit. The hat worn by Runic shamans in Scandinavia with the inside out symbolized that with regard to the totality of our being we ourselves are 'inside out'. Our Soul body, which has faster vibrations and is the vehicle of the innermost Self, is on the 'outside' of our energy-system, and our physical form, the densest and slowest vibratory body, is on the 'inside'. It is through the more subtle energies of the Soul Body that communication with trees becomes possible.

The trees that are linked with the Runes in the following pages are a means of coming into a fuller awareness of the true nature of the Runes, because the qualities of a particular tree are in tune with the qualities of a Runic potency with which they are harmoniously associated. This relationship is a reminder that the abundance of the Universe is there to support us in the quest to discover our true identity and to sustain those qualities which we each bring into the world and are inside us waiting to be released and shared with others.

Tribal groups lived close to the forces of Nature and their lives were entwined with their all-pervading presence. Trees were perceived not only as members of the Plant Kingdom, with their own unique awareness and purpose for being, but also as guardians of other realities which provided an understanding of the greater Whole.

TREES AND THEIR RELATED RUNES

Silver Birch	UR	*Yew*	EOH
Blackthorn	THURS	*Reed*	ALGIZ
Ash	ASS	*Spindle*	SOL
Oak	REID	*Holly*	TYR
Pine	KEN	*Hornbeam*	BJARKA
Elm	GIFU	*Ivy*	EH
Fir	WYNJA	*Vine*	MADR
Rowan	HAGAL	*Willow*	LAGU
Beech	NAUD	*Apple*	ING
Alder	ISS	*Gorse*	ODAL
Hazel	JARA	*Honeysuckle*	DAGAZ
Aspen	PERTRA	*Elder*	FEH

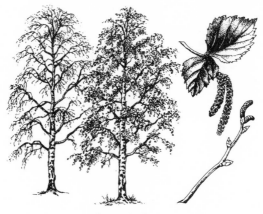

UR

Silver Birch

The Silver Birch (*Betula pendula*) is a slender and graceful tree which grows in profusion in Scandinavia and is regarded there as 'the shaman's pillar', providing access to inner-worlds. The word *birch* is derived from a root which means 'bright, shining, or shimmering', referring not just to the glittering bark but to the tree's inner light. Its resilient wood was often used to make cradles, indicating its protective properties and symbolic of rebirth and new beginnings.

The tree's silvery-white trunk symbolizes purity and clarity, indicating that purity of motive and clarity of intent are essential in any shamanic endeavour.

Like UR, the Rune with which it is associated, the Silver Birch characterizes new beginnings and the upsurge of energy usually associated with things that are fresh and new. It also stresses the need to be free from those things that have now served their purpose and might block progress if they are held onto. Silver Birch and the U-Rune can help to strengthen the image of what is desired and bring into sharp focus the intention. Furthermore, they guard the image from diffusion.

Silver Birch can be a helper in guiding you along the rightful path of your Soul's journey. It can help you to release things that are limiting your progress, teaching you that endings are part of the cycle of growth, and providing you with the stimulus to accept the challenges of a fresh cycle of activity and the opportunity to forge new relationships.

Blackthorn

ᚦ

THURS

The dense and thorny Blackthorn (*Prunus spinosa*) is also known as the sloe tree – its black fruits, which ripen after the first frosts of winter, are often used to make sloe gin, a potent wine. In olden times its branches were used to make staves and for fighting sticks as a protection against attack. So Blackthorn, like THURS with which it is associated, is concerned with the strength to cope with unexpected and sometimes inescapable happenings, and as a help when disruptive influences are at work. It helps also to strengthen the quality of persistence during periods of patient waiting for new opportunities to develop and to reach fruition.

Ash

ᚨ

ASS

The Ash (*Fraxinus excelsior*), with its deep roots and thick, strong branches, was used as a representative of the Cosmic Tree, whose roots penetrated down into the Lower and Under worlds and whose branches reached up into the Upper worlds, thus connecting all realms of existence. So shamans regarded the Ash, like its associated Rune ASS, as a key to understanding the holistic nature of the Universe and comprehending how the physical and the spiritual are connected and how what is 'hidden' in the invisible will come into manifestation and find expression. So the Ash, as with ASS, is a link between the inner and the outer and can teach us how to have a correct relationship with the Earth by being well grounded and practical.

Being in the presence of an Ash tree and meditating on the A-Rune will help to calm the mind and sharpen the awareness so that thought-patterns come more into harmony with your spiritual nature.

Since the wood of the Ash tree is tough and elastic, shamans also associated the tree with the qualities of resilience and endurance.

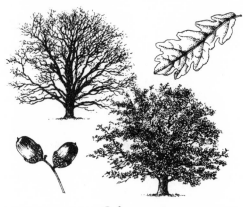

REID

Oak

The sturdy Oak (*Quercus robur*) was regarded in olden days as the king of the forest and as a refuge, and it has long since been associated with strength and durability. As its wood provided timber for sailing ships and wheels, it thus played an important part in travel and the means of conveyance from place to place. Oak was also used for making doors. An Oak tree was often used to mark boundaries, and sometimes appeared on shamanic journeys to indicate the border of another level of existence. It was associated with REID – the Rune of the travelling shaman. Runic shamans thus regarded the Oak and the R-Rune as providers of the strength to fight against the limitations of logic, which can smother our hopes and aspirations, and the courage to go beyond self-imposed boundaries.

Oak is a tree that grows slowly, but its development is sure. So it stresses the importance of not being too hasty, and minimizes the importance of relatively 'small' things, for the mighty Oak itself has grown from a tiny acorn. Oak and REID can thus help you to be expansive and to recognize that the power of achievement is inherent in you, for your greatest resource is yourself, and the connection with the Infinite lies within you.

KEN   *Pine*

The Pine tree (*Pinus sylvestris*) is a tall evergreen which spreads its branches wide and grows sharp needle-like leaves that exhude a sweet and refreshing aroma. Its cones release seeds that are prized by squirrels and birds.

Runic shamans associated the Pine tree with persistent endeavour towards a particular aim – by learning to go beyond 'appearances' and to look for the underlying energies that can open up to clarify our sense of direction and enable a fulfilment of the Soul's purpose. As with the Rune KEN with which it is associated, the Pine tree can help us to value knowledge yet look beyond it by activating our own inner light to obtain understanding, which is the greater prize.

X

GIFU   *Elm*

The Elm (*Ulmus procera*) is a stately and graceful tree whose branches fan out to provide shade and replenishment on hot, sunny days. It was sometimes referred to as 'the tree of trust and compassion'. Trust is a confident reliance on an inexhaustible Source that is contactable within, and an expectation that energy exerted will be returned in full measure through the natural process of giving and receiving. Compassion is a supportive energy that strengthens endurance and projects empathy.

Runic shamans associated the Elm tree with caring – not only in the sense of concern for others, but also of attending to our own personal needs, which is another facet of caring. So the Elm and its associated Rune GIFU can help you to attain balance and equilibrium in your life and a sense of self-esteem, which is a recognition of your own value and need to nurture the light that is within you.

WYNJA

Fir

The Fir tree (*Abies grandis*) is a slender and lofty conifer. Since it thrives in mountainous regions and high places, it is shamanically associated with clear air. It was the original Christmas tree of ancient times and was danced around during Yule-time to evoke tree spirits to impart their gifts. So it is an expression of joy and of WYNJA.

The Fir is the Plant Kingdom's equivalent of the Eagle, and is associated with being rooted to the Earth whilst also seeing distant horizons. Runic shamans considered it to be the protector of distant vision, which helped one to become intuitive of the likely outcome of present and intended actions, and also to broaden one's perspective.

The energies of the Fir tree and its associated Rune can help you to value what you are feeling inside and to trust this inner nature as a means of understanding your own spirituality. The presence of a Fir tree and the carrying of the Rune WYNJA can help you to release emotions that you may be blocking and that are causing rigidity. The Fir and WYNJA help you to let go – to let *be* and find satisfaction.

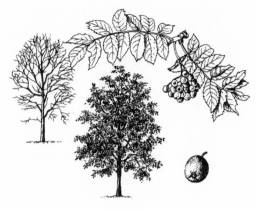

╟ HAGAL

Rowan

The Rowan (*Sorbus aucuparia*), or Mountain Ash, was regarded by Runic shamans as a feminine equivalent of the Ash and therefore a Tree of Life. It radiates a powerful aura and because of this was often planted near a door as a protector of the home. In Scandinavia it is sometimes referred to as 'the Lady of the High Places'. Rune-sticks were often fashioned from the Rowan, which was closely associated with 'whispered secrets'. In ancient Britain it was sometimes called 'the Druid's tree' and related to knowledge and wisdom that comes from 'above' – meaning inspiration derived from the Higher Self.

The red berries of the Rowan have a dimple opposite the stalk which is in the form of a five-pointed star – considered a sign of protection. Rowan teaches you the need to protect yourself from adverse influences and to learn discernment.

Runic shamans associated Rowan with HAGAL because it was considered to be a bridge to the creativity that incites beauty, and because it had an ability to allow what is beautiful in thought, word and deed to flow forth in one's life.

↑ NAUD

Beech

Beech (*Fagus sylvatica*) is associated with food because in olden times its foliage was used as fodder for pigs and other animals. It is also suggestive of knowledge because its fine-grained bark is so smooth that it provided an excellent writing surface. So Beech is indicative of a knowledge that not only feeds the mind but nourishes the Soul.

Runic shamans regarded the Beech as a guardian of ancient wisdom and also as a door that provided access to it – for the person with a questing spirit and with love in the heart. The Beech was regarded as reflective and, like the Rune NAUD with which it is associated, enabled one to learn what one needed to know from an experience and to avoid repeating past mistakes.

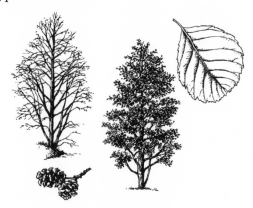

| ISS

Alder

The wood of the Alder (*Alnus glutinosa*) is so oily that is water-resistant. It was used for building bridges and lock gates and for making clogs, whistles and flutes.

The Alder signifies an ability to cross turbulent times with serenity and calmness and, like ISS its associated Rune, imparts the power to avoid being swept away on tides of emotion. The Alder is associated with transformation, indicating that adversity contains within it the opportunity to convert present weaknesses into new strengths.

JARA

Hazel

Shamans used the more pliable branches of the Hazel tree to make dowsing tools, and its thicker branches to fashion wands, which were symbols of authority in olden days. Hazel (*Corylus avellana*), like JARA its associated Rune, stresses an ability to come into attunement with Nature's cyclic changes and to discern its subtle influences. Hazel nuts are symbols of inspiration and wisdom gained through an understanding of the cycles and rhythms of life.

Like JARA, Hazel draws one's attention to the need for taking care of those things over which one has stewardship. The power that is in Hazel is that of balance and the importance of meeting the needs of others as well as fulfilling one's own needs.

Hazel and the JARA teach the value of meditation in the development and direction of creative energies.

PERTRA

Aspen

In olden times the Aspen (*Populus tremula*) was known as 'the trembling tree' because its leaves appeared to quiver in the wind as if they were conversing. So the Aspen encourages you to whisper your own silent thoughts and to express your feelings with a similar gentleness. The Aspen is an expression of collective energy that is both strengthening and protective.

The wood from the Aspen tree was made into shields, indicating that the tree not only resists attack but also strengthens resolve in the face of difficulties. The Aspen is also a symbol of hope – an expression of its quality of encouragement for doing what the heart tells you is right.

EOH

Yew

The Yew (*Taxus baccata*) is associated with longevity and eternal life because it is one of the longest-living trees and can live for well over a thousand years. So it is associated with ancient wisdom, with ancestry, and with reincarnation, indicating continuity in the face of dramatic change. Yews are prominent in graveyards as a reminder that death should be regarded as an advisor rather than an enemy, that every change is a death of what has gone before, and that every death is a transition to a new beginning.

The Yew connects to the past and to things that may have been forgotten or ignored so that the lessons they contain can now be learned and progress furthered as a result.

The Yew tree is associated with the Rune EOH which, like trunk and spine, is the central structure connecting roots to branches, feet and legs to head, Earth to Sky, death to rebirth.

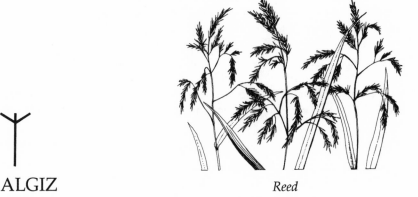

ALGIZ

Reed

Reeds, often man-high, once covered the ancient marshlands and were associated with secretiveness and inner depths because although some trees could be uprooted by strong winds, only the top of the Reed bent and there was little disturbance at water level. So Reed is associated with the strength and endurance that can withstand the storms of life. The stalks of the Reed are hollow and were once used to make wind instruments, especially reed pipes, so Reed is related to the Element of Air, to thought and ideas, and to the vibratory force of the Universe.

The long, straight stalk of the Reed was compared to the shaft of an arrow, which the warrior hunter needed to choose with great care for it had to be as true as his intentions. So Reed teaches the importance of having a sense of direction in life, coupled with a willingness to be flexible and to adjust to change as a protection against being broken through stubbornness and rigidity.

Reed is associated with ALGIZ, a Rune which suggests an inner strength through being rooted firmly in the ground of practical reality whilst adjusting also to change.

SOL

Spindle

The Spindle tree (*Euonymus europaeus*) is small and delicate with a smooth grey bark and tiny white flowers. In the autumn its leaves turn red and it produces pinkish-red fruits which attract the birds and thus spread the seeds. Its wood is hard and was used for making pegs and bobbins and spindles for wood turning, hence its common name.

The Spindle tree is associated not so much with thunder but with the flash of illumination and sudden, vibrant power that can bring out the best in us. It is associated with SOL, a Rune of enlightenment.

Spindle stresses the delight that comes from persistent endeavour and the creativity that stems from within, and honour that results not from obligation or duty but from unselfish service.

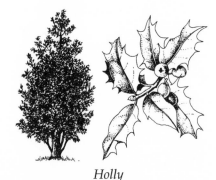

TYR

Holly

Holly (*Ilex aquifolium*) is an evergreen whose leaves are soft in summer and hard with protective spikes in winter, when the tree bears its fruit and is likely to be attacked by browsing animals. In former times its wood was used by some tribes for making spear shafts so, like the Rune TYR, it is associated with the battles of life, with courage, and with eventual victory over malevolent forces.

Holly enhances the qualities of masculine potency and drive. Its qualities are vigour and aggressiveness, direct action and balanced judgment. It stresses the power in the moment – the need to accept the reality that is now, and to learn from it.

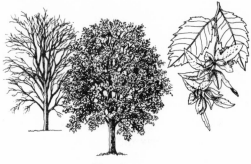

BJARKA

Hornbeam

Hornbeam (*Carpinus betulus*) was once known as 'the great provider' because of its great fertile qualities and inner strength. Its strong, smooth white wood was used in olden times for ox-yokes and the cog-wheels of water mills and windmills. When cut back, its twigs were used for fire lighters. The pale-green vagina-shaped leaves turn brilliant yellow then fade to pale brown in autumn, adding much beauty to a woodland scene.

The tree bears separate male and female catkins. The male catkins droop down and are sometimes referred to as 'lamb's tails', while the much smaller female catkins are set in pairs with red stigmas. These ripen into a nutlet with a papery brown wing which carries the seed in the wind. The nutlet seeds are attractive to birds and squirrels who carry those they fail to eat further afield to produce 'offspring'.

Hornbeam has the resilient qualities of BJARKA with which it is associated and, like a mother who ultimately releases her offspring to find their own way in the world, encourages us to discover and live our own uniqueness for the 'mother' cannot walk our path for us.

Ivy

ᛖ

EH

Ivy (*Hedera helix*) is a tenacious creeper which spirals its way towards the light. It has both a positive and a negative aspect, for it was regarded as an emblem of regeneration and both a bringer of death to some trees. Ivy is female and is frequently paired with Holly, which is male.

Ivy pushes itself between cracks and crevices and is symbolic of soul searching and the way that conscious awareness during shamanic journeys is able to push through the cracks between dimensions of existence so that non-ordinary realities can be experienced. Ivy is associated with forward vision and with perception that goes beyond what is immediately to hand.

Ivy is associated with the EH-Rune, which is concerned with exploration and fresh experiences through which further development can take place. Ivy's energy is that of the wanderer who must impart some of his substance to wherever he passes, and absorb also something of what each place has to impart.

Vine

ᛗ

MADR

The vine (*Vitis*) is an evergreen creeper whose fruits have traditionally been associated with winemaking. Wine is a great relaxer, smoothing out the creases of the day, enhancing what has been consumed and providing a pleasant glow of well-being. These physical characteristics can be applied spiritually to indicate the dissolvement of inhibitions, the stimulation of inspiration, and the satisfaction of achievement. The vine is associated with MADR and teaches the need to dispense with those things that are blocking progress and to draw upon inner resources that will enable you to push forward in all directions.

The vine is an expression of energy that must be trained and its growth pattern is spirallic. It emphasizes the need for proper training and strength of effort in order to grow and develop.

LAGU

Willow

The graceful, water-seeking Willow (*Salix alba*) thrives near lakes and streams and in low-lying areas. In olden times it was associated with the lunar cycles and female rhythms.

Willow emphasizes the importance of receptive and nurturing qualities and of drawing things together into proper balance. Willow furthers the development of the intuitive senses, which is one of the secrets of the Rune LAGU.

ING

Apple

The Apple tree (*Malus pumila*) has figured in the myths and legends of many peoples and has been associated with sexual symbolism and with knowledge and beauty. Spiritual sexuality is concerned with the separation of vital energies and the tremendous force of attraction caused by their urge to merge and to bring into being the beauty of individual expression. At the core of its fruit is a five-pointed star, which anciently symbolized the five primary Elements behind all physical manifestation – Air, Fire, Water, Earth and Aether (or Spirit), and from which the other four are derived. It was the ignorant who were forbidden to eat of the fruit, because it contained the knowledge behind physical existence.

Association of the apple with evil and sin is utter nonsense. In the biblical Adam and Eve myth, neither an apple nor an Apple tree is mentioned or indicated. The concept of sin had no place in shamanic thought. Sinfulness in the sense of defying Cosmic and natural laws is not possible without immediate consequences, and sin in the sense of 'missing the mark' or failing to do what needs to be done can be rectified by the individual. So can the 'sin' of doing something in excess and becoming addictive or disturbing the peace. To the shaman, 'evil' is doing intentional harm to another – and that includes animals, plants and the Earth itself – for such intention is violence against the Life-force itself. According to shamanic understanding, we are each responsible for our own actions and the subsequent consequences, sooner or later, of those actions. The Cosmic law of Karma was understood by shamans not in the moralistic sense of 'what you sow you reap', but as the very nature of life itself. In other words, violence begets violence. What you do to others will be done also to yourself in due course, because experience follows intent.

Shamans associated the Apple tree with making decisions from a number of options, so it became concerned with making right choices. And because the trees were usually cultivated in orchards, they were regarded as being particularly protective and helpful in those areas of human activity where talents and skills need to be carefully nurtured and developed through constant care and persistent practice. So the Apple tree is an aid to concentration, satisfaction and well-being, and is associated with the Rune ING.

ODAL   *Gorse*

The gorse or furze bush (*Ulex europaeus*) was traditionally burned at autumn to rid it of the dry old spines and to promote new growth in the spring. So it is a tree associated with purification and replenishment. Its rich yellow flowers bloom throughout the year and attract the first bees of the year. Their affluence of pollen and nectar is understood shamanically as being indicative of the rich rewards that await the diligent seeker.

Gorse is a tree that protects one's endeavours in gathering the skills and whatever else is necessary to attain a goal. It indicates forthcoming abundance that needs to be shared or distributed fairly and wisely, for if hoarded it will have adverse effects. Its associated Rune is ODAL.

DAGAZ
Honeysuckle

Honeysuckle (*Lonicera periclymenum*), with its entwining branches, was associated with sensuousness and eroticism and the gradual revealing of hidden secrets. It was also an emblem of the labyrinth and of the quest for hidden secrets of the Soul. So Honeysuckle is concerned with finding a way to your own spiritual centre and with enjoying the thrill of the experience as well as its eventual revelation. Its associated Rune is DAGAZ.

Honeysuckle helps to guard against distractions; it can also help you to put passion into your interests and to distinguish what is of true worth. Honeysuckle stresses the Cosmic principle that if a thing *feels* right, then it's okay to do it, so long as no one gets hurt. Life, in the main, is intended to be pleasurable.

FEH
Elder

In the British Isles and northern Europe in former times, the Elderberry tree (*Sambucus nigra*) was associated with fairies, and there was an old wives' tale that if you slept under the branches of an Elderberry tree on Midsummer's Day you might see the King of the Fairies! This was because shamans associated the Elder tree with the spiralling Life-force at a cusp where dimensions merge – like twilight in the daily cycle and Halloween in the yearly cycle. In other words, it indicated where one sequence ended and another was about to begin.

The Elder is a teacher of renewal and helps one to regard endings as opportunities for new beginnings. The Elder indicates the imminent beginning of a new relationship, the culmination of one cycle of activity and the beginning of another. Its associated Rune is FEH.

Since the Runes are closely associated with trees, in extending your knowledge and understanding of them, you will find it helpful to make the effort to visit woodland sites fairly frequently to help your 'inner' learning.

In ancient times trees were venerated because they were recognized as a source of wisdom and understanding. Indeed, woodland glades and groves were often sanctuaries of spiritual learning. Trees that are associated with Runes can help us to understand that although physical growth is expansive – from a 'seed' outwards – spiritual development is *inward*, towards the source at the centre. Spending time among trees in a meditative and receptive frame of mind also helps us to come to an awareness of an unseen spiritual ecology that exists beyond the physical ecology we can see.

Native American shamans recognized two principal realities – physical reality, which some called the *Tonal*, and spiritual reality, which was called the *Nagual*. Runic shamans had a similar understanding regarding a world of matter and a realm of the Spirit, and of how the energy of the Life-force becomes matter in an infinity of forms and how physical form is an expression of divine consciousness. Consciousness, or self-awareness, was understood as the Life-force energy functioning at spiritual level. These two principal realities were not separate but interrelated and interdependent. Recognition of the Runes' association with trees can help us to better understand the nature of physical reality and to comprehend also the reality of the Spirit.

A British physician and bacteriologist, the late Dr Edward Bach (1886–1936), through his recognition that these two realities were interdependent, developed a range of oral remedies based upon his understanding of the healing qualities of certain trees and plants. He considered that physical disorders were caused primarily by a way of life that conflicted with Nature, but that they could be rectified through contact with the Life-force inherent in the natural world. His remedies were prescribed in accordance with a patient's state of mind, whether it was fear, anger, depression, anxiety, lethargy, and so on, rather than with regard to physical symptoms. Bach Remedies, which play a principal role in Complementary Medicine today, treat the unseen psychological causes with the unseen essences of trees or plants.

For instance, among the tree remedies, Red Chestnut was found to be effective for relieving anxiety, Larch for feelings of inadequacy, Gorse for chronic depression, Holly for anger and bitterness, Willow for resentment, and Pine for guilt.

Dr Bach's work has helped in the movement to bring about a greater awareness of the healing powers within Nature. By learning to co-operate with Nature rather than exploit the natural world, we can come to co-operate better with each other.

Rune-work: Assignment 16 Linking with Trees

Visit a location, a woodland or forest, where trees have grown naturally, rather than a garden or park where they have been planted by humans. Take with you a notebook and pen, your bag of Runes, and a packet of mixed herbs (obtainable from any supermarket).

You will notice after even a few minutes of walking among trees that you experience a feeling of relaxation and a clarity of mind. This is not just due to an increase in oxygenation but because of a prevalence of Life-force energy in the natural environment.

Pause to consider the affinity you have with trees. You each take nourishment from the Earth and from the light and air above and around you. You each circulate energy throughout your entire physical structure.

Then allow yourself to be drawn to a particular tree, for then you will be provided with the qualities you need at that moment. Appreciate the tree's shape and the beauty of its form. Talk to it and tell it how beautiful it is. If you find that idea ludicrous and even embarrassing, remember that the tree is 'alive', and although it does not have physical ears like you it does have a spirit – a vital essence – which is contactable by *your* Spirit. The real communication takes place spiritually and telepathically. Just express your feelings *mentally* if that makes you feel more comfortable.

Then move closer to the tree and hold its trunk between your hands. Close your eyes and focus your attention on the soles of your feet. Visualize each foot putting down roots into the ground, like the tree, descending deeply to where subterranean springs can be tapped into to nourish and sustain you. Sense that connection. Experience it.

Breathe in slowly and as you do so experience energy being drawn up from beneath your feet and rising like sap through your legs, into your torso, up through your chest and into your throat and head and reaching a point just above the crown. Pause for a few seconds as you hold your breath and *feel* that energy being suspended there.

As you breathe out slowly, experience that energy jetting out from that point above the crown of your head like a fountain and cascading around your entire body like a gentle waterfall.

Visualize the 'water' as amber light invigorating your entire being and forming a pool by your feet before being absorbed into the ground as you pause before the next in-breath.

Repeat this sequence as you breathe up more of that energy. 'See' globules of golden light cascading around you and penetrating through you before being absorbed into the ground to be filtered and purified.

Continue this sequence of inhaling, pausing, exhaling, and pausing, until you feel invigorated.

Open your eyes and with your hands still grasping the tree trunk ask the tree to give you a personal teaching. Now sit, and with your back supported against the tree trunk, select at random a stave from your Rune-bag.

The teaching is in the Rune. Consider the qualities of that particular Rune. What 'message' has it for you? Write down that message in your notebook.

When you have finished, get up, stretch your limbs and move around for a while so you are grounded back into ordinary reality. Before departing, thank the tree for its help and sprinkle the mixed herbs around the base of the tree as a token of your appreciation. The 'Give-Away' is an important principle in shamanic activity for it demonstrates recognition of the necessity for an equal exchange of energies in order that balance and harmony are maintained. It teaches us the need to *give* as well as to *receive*, for giving and receiving are of equal importance.

In doing this Assignment you will find yourself getting closer to Nature, and thereby getting closer to the Source that we sometimes call God. You don't need a university degree in psychology to enjoy a close personal relationship with another person, nor do you need to become a botanist or a naturalist to get closer to Nature. Getting close to Nature is like getting close to a person you admire or respect. It simply requires spending time with them.

Rune-work: Assignment 17 Rune-work with Trees

Once you have established a link with trees, as in the previous Assignment, you can make further visits, taking with you your Runes, a notebook and pen, and some 'Give-Away' herbs.

During your meditative walk focus on the intention to work with a Runic tree. On this Assignment you are to link with a tree that is associated with a Rune and allow it to connect you with the potency of that Rune and to obtain a teaching on it. For instance, a Silver Birch will extend your understanding or UR Γ, an Oak will help you with REID $\mathcal{R}$, Rowan with HAGAL H, Willow with LAGU Γ, and so on.

As with Assignment 16, stand facing the Runic tree and affirm your affinity with it. Tell it you seek its help in furthering your experience of the Rune with which it is associated.

Take the appropriate Rune from your Rune-bag and hold it in your left hand (your *receiving* hand). Then put your arms around the tree trunk with the Rune clasped firmly in your hand and your forehead resting gently against the tree.

Perform the rhythmic breathing you did on Assignment 16 but this time focus your awareness on experiencing the energy of the Rune in your hand. You may sense energy being drawn up from the ground beneath your feet, or flowing down from above. Again, simply be attentive and receptive.

The 'teaching' can come from the physical sensations you may experience, from mental impressions or thoughts that come into the mind, or from 'feelings' you have, or a combination of these things.

You will know intuitively when the session has come to an end. Then sit with your back to the tree and write notes of what has been experienced and learned.

When you have done this, get up, and in thanking the tree for its help look for an offering from the tree – a leaf perhaps or a twig that has fallen to the ground. Do not take from the tree anything that may damage it in any way. Then perform your 'Give-away' before returning home with your gift.

The gift from the tree will be a further help to you in any meditative work you do with that particular Rune at home.

16 The Cosmos of the Shaman

THE COSMOS MIGHT BE DEFINED as the entirety of existence. It can be experienced only in part, and in different but limited ways, by different beings whose aliveness and state of awareness is determined by the way they are fashioned and organized. So each species of being – whether human, animal, bird, marine creature, extraterrestrial or celestial – perceives life through its own unique awareness, which is limited by the natural laws that determine its existence. The Universe, on the other hand, is a sphere of activity and influence. So whilst there may be many 'universes' there is only one Cosmos.

The Cosmos includes many domains of activity and influence and may be described as a multiverse containing many universes. The Cosmos, therefore, is the Whole, and the Whole is organized into different layers, levels, or planes. These graduations, or 'dimensions', are not only arranged in layers which merge into and penetrate one another, but they also extend outwards and inwards. Furthermore, the Cosmos not only embraces Time and Space, it also transcends them.

The 'Wise Ones' of the ancient Northern peoples represented this multidimensional Cosmos as a Tree. The concept of a Cosmic Tree was shared by visionaries of other races and traditions and was referred to as the 'Tree of Life', the 'Tree of Knowledge' and, in Jewish mysticism, the 'Kabala'. In Scandinavia it was known by the Norse word *Yggdrasil* meaning 'Ygg's steed' or 'Ygg's carrier', but is, perhaps, more meaningfully translated as 'the carrier of *I*'. The Cosmic Tree is thus a multiverse in which the essential *I* – the Spirit – is enabled to explore on its own journey of cultivation and development through the experience of many lifetimes.

The myths, legends and poetic sagas of the Northern peoples, like those of others, were a means of imparting understanding of the way the Cosmos came into being and is structured. They were stories which had been passed from generation to generation by word of mouth long before they were put into writing. The tales that were woven around them might be compared to today's novels, plays, films and television dramas which contain beneath the surface a social message or statement which the author is attempting to convey in an absorbing and entertaining format, engaging the recipient's emotions as well as the mind. In other words, the story itself is a means of conveying an inner message. A problem arises, however, if the fiction is taken as literal truth and the inner truth itself is then misunderstood or not even comprehended. This can also apply to those sacred writings which contain spiritual truths packaged in allegory and symbolism. These truths are not perceived by those who mistake the stories that convey them for literal historical events.

The great quest of Runic shamans in pre-Christian times was that of winning the 'poetic mead'. The poetic mead was considered to be the nectar of the 'gods', enabling those who partook of it to experience a state of inspired consciousness that went beyond the powers of human reason, to access a source of 'higher' wisdom, and to be creative with words. Like an alcoholic drink, it expanded the mind and tapped into a memory bank of hidden knowledge which imparted understanding.

In the Norse myths this nectar was protected by a type of 'giant' – a being of great strength called an *etin*. An etin might be described as a non-evolving being that remains the same as it has always been. This implies that there is an ageless strength guarding this memory bank so that it is neither lost nor diminished – a power that does not change as we do. Although it is 'hidden', this information is neither unknowable nor denied, rather it exists in another state of existence and requires a stimulus to expand the consciousness in order to be reach it. The Eddas – the *poetic* tradition of pre-Christian Scandinavia and on which much interpretation of the Runes in modern times has been based – were compiled in writing between the 9th and 13th centuries. They contain Runic poems which themselves are mythical stories and teachings conveyed orally to an illiterate society to impart knowledge of the mysteries of life and the unseen powers of the Universe, and their relationship to the human condition. Historical knowledge of the myths has been derived mostly from these anonymous poets, who were the professional entertainers of their time. The myths we know today, compiled and retold in the written word of historians, are but the remnant of a past understanding.

Unlike the Creation stories of Middle Eastern traditions, the Norse myths do not present the Universe as having come into existence out of nothing, but suggest that it is a manifestation of what was already *there*. In other words, the Intelligence that fashioned the Universe did so by reshaping what had previously existed but had been in a state that was neither conditioned by the laws of physics nor by duration, which we call 'time'. The Creation message of the myths is that before the Universe came into existence a vital essence occupied cosmic 'Space', but it was unordered and chaotic.

Movement brought about a polarization which divided the essence into two extremes, likened to hot and cold, fire and water – Cosmic Fire and Cosmic Ice – equivalent to the Ying and Yang of Taoist understanding. Between these two polarities, the powers of expansion inherent in one and of attraction inherent in the other, came together and released a great force of energy which became a third influence. This third power was capable of creating unmanifest seed patterns which, when nourished with the appropriate energies and elemental substances, became manifest in an infinity of possibilities and a myriad of forms. This triad of powers which together create, bind together and utilize.

In the Northern myths an androgynous being arose out of the primal substance which formed when the forces of Cosmic Fire and Cosmic Ice met in the Void – the black abyss of Chaos called *Ginnungagap*. The giant was called *Ymir*, a word which means 'roaring sound' and conforms with the understandings of other traditions that in the 'beginning' there was first movement and sound. Creation was thus a natural and organic process which came out of Ginnungagap and divided into expansive energy (Fire) and primal matter and anti-matter (Ice). So manifestation out of primal essence was perceived as taking two principal forms – what we call energy and matter.

Energy and matter are interchangeable and both return to primal essence. Materialistic science did not 'discover' what was known anciently by the visionaries until well into the 20th century!

The slaying of the giant Ymir and the reshaping of his body was an allegory intended to impart an understanding that the Universe was fashioned out of 'living' substance, or essence, into an ordered and evolving structure, patterned like a snowflake and organized like a tree – although centuries ago it may not have been understood that due to the fixed shape of the water molecule, a hexagonal shape is the only crystal arrangement that can be formed. However, no two snowflakes are identical. Runic shamans were well aware of the significance of the hexagonal shape of the snowflake in understanding the structure of the Cosmos.

In the myths four dwarfs were depicted as guardians holding aloft Ymir's skull. What does this symbolize? In ancient times, and to pagan peoples, the skull was not perceived as a sinister object and a grim reminder of death, which is how most of us have been conditioned to regard it. The skull was looked upon as the container of the conscious awareness of the Spirit. It symbolized that when the 'flesh' of the earthly personality no longer 'appeared' to the world, the individuality remained, for it outlived mortal flesh – the 'face' presented to the world. So the skull indicated that behind the outward world of appearances were other realms which could be experienced only from *within*. The Four Guardians of Northern mythology and the Four Spirit 'Keepers' of Native American cosmology were symbolic representations of the powers which connect that which is above – the 'Heavens', or unmanifest Reality – with that which is below – the Earth, or physical reality.

Another interesting point is that the human skull is made up of eight plate-like bones which surround and protect the brain. This is significant because it is a design that is in accordance with the harmonic Law of Octaves. In numerics, the number Eight represented the Law of Cycles and the way things are held together and relate to one another. Eight symbolized the closeness of the relationship between the seen and the unseen, the tangible and untangible. Its form is two circles connecting at a cross-over point where the direction of movement changes from clockwise to counter-clockwise. This cross-over point at the centre of the figure is the point of balance and represents the change in energy-movement where transformation takes place. In Taoist understanding, the Figure of Eight symbolized a coming together in balanced unity of the two complementary polarities – Yin and Yang, Earth and Heaven – in a mutual act of giving and receiving for the purpose of creating beauty and harmony.

Ymir thus represented the crystalized seed that contained within it the collective pattern from which the manifest can take form out of unmanifest forces in accordance with Cosmic order. The Runes were the powers inherent in that process and thus came into being from the *inside* out and, not as has been commonly assumed, as a revelation from the *outside*, or as a product of the human mind. They were unfolded in spherical impulses or complementary pairs in accordance with the Yang and Yin polarities. First came UR and FEH, indicating a beginning and a culmination – the alpha and omega, paired together in a cyclical arrangement, the first and the last, demonstrating that every ending is but another beginning.

Yggdrasil was sometimes represented by the symbol of the snowflake pattern ✳ to indicate that the Cosmos is similarly structured, like a tree with a vertical axis bisected by energy systems orbiting a central pillar. The structure is dynamic for vital force is enabled to flow up the central column and outwards from its source, which is *within*, as sap rises from a tree's roots, circulates out to the branches and furthermost leaves, and is then drawn back to its source for replenishment and renewal. The Cosmos was thus portrayed as a dynamic, interacting infinity of essence and energy.

The snowflake pattern symbolized also that the central point where the planes meet in the 'middle' is one of dramatic change and development. This 'middle' plane was likened to our everyday life on Earth, for Earth is a realm of activity which appears to be our one and only reality. The vertical pillar, however, suggests the possibility of ascending higher – to more sublime levels – or descending lower into a state of living death. Living death is being dead to the nobler aspects of the Spirit. Human beings in that state *are* the living dead!

Yggdrasil thus unlocked the mystery of the Dimensions and helped in the understanding of the real relevance of Earth life and our own existence.

Out of the Great Nothingness – the No-Thing which is without form or duration – arose the single point. This can be understood as perception without measurement of point of view – the 'I' which has infinity of potential before the becoming of qualities. Existence in the 'nothingness' of Space was represented by a single dot or point:

●

The 'aliveness' of the single 'I' generates a resonating pulse which extends the point into a reflection of itself within its own 'substance' to become an 'I Am'. It thus establishes a dimension in space. This dimension has length, but no breadth or height. It was represented by a line, the **First Dimension**:

————

When that which is reflecting or reflected is considered from a 'higher' perspective, a 'surface' is established – a **Second Dimension**, which has length and width but no depth. This was represented anciently as a triangle:

By a shift of the awareness above that of length and width, the reality of a **Third Dimension** comes into being – that of *depth* which provides 'solidity' and form. This was represented by a triangle on a square base and expressed the concept of form arising out of a single point in the 'nothingness' of Space:

The notion of 'distance' introduces a **Fourth Dimension** – that of duration, or what we call Time. Time provides the duration in which form may have duration in manifestation. Physical reality exists within the Four Dimensions yet has the 'appearance' of being on the 'outside'. A symbol of the four Dimensions was a pyramid:

The **Fifth Dimension** is that of the Mind, which is 'outside' matter and has no duration but functions in and through matter and the Dimension of Time. It is through the Mind that choice is exercised.

The **Sixth Dimension** is that of the Soul. It is the dimension of *creativity*. It is not the mind that is the source of creativity, but the Soul. The Mind is a process through which creativity can be patterned, shaped and formed.

The **Seventh Dimension** is that of the Spirit, which is an essence that has no form but finds expression and cultivates experience *through* form and is the primary intelligence functioning within form.

The **Eighth-Dimension** is the No-thing out of which individuated Spirit arose. Native Americans called it 'the Great Mystery'. In China it was known as the Tao.

There is a further 'dimension' – one in which all the others come together in one place. The **Ninth Dimension** is the Earth: 'Middle' Earth in the 'middle' of the Eight Dimensions! It is the place where all the dimensions can be experienced together. That is why cultivation of the Spirit takes place here on Earth and not in some ethereal realm beyond practical reality! It was represented in ancient symbology by two interpenetrating triangles – one pointing upwards and the other downwards, each with a point above its apex – and an eye in the middle:

There were thus nine emanations or viewpoints of the single unity – the 'I' – within the Greater Whole. In other words, it was a symbol of multidimensional existence. Human life is where dreams aspire to 'heavenly' things – to the so-called 'god' – and its realities are themselves the dreams of the 'god'!

This concept is the same as the 'Cosmic Tree' of the Northern tradition, with its perception points of nine 'worlds' or states of being.

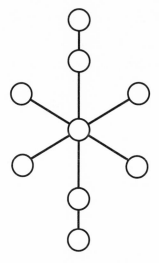

Figure 18 The Cosmic Tree pattern

Although each of the nine 'worlds' has its own identity and functions in a different way from the others, each makes an essential contribution to the well-being and harmony of the composite whole. This also applies to the Universe, and since human beings function as a miniature universe, we are structured similarly in the entirety of our being.

Through Germanic influences, these nine 'worlds' or 'enclosures' came to be likened to 'homes' or 'mansions', meaning 'dwelling places'.

We will start with the one that is familiar to us – the Middle World, whose name MIDGARD means 'Middle Land'. It was so called because it is at the centre of the cosmic structure, where all the other 'worlds' interreact. It is where every aspect of our total being – physical, energic, mental and spiritual – is in dynamic relationship, each affecting and influencing the other. It is the realm of physical manifestation and practical reality, of reason and emotion. it is the realm of the temporary personality 'self' and its Ego-consciousness, where everything

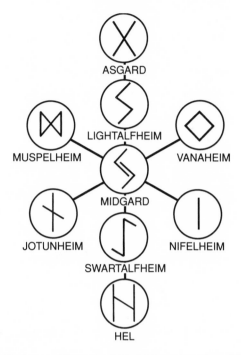

Figure 19 The Tree of the Nine 'Worlds' has Earth reality at its centre

is conditioned by Time – that is, limited by duration. It is where
the powers of what we call good and evil are present in equal
quantities and where every act is one of choice or consent.
Midgard is the dwelling place of humanity – an 'enclosure' that
is in the midst of everything.

Midgard's key Rune is JARA $\diagup$ which is closely related to
the Element of Earth. Its particular emphasis is the 'turning' of
Time, for it is the power that turns the Wheel of the Year and
regulates the seasons. It is expressive of gradual change and
development and provides a clear indication of the true *purpose*
of our Earth life – a period of opportunity to develop every
facet of our being and to cultivate the Spirit.

Above Midgard on the vertical axis is LIGHTALFHEIM,
which is usually abbreviated to ALFHEIM, a word meaning
'Place of Enlightenment' because it brings light or brightness to
the intellect. It is the realm of the Mind and the imagination. It
is our *mental* universe, so we are familiar with it even if we
have not recognized its existence as an alternative reality. In
Northern myths it was projected as the abode of beings called

elves. Elves were described as tiny figures because they were rarely seen, although they had an effect on the minds of humans. The reason for this is that they are collective thought-forms which are rarely 'seen' but have an influence on the human mind, beneficially or adversely.

Alfheim's key-Rune is SOL S – the potency of solar-energy that enables what was previously hidden to be comprehended. This Rune is usually associated with the rising Sun and the Element of Fire, but in Northern mythology the deity associated with the Sun was a goddess, *Sunna*, who was regarded as the nurturer and carrier of the Sun's light-energy. What is implied here is that the Sun has a *feminine* aspect – not the full power of the Sun as in the heat of day, but its light which is *reflected* by the Moon in the cool of the night! In other words *moonlight* – the reflected light of the Sun providing the means of seeing in the dark! Alfheim is the Realm of the Mind, and the mind is an extension or emanation of the Soul and reflects the light of the Soul. The S-Rune SOL S , though related to the progress of both the Sun and the Soul, is here associated with the *mind* as a *reflection* of the Soul.

Below Midgard on the vertical axis is SWARTALFHEIM, which means 'Realm of the Dwarfs'. In Northern mythology, dwarfs are the counterparts of elves but are the *fashioners*. They transmute the raw, base materials of inner Earth into more refined forms such as gemstones. The classic Disney cartoon film *Snow White and the Seven Dwarfs* presented the dwarfs as working in a mine and doing precisely that. The mythological dwarfs represent the formative intelligences of the Lower World – the formulators that shape whatever is coming into manifestation in Midgard. Swartalfheim is thus a realm of 'patterning'. It is where the future is being formed from the thought-patterns of the present, and is associated with the *subconscious* activity that is taking place just beneath the surface of our normal awareness and which supports the structure of our 'ordinary' reality. It is the province of *Unihipili*, the silent, servant 'self' of the understanding of the kahuna shamans of Polynesia, supporting and serving the Ego-self that predominates in Midgard.

Swartalfheim's key Rune is EOH $\int$, whose stave shape is indicative of the spinal column – the supporting structure of the physical body, and of the trunk of a tree or stem of a plant.

So Swartalfheim represents a level of awareness that might be likened to the subconscious aspect of the Mind, which is a servant of the conscious 'self'.

At the very base of the column, at the deepest level which was sometimes referred to as the Under-world, is HEL – but not the 'Hell' of Christian theology. The Christian 'Hell' is an interpretation of the Hebrew 'Gehenna', a waste disposal facility where dead vegetation and garbage was burned in ancient Israel, and a distortion of the Northern concept of a reality of the dead. According to the way our Northern ancestors perceived things, Hel was the Abode of the Dead, because the realm of the Unconscious was regarded as the gateway to new life. In the cyclic scheme of things, life leads to death, and death leads to life, or rebirth. Hel was never visualized as a fiery place. Fire was not so life-threatening to the ancient Northern peoples as it was in the hotter regions nearer to the equator. In the lands of the North it was an excess of *cold*, not heat, that threatened survival!

The word 'Hel' means 'covering'. Hel is that which actually 'covers' the natural forces that function at the deepest levels of the unconscious. It is a realm of apparent stillness and inertia, a place of *rest*. That is why it was associated with death. It is a realm of instincts and impulses, the level at which the intelligence of the physical body – the Body Self – functions.

In the pre-Christian Northern religion, Hel had a dual nature, as represented by the goddess *Hela*. Hela was represented as a corpse on the one hand, and as a beautiful and desirable woman on the other; one aspect thus indicating the entrance to the tomb, the other suggestive of the entrance to the womb. Her dual nature thus revealed that that which was considered 'dead' is brought forth into newness of life again.

Hel's key Rune is HAGAL Ⴕ the transformational power that is within the seed and within its eventual manifestation to fullness. This Runic potency is the power of *becoming* in a state of suspension. It is like a bridge which enables a cross-over to be made.

At the top of the vertical column of the Cosmic Tree is ASGARD, a celestial realm of the 'gods' or 'Shining Ones' who, in mythology, were represented as shedding light on all that is hidden. Although Asgard is indicated as the uppermost location almost beyond reach, it is actually the one that is the innermost 'enclosure' of the human being.

Native American shamans had an understanding similar to their Northern counterparts: they believed that they had a Spirit that lived both in a spiritual reality (the *Nagual*) and the *Tonal* world of physical reality. According to this understanding, after death, and lacking a mortal body, 'aliveness' is experienced in a spiritual realm where we are surrounded by energy-patterns that have been created *within* us during our life on Earth. We thus create our own Hell!

Asgard's position 'Above' was to indicate also that this was a place accessible only through determination and persistence and – in the understanding of the Northern shaman – with the aid of a *valkyrie*. In mythology, valkyries were the daughters – the offspring – of Odin, who were presented as accompanying the souls of Viking warriors to a happy eternity. The word *valkyrie* means 'chooser of the slain'. Valkyries are symbolic of the perfecting 'self' which, having battled with valour through Earth life, has created for itself a happy afterlife! Asgard's key Rune is GIFU ᚷ .

On the horizontal plane there are four 'outer' realities:

NIFELHEIM – the name means 'Abode of Mist' – is a place of illusion where what is seen in a search for meaning is in accordance with one's own nature. It has a magnetic power that draws things to itself like a Black Hole in Space. It was said to be the place where water 'originated'. Mist is vaporized water, and water has the potential to become solidified as ice, so what is implied here is a state of being that is between the tangible and the intangible. The key Rune is ISS ᛁ .

MUSPELHEIM – meaning 'Abode of Fire' or 'Realm of Passion' – is Nifelheim's complementary opposite. It is likened to electrical energy that is constantly expanding away from itself. In mythology, the beings associated with this realm were called *Thurses* – perceived as beings of great age and possessing both transformational and destructive power. Muspelheim's key Rune is DAGAZ ᛞ , the power of transformation.

VANAHEIM is the Abode of Wanes. *Wanes* are the forces and intelligences governing organic patterning – that which produces in plenty. So Vanaheim was sometimes referred to as 'the Place of Peace and Plenty'. Its key Rune is ING ◇ , a Rune of gestation and organic growth.

JOTUNHEIM is the Abode of Giants. A definition of the Norse word for 'giant' is 'an entity of great size and mighty power'. It is the realm of the intellect and the imagination, both of which have formidable power. The key Rune is NAUD ⊬ , which is associated with necessary change.

As well as existing outside ourselves, the nine 'worlds' also comprise our inner universe. So there are subjective, non-ordinary realities as well as 'ordinary', objective reality. The Cosmos – the entirety of existence and of our own individual existence – includes the internal as well as the external, and that which is unknown as well as that which is known.

According to the understanding of some mystics, the nine 'worlds' are connected by 24 pathways or 'bridges' that hold the Cosmos together as a unified, ecological whole. Each is dominated by a non-invertible Rune which, like a door or gateway, protects the entrance and makes access possible. A non-invertible Rune is one that looks the same whether upright or upside down. There are nine such Runes: GIFU X , ISS | , HAGAL Ⴉ , NAUD ⊬ , JARA ⧫ , SOL ⟨ , EOH ⌠ , ING ◇ and DAGAZ ⋈ .

These 24 'paths' are said to be explorable by methods called 'pathworking' – similar to those employed by cabbalists and those who are engaged in the deeper esoteric aspects of the Tarot. Pathworking should not be attempted without an Inner Guide. An Inner Guide is not a spiritual leader, a guru, a person in the 'outer' world of ordinary reality, nor an outside entity like the spirit guides of spiritualism, but one whose 'alive-ness' is on the inner planes. The Inner Guide is an Intelligence that serves the individual's essential Spirit by guiding and protecting the physical Ego-self during its incarnation; it exists as an energy within the totality of one's being and functions at superconscious levels.

You cannot find and communicate with your Inner Guide by *seeking* or invoking it, because that Inner Guide is already with you. You simply *allow* that Inner Guide to be revealed to you, and that can come about only through your intention to allow that presence to be *experienced* through a shamanic 'journey' – an altered state of awareness to a 'higher', more refined level of multidimensional being. Your Inner Guide has a loving concern for you and is a friend, companion, counsellor and protector who delights in your achievements that further your

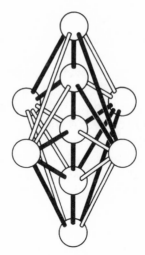

Figure 20 The 24 Pathways on the Cosmic Tree of Yggdrasil

inner spiritual development. As an example, my wife's personal experiences of coming into contact with her Inner Guide is expressed beautifully in words and music in her orchestral poem *Powers of Love* (*see* Resources).

The Nine 'worlds' are also levels of awareness which the Runic shamanist may begin to experience through shamanic 'journeys' on the Runes. A shamanic 'journey' is the movement of the awareness into a non-ordinary reality, usually with the aid of drumming or rattling, or a combination of the two. The Runic shamanist has a Rune with him or her as they embark on such an endeavour. Shamanic 'journeying' is a willing shift of the awareness into another region of multidimensional existence in order to attain empowerment from the deeper levels of one's being in order to undertake certain tasks or face particular challenges, or to obtain knowledge from an inner or higher source. 'Travelling' in this way is to experience in a dreamlike state something of a Rune's characteristics and attributes – as visual images, sounds, feelings, and even physical sensations. Such 'journeys' can be just as 'real' and as vivid as experiences in everyday reality.

The sacred quest of initiatory systems was to pass through the portals which led to other levels of reality, finally coming face to face with one's own *innermost* Self. By so doing the initiate found Truth – which lies *within*.

In the myths, the roots of Yggdrasil, although firmly established in the soil of practical reality, reach down to obtain water from subterranean or 'unconscious' levels. The first of its three roots obtains water from the Spring of *Mimir* – a name which means 'memory'. But this is not a retrieval of information which is an activity of the mind and the concerns of the temporal Ego-self. Rather, it is an activity of the Soul, where the memory of prenatal existence is stored. It was in order to drink from this 'water' that Odin was willing to sacrifice the eye of reason, which is 'connected' to the Mind, in order to strengthen the intuitive eye, which is 'connected' to the Soul, and thus be enabled to 'see' what cannot be perceived through the exercise of the intellect alone. The 'memory' to be obtained from the Spring of Mimir is the knowledge to re-awaken the potential talent inherent within the totality of our own individual energy-system – it had expression in previous incarnations and is capable of being revived in order to nourish us now.

A further understanding is that the waters that are drawn up through the root are a means of bringing what is contained in the unconscious to the surface of conscious existence. The branches of the Tree of Yggdrasil, reaching upwards into the less dense substance of the atmosphere, are suggestive of the realm of the Mind and of thoughts which move like air and are similarly elusive. The topmost branches touch the sky and reach up to the heavens, suggesting realms of even finer energies – those of the Soul and the Spirit, and accessible through the vertical pillar which connects that which is above with that which is below.

Mimir was the mythological name also of the wisest of the *etins*, who gained wisdom from drinking of these waters. The waters might be likened to the occult concept of Akashi Records, where the memory of past lives is said to be kept. The memory referred to is ancestral – our own individual ancestry or past lives, each of which has influenced the next, and all of which have contributed in some way to the life now being lived. Each mortal life may be perceived as a separate cultivation of the one immortal Spirit – like an individual pearl on a necklace of pearls – strung on a continuous line which is symbolic of the Life-line, or *lives*-line, of the Spirit.

The second root of Yggdrasil drew water from the Well of *Urd* where, in mythology, the three Norns dwelt and tended the needs of the tree. The Norns were regarded as the 'weavers of the Wyrd' – a name which became interpreted as 'fate'. It did not, however, mean that which is predestined to happen and, therefore, beyond control, nor was it identical to the concept of karma, which advances the view that certain privileges or ordeals experienced in this present lifetimes are the rewards or punishments for deeds or misdemeanours of a previous life. Indeed the Norns are not causal influences at all but a combination of natural processes by which the energies expressed through individual actions are given out, received, transformed and returned to their source, where they will have their effect. In other words, we each shape our own destiny by our thoughts and deeds.

The third root of the Cosmic Tree reached down to the Pool of *Hvergelmir* – a fathomless cauldron where a dragon knawed unceasingly at the root, suggesting a never-ending process where that which *was* is consumed by that which *is* becoming that which *shall be*.

The water drawn up through the roots into physical manifestation shapes even the growth of the leaves the tree bears. Water then drips from the leaves and back through the soil into the waters beneath to further the means by which the next cycle of activity may be patterned and nourished. We thus each have our individual wyrd, which is the totality of the patterns of our own past lives and the conscious actions undertaken in our present lifetime. So we are each the weavers of our own web of wyrd – our own fate.

17 The Runic Talisman

A TALISMAN IS NOT A LUCKY charm but an energy-pattern which attracts the effects for which it is fashioned. It is usually an object which can be worn or carried on the person – a pendant, perhaps, or a token on which is written or engraved runic characters or symbols of magick to indicate what the talisman is intended to achieve.

The word *talisman* is derived from the Greek *talisma*, meaning 'completion' or 'payment'. On a Runic talisman the Runic characters form a sigel, which serves a similar purpose as a signature on a cheque authorizing payment for work done or for goods received. The word *sigel* is derived from the Latin *sigmum*, meaning 'emblem' – in this case an emblem of an inner, spiritual potency seeking to find expression in manifestation.

Contrary to some modern representations, a talisman cannot be made for another person. Objects made for another person are amulets or so-called 'lucky' charms. A talisman must be fashioned by the person for whom it is intended to work – *you* – because a talisman performs its work *whilst it is being made*. When the fashioning is completed, its work is done and 'payment' can be expected. The carrying of the talisman on your person is a tangible 'link' with the intangible forces involved – a contact point with the 'inner' world allowing energies to flow from the inside to the outside.

The combination of Runic characters drawn or inscribed on the talisman is a representation of an energy-pattern which needs to be forged at a subjective level in an 'inner' universe. It then flows 'outwards' so its effects may be experienced at an objective level in the 'outer' world of physical reality. The 'outer' and the 'inner' are thus brought into harmony. The talisman itself is an *affirmation* of a *process* which is set in motion by its fashioning.

There is a Cosmic Law that energy follows intention. What happens with a talisman is that the thought-impulse of the desired result – the intention – if properly focused, provides a channel along which the potencies can be routed. *Intention* is the means by which what is desired can be brought about. It provides a channel into which the potencies can be released so that when they are activated they can find expression and fulfilment in physical reality. Manifestation thus takes place from the inside out. This is why purity of intent – clear, focused intention – is so important in shamanic work.

The intention in making your Rune-work talisman is to bring your 'outer' life into harmony with your essential 'Self' – the 'You' which 'purposed' your life and determined your basic personality traits and the perception point on the Wheel of the Year – the period of your birth – from which you would experience physical reality. It is to enable this 'You' – the *real* 'You' – to shine forth and find creative expression in everyday living so your life can become more meaningful and fulfilling. Involving Runic influences prevalent in the Time segment in which you were born – your Birth Runes – in your talisman will accentuate the positive qualities inherent in your personality and enhance your ability to *be yourself*!

Physical reality is derived in its entirety from primary impulses or *fluctuations* and their combinations. These fluctuations are not physical substance or, initially, even energies. They are qualities which are in being *before* manifestation takes place. Runes are the patterns or *signatures* of these qualities. Your Birth Runes are qualities prevalent in the dimension of Time when you were born and which have an effect on the subtle energies that determine your personality.

The Soul puts on the garment of a physical body at birth in order to experience matter and thereby cultivate the Spirit on its evolutionary path. The personality expression of the individual – the word *personality* is derived from the Latin *persona*, meaning 'mask' – is the 'face' the individual Spirit presents to the world, and through which it perceives the physical universe. The personality expression is determined to some extent, though not wholly, by the segment of Time in which the individual is born. The birth-time place on the yearly cycle also indicates Earth forces which are helping to shape the individual. I have called a method of personality profiling based upon Medicine Wheel principles 'Earth Medicine', and it is described comprehensively in my book *Earth Medicine*, which gives a detailed analysis of each birth 'month'. An understanding of the 12 time periods can help us to see things from the perspective of other people and is, therefore, an aid to human relationships as well.

Runic potencies flow with the yearly cycle, the seasons of the year and the directional forces. Together they infuse a Time period with their specific qualities. So Time itself embraces Runic qualities. By identifying the Runes which were prevalent at the time of the year in which you were born, knowledge of the Runes will enable you to come to a deeper understanding of yourself. And by combining these Runes into a Bind-rune in the form of a monogram and crafting it into the talisman, you will be making a powerful conscious link with your essential Self – the Spirit 'You' – and with the essential *purpose* of your life in this incarnation.

The Birth Runes Chart in *figure 21* indicates which Runes have the strongest influence in each of the 12 Time 'segments' or 'months' of the year. The Runes indicated in the Time period of your birth as your Birth Runes will form part of the design of your talisman.

Rune-work: Assignment 18 Making a Runic Talisman

First you must decide the material from which your talisman is to be fashioned. It can be a small slice of wood cut from a branch, or a slither of agate, about 8 or 9 centimetres (about 3 inches) in diameter. It can be made into a flat, oval shape from clay or Das compound and baked. For either of these you will need to drill a small hole near the top edge so that a cord or chain may be passed through it when completed so that it may be worn round the neck. Alternatively, your talisman can be made from a small piece of genuine parchment of a similar size which, when completed, can be wrapped in a piece of silk and carried in a wallet or purse. Genuine parchment is the skin of a

Figure 21 The Birth Runes Chart, showing the Runes which influence each of the 12 Time 'segments' of the Wheel of the Year and the Medicine Wheel, which it complements. UR thus begins the year on 1 January and FEH completes it on 31 December

goat or sheep and as well as being a 'traditional' material for talismans has greater permanence than paper. The permanence factor is important because it is a reminder of the permanence of the Reality that produces patterns out of which 'that which becomes physical' has materialized. That which is in physical reality is temporal and has no real permanence, because all material things are subject to change and transition. What *is* permanent is the unseen Reality out of which manifestation takes place.

If you have chosen to fashion your talisman from a slice of a tree branch, polish both surfaces by sanding them smooth with fine sandpaper. Then seal the surfaces with a thin coat of clear vanish or beeswax and allow to dry thoroughly before undertaking the Rune-work.

Identify a quality which you consider you possess and express through your personality, then look for a Rune that matches that quality. Scan through the commentaries in Chapters 5–9 if you need to. Then combine all three Runes into a single Bind-rune. For example:

The Birth Runes for someone born on the 28 October are LAGU ┌ and ING ◇. If that person considered that determination and singleness of purpose were among his or her prominent qualities, the Rune TYR ↑ would be appropriate. These three Runes could then be combined as:

The Birth Runes for someone born on 17 March are REID ʀ and KEN <. If a primary quality of that person was caring concern for others and an empathy toward other people's problems, then GIFU X might be appropriate. All three Runes could be combined as:

For a person born on 25 June, the Birth Runes are EOH ∫ and PERTRA ⌊. Let us say the person worked in the communications field and persuasiveness was one of the skills employed consistently. If he or she particularly wanted to express persuasiveness and develop communication skills, then Ass ⊦ or MADR ⋈ would be appropriate.

Now we will construct a monogram in the form of a Bind-Rune for the reverse side of the talisman. A Runic monogram, like the combined initials of someone's name, identifies the person it belongs to. It can be a combination of the Rune-stave equivalent of the initials of your forenames and surname – for example, KWM <ⲣⲘ, AFH ⊦⊦Ⲛ, JCB ᛋ<ᛒ, MCB Ⲙ<ᛒ, or abbreviations of your first name – Ken for Kenneth, <Ⲙⲭ Tom for Thomas ↑ⲬⲘ, Kate for Kathryn, <⊦↑, and Jo for Josephine ᛋⲬ.

The Rune-staves of the above examples could then be combined, like this:

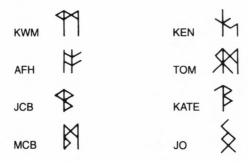

KWM		KEN	
AFH		TOM	
JCB		KATE	
MCB		JO	

A monogram has the effect of drawing Runic powers into yourself – including those of any 'hidden' Runes that are perceived in the Bind-rune once it has been completed. Connecting with them in this way draws out the powers so they can find outward expression through you, because they are qualities which are potentially 'there' all the time – they merely need to be recognized and awakened. This is what the preparation of a monogram does. Its construction, fashioning and eventual consecration, activates dormant energies so they can find positive expression through you. Like your name, they are personal to you and an essential part of who and what you are. Fashioning your monogram will begin to unlock and release those powers.

To be effective, your talisman now needs to be activated. Activated by what? By forces on the 'inner' planes. It means charging your talisman – an otherwise inert object – with powers of motion from the 'inner' universe of non-material existence, enabling the manifestation of those qualities that are impressed into the talisman through the intention of the 'working'.

Consecration of the talisman – that is, setting it apart for its special work – should involve the Four Elements of Air, Fire, Water and Earth, before it is activated by being 'charged' with the life-energy of Chi in accordance with the principles I outlined in Chapter 13.

AIR: Smudge the talisman by passing it through the smoke of a smouldering smudge stick or through the smoke of incense.
FIRE: Pass the talisman through the flame of a candle several times, or alternatively place it in sunlight for an hour or so.

WATER: Gently sprinkle a few drops of clear running water.
EARTH: Leave the talisman on some earth overnight.

When the consecration is complete, hold the talisman carefully between the forefinger and thumb of both hands and blow forcefully into it four times with the intention of blowing Chi – life-energy – into it. It is the charging with Chi from your own energy-system that activates the Runic forces associated with your talisman.

If your talisman is in the form of a pendant, it can be hung on a suitable cord or chain so that it can be worn round your neck and at a level close to your heart. If it is a parchment talisman, wrap it in a small piece of silk or cotton cloth and put it in a safe place where it can be carried with you at all times.

18 Runic Divination

USE OF THE RUNES FOR fortune telling is a trivialization of their true function and purpose as an oracle. An oracle does not predict the future or give instructions on what to do. An oracle draws attention to intangible energies that have influenced what has come into manifestation, and indicate the direction in which those unseen forces are flowing and shaping what is coming into being. The Runes of the Northern peoples and the *I Ching* of China are two of the world's greatest oracular systems because each is derived from Nature and the cycles of life.

The word 'divination' means 'insight from the divine'. It is a way of seeing from a higher perspective. It is obtaining an overview not from spirits or 'gods' but from within *you. Divination is the submission of a problem to the Spirit that is you* – the 'permanent' you that has an overview of life, looking down, as it were, to the 'you' on the ground, the temporary 'you' that is too close to the everyday world of appearances to see the bigger picture and to comprehend where all the separate circumstances and bits and pieces of one's life 'fit together' to make a comprehensive 'whole'. It functions in what modern psychology calls the 'Unconscious', so divination can be regarded as a method of exploring the unconscious and obtaining relevance from it.

Divination, like any other skill, can be learned through practice. It requires patience and persistence in addition to diligent personal effort. The potential ability is within you already, otherwise you would not be reading this book. Once generated by Love and Harmony, it merely takes a while for the channels of communication to open. It is like learning to ride a bicycle. It takes concentrated effort and application at first, but before long you find you can do it without having to 'try'.

An oracle is a means of connecting with inner forces that are shaping the future in accordance with the decisions and choices that have been made in the past and with what is being determined in the present. It provides insight into how these energy-patterns are forming so that changes can be made that may affect the way their consequences are to be experienced. An oracle works by relating the outer situation affecting the realm of the Body Mind – the Ego-self – to the inner reality which is of the Soul and Spirit, and perceiving what is in the process of coming into being through the transformation of energy. In Runic divination the spiritual forces inherent in the Runes are inherent also in the situation which one is seeking to resolve – it is a part of the same process which is taking place at an unconscious level. The Runes that are selected in a Rune-cast provide a reading of energy-fields prevalent in the dynamics of Time and actions that are associated with them. The Runes indicate not what is going to happen but the *direction* of specific actions and their potential consequences. The future is thus not immutable, for by changing the way a situation is perceived, or the way that one responds to it, the potential itself is changed.

A Rune-stave, like a totem, is a *connector*. It connects movement in the reality of 'appearances' with the movement of energy in a reality that cannot be seen. Runic divination sets in motion a process which indicates in that moment of Time the direction in which those unseen energies are moving and taking shape. The stream of Time has its source within and it flows in each of us. The Rune-Staves are patterns which link 'ordinary' reality with the non-ordinary reality in which spiritual powers bring energies into existence. They are a means of connecting with forces that govern Nature, which itself is a process of orderly change.

Oracular divination is, therefore, not a superstition, nor does it depend on belief. It has its roots in the oral traditions of shamanism and, as with all shamanic work, functions at different levels – physical, mental and spiritual.

Divination is a very ancient method of finding ways to cope with the challenges that human problems and situations produce. Most of our problems are self-inflicted – that is, they are inflicted by the Ego-self, which rarely sees beyond the limitations it imposes on a situation. Divination helps us to see things from another perspective so that by our choices and actions we can reshape the likely outcome. Divination is not fatalistic. The future is not fated to happen. The idea of a fixed destiny is a belief derived from religious conditioning. The presence in the Cosmos of a random factor – a chaotic movement of energies that is neither law-abiding nor pattern-forming – has also to be taken into consideration. It is recognition of this random factor that is behind the wise saying: 'Expect the Unexpected'.

There are many methods of Runic divination, because the Runes themselves communicate their essence to different individuals in different ways. In this book I shall give an example of each of three broad methods of Runic divination, which should help you to establish for yourself an effective dialogue with the Runes. But before we examine these methods it is important that we recognize an essential difference between a shamanic approach to Runic divination and a 'magickal' one. Magick is essentially an activity of the mind and an expression of the Will of the one who performs it. Changing things in accordance with the Will is to enforce the desires of the Ego. Ceremonial magick is a highly disciplined system and requires an ability to establish relationships – called 'correspondences' – between tangible objects and intangible forces. It also requires a compensation of energy from the person or persons involved in the working, which sets out to bring the intangible energies under the control of the Will. A shamanic approach, on the other hand, is essentially an activity of the Spirit generated by the motive of coming into harmony with the natural forces of the Universe. It is directed by an intention that leads the shamanist to experience what is sought in a very personal way and in another reality, and a bringing of that knowledge through into conscious awareness where it can then be examined by the mind. It is important to recognize this essential difference.

Divination should be motivated by the principles of Love and Harmony and conducted in accordance with the Sacred Laws which are concerned with the evolutionary development of the Universe and of life forms within it. Evolution is a natural process of growth, development and transformation which promotes the well-being of body, mind, Soul and Spirit. The opposite of evolution is a breakingdown process called entropy, which is also at work in the Universe. Malicious intent and manipulative practices for the purpose of personal gain, self-gratification or revenge, are in discord with harmonic laws and lead to entropy. This issue is not a moral one. Manipulative practices create discord and deprive others.

The three broad systems of Runic divination are:

A Rune-lot: This entails a random selection of a Rune or Runes as a means of determining the quality of the moment of Time and the nature of the situation or problem.

A Rune-spread: This is an arrangement of Rune-staves that have been selected into a pattern in order that the flow of energies at an unconscious level can be discerned sequentially.

A Rune-cast: This is a method of divination which entails allowing the Rune-staves to fall on a flat surface – preferably a white casting cloth – in an apparently random fashion, and interpreting them in accordance with their place on the surface and their positions in relation to one another in the light of the question that has been asked.

Whichever method is used, it is important that a record be kept of the work. Make a note of the intention of the working and the Rune or Runes which appeared and in what order, and, finally, the outcome deduced. Refer to the Runic qualities given in the Commentaries and the Divination Indicators, which provide *suggestions* of likely meanings and serve as guidelines. You must develop your own interpretive skills through practice and experience. Should a 'reading' seem obscure and not make immediate sense to you, let it rest for a while. Shamanic understanding does not necessarily come instantly. Sometimes it unfolds over a period of time.

This is why it is important to keep notes, for further understanding often comes when they are reviewed. Sometimes it may come in a sudden flash of illumination whilst you are engaged in some other activity. Sometimes a full meaning may come unexpectedly through synchronicity. Sometimes it may come in a dream. Learning to 'read' the Runes is no instant process, but will grow and develop in a natural way.

As with all shamanic work, Runic divination must be carried

out with purpose. There needs to be a clear, single intention with each 'working', which is a mission into the unknown. In order to focus the intention and ensure that it is not obscure, it is advisable at the outset to write down the intention. You can then scrutinize what you have written to make sure that it is clear and that it expresses a single purpose rather than a combination of intents.

DIVINATION INDICATORS

UR	ᚠ	Advancement. New conditions. Assertiveness. Perseverance. Endurance. Maintenance. Health. Physical power.
THURS	ᚦ	Strength. Drive. Assertion. Defence. Conflict. Breaking-up. Barriers to be cleared.
ASS	ᚨ	Mind power. Intellect. Verbal expression. Inspiration. Messages. Communication. Confidence. Wisdom. Opening.
REID	ᚱ	Control. Direction. Movement. Balance. Co-ordination. Reunion. Travel. Decision.
KEN	ᚲ	Discernment. Insight. Guidance. Learning. Knowledge. Truth. Opportunity.
GIFU	ᚷ	Give and take. Exchange. Sacrifice. Generosity. Love. Contracts. Time.
WYNJA	ᚹ	Happiness. Pleasure. Enjoyment. Contentment. Satisfaction. Accomplishment. Success.
HAGAL	ᚺ	External influences. Dramatic change. Liberation. Linking.
NAUD	ᚾ	Necessity. Needful. Needs. Constraint. Restriction. Caution. Arguments. Paradoxes.
ISS	ᛁ	Holding. Formation. Waiting. Fixation. Privacy. Coolness. Delay. 'Higher' Truth.
JARA	ᛃ	Gestation. Gradual change. Turning point. Commitment. Timing. Expectations. Plenty.
PERTRA	ᛈ	Recollection. Receptiveness. Humour. Investment. Promotion.
EOH	ᛇ	Motivation. Enterprise. Management. Mastery. Durability. Longevity.
ALGIZ	ᛉ	Protection. Guidance. Caring. Grounding. Continuance.
SOL	ᛋ	Healing. Wholeness. Confidence. Restoration.

TYR	↑	Courage. Leadership. Authority. Loyalty. Trust. Success. Justice.
BJARKA	ß	Close relationships. Family. Partnerships. Nurturing. Renewal. Growth. Fertility. Fruition.
EH	ᛗ	Co-operation. Adaptability. Progress. Transportation. Increase.
MADR	ᛉ	Attitudes. Compatibility. Individuality. Understanding. People. Family.
LAGU	ᚱ	Emotions. Feelings. Love. Affections. Intuition. Flexibility.
ING	◇	Well-being. Fulfilment. Integration. Realization. Anticipation.
ODAL	ᛩ	Property. Social life. Heritage. Establishment. Home.
DAGAZ	ᛝ	Transformation. Break-through. Security. Initiation. Certainty. Day. Meditation.
FEH	ᚠ	Culmination. Abundance. Success. Luck. Possessions. Finance.
BLANK RUNE		The random factor. Destiny. The unknown. The unexpected. Wish. Challenge. Faith.

Figure 22 Divination indicators for each of the Runes

Rune-work: Assignment 19 A 'Sacrifice'

Before using your Rune-set for divination purposes, take it in its pouch to a river, lake or stream, and have with you nine coins. They can be copper or silver – the denomination is not relevant – but do not mix them. Hold the pouch containing your Rune-set in your left hand and the nine coins in your right hand. Then cast the coins three at a time into the water as a 'sacrifice' to the three Norns. A sacrifice is a letting go of something of value in exchange for a blessing of greater value. The word 'sacrifice' is derived from a Latin word meaning 'to make sacred' – that is, separating something from mundane activity and setting it apart for a 'higher' purpose. A blessing is a merging of the nature of divinity with human nature. The quality of human existence is thus raised, bringing it into attunement with the natural order of the Universe so that the immediate 'world' may be a more hospitable place in which to exist. As you cast each set of three coins into the water say: 'Let the Runes speak truly through me.'

We will now look at how to read what the Runes have to say about the issue on which they were consulted.

In divination, each Rune is a separate *thought* so a sequence of Runes is like related thoughts that make up a paragraph in writing. Reading the Runes requires not the skill of the intellect to *interpret* their message, but, rather, the application of *intuition*. The Runes are, therefore, read by *intuiting* and not by *interpreting*.

All divinatory work should be regarded as a meditation, since both the conscious and unconscious aspects of the mind and the active and latent qualities of the personality are being exercised. In losing the eye which is related to the logical and reasoning function of the brain, Odin symbolically set aside that which provided only a limited perception. A true reading of the Runes is achieved first through the 'eye' of the intuitive senses and then is examined by the mind in order to obtain understanding. In this way, both hemispheres of the brain are engaged and brought into balance and harmony.

Let us examine each of the three broad methods of Runic divination in turn and consider some examples.

THE RUNE-LOT METHOD

A Rune-lot is a quick and simple method of discerning the quality of the present moment and the way the dynamics of Time are flowing. It provides an overview of a situation so that an issue or concern can be perceived in a shamanic context – that is, as a furthering of personal development as an individual.

The first essential is to determine the problem and to see it from a *shamanic* perspective. The question provides a route along which energy can flow, so in order for it to be clearly focused it should be carefully worded in order to avoid a simple 'yes' or 'no' response. A pendulum is the tool to use when 'yes' or 'no' answers are required. With a Rune-lot it is best to focus on an *issue*. Rather than asking 'Should I accept this job offer and move to another place?', present it more open-endedly as: 'The issue is a new job'. So consider the problem as an issue: 'The issue is my health', 'The issue is my personal finances', and so on. This statement should then be followed with your purpose for consulting the Runes: 'I need help in seeing what this experience is endeavouring to teach me for my ultimate good.'

Selecting a Rune-for-the-day is itself a Rune-lot method. So is choosing a Rune at random for the purpose of meditation. But for this particular Rune-lot method you should select at random *four* Runes, since Four is the number of balance and harmony, which essentially the drawing of lots is intended to bring about.

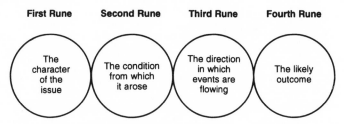

Figure 23 A Rune-lot employing four Runes chosen at random

Close your eyes and consider carefully the issue and the request for guidance. Repeat them to yourself *four* times. With your eyes still closed select a Rune from your Rune-bag. Open your eyes and look at the Rune-stave.

This *first* Rune identifies the essential *character* of the issue. Place it face upwards in front of you.

Close your eyes and select another Rune from the bag. This *second* Rune describes the *condition* out of which the issue has arisen and indicates its possible cause. Place it on the right of the first Rune.

Now, with your eyes closed again, choose a *third* Rune. This Rune is placed next to the two other Runes on the Rune-cloth and shows the *direction* in which the energies are flowing and its essential *purpose*.

Finally, close your eyes and select a *fourth* Rune to complete the sequence. This fourth Rune indicates the likely *outcome* of the issue.

Example 1 How Sarah Saved Her Marriage

Sarah was anxious about her marriage which was in danger of breaking up. The domestic atmosphere was so tense that she and her husband found it difficult to talk to each other, even about events of the day. Sarah consulted the Runes by performing a Rune-lot. Her question was phrased quite simply: 'The issue is my marriage. I desperately need advice.'

This is the sequence of the four Runes she drew:

EOH   DAGAZ   UR   ISS

The first Rune, EOH ς, indicated the nature of the issue, which she read as strength and assertiveness. These two qualities described precisely what her marriage lacked.

The second Rune indicated the condition out of which her marital problems arose. She read DAGAZ ⋈ as transformation and change. She recognized immediately that her marital difficulties, and particularly the lack of real communication and understanding between the two of them, had become more acute since she had devoted time to a home study course with a view to attaining a qualification in a subject that interested her. She recognized that in the 18 months she had been involved in this study, which required her to spend an occasional day or two away from home attending seminars and workshops, she had changed. Her interests had widened. She was engaged in many new things. She had developed new friendships. Her husband was not only unwilling to share in her interests but appeared incapable of understanding why she wanted to undertake this course in the first place. So they no longer talked about it.

The third Rune, UR ⌐, suggested to her the need for a new approach – a fresh start, perhaps.

The fourth Rune Sarah pulled was ISS |, and this indicated the outcome or purpose, which she understood as clarity – making things clear would lead to a more solid relationship.

After completing the Rune-lot, Sarah experienced an inner 'reminder' that her husband was dyslexic. His difficulty in reading had prevented him from pursuing so many interests and she realized that her enthusiasm to explore new horizons left him with a feeling of total inadequacy.

Sarah told me: 'I had really despaired at times that our relationship could ever be the way I wanted it. After the Rune-cast I had a long chat with my husband. It showed me how bewildered and confused he was at feeling incapable of sharing my interests. He had felt more and more isolated, more and more "abandoned". This talk strengthened my resolve to stick with it and make the marriage work.

'This may seem strange, but what has come out of the Rune-lot and my resolve to make a fresh start with my husband is that I have fallen in love with him again.'

Example 2 How Jane Conquered Her Fears

Jane was concerned about her reluctance to start a new project. She was enthusiastic about the project itself, but had doubts about her ability to see it through because of a health problem. Her question was 'The issue is my *hesitancy* in starting a new project because of my health. I need advice.' She drew four Runes in the following sequence:

| SOL | LAGU | BLANK | KEN |

This was her analysis.

⟨ The *nature* of the issue has to do with doubts about my *vitality*.

Γ The *condition* is *emotional*. I have so many fears – about my health, my failures, even about success – it might take over my life!

○ My fears are blocking the flow of *unmanifest* energy. It is for me to *choose* whether to begin a new project now or later or not at all. My *choice* is what determines how the energies flow!

⟨ Inner light. Inner guidance. Inner *knowing*.

Realization: It is how I feel *inside* that should determine whether I go ahead or not. The confidence and vitality I need can only come from within *me*.

Example 3 How Paul Cut the Shackles of Addiction

Paul, a teacher living alone in a small two-room apartment, was concerned about his life-style, which was cramping his desire to develop the abilities he knew he had and blocking his career prospects. He considered that his life was being restricted by three factors: lack of space in his domestic environment which made him feel 'closed in', lack of time to pursue his real interests, and lack of money.

He performed a Rune-lot on the issue of his life-style and sought help through the Runes to know how to break out from the conditions which were dragging him down into deep depression. The runes he knew were:

| ODAL | THURS | REID | DAGAZ |

The first Rune ᛟ is not only associated with the home but also with *social* life. It was this latter factor which impressed itself on Paul and he recognized this was at the heart of the issue.

The second Rune ᚹ indicated the condition out of which the issue arose, and he saw this as an inner *conflict* between his desire to be creative, productive and fulfilled, and his need to socialize in order to escape from the lonely confines of his domestic environment. He spent most evenings in a pub or tavern and had become a heavy drinker and smoker.

The third Rune ᚱ indicated that the solution was one of *control*. Paul saw the need to take control of his life, rather than his addiction to drink and cigarettes controlling him. But how? The power was in the Rune. The Rune was the power to assert *control* and to determine *direction*. REID was the power to enable him to succeed in a determination to stop smoking and to give up drinking, and that power was *within HIM!*

The final Rune Paul selected was ᛞ, a *transforming* power – indicating a break-through to a more secure and fulfilling life-style; the ending of one cycle of activity that heralded a new 'dawn' in his life.

Paul fashioned for himself a pendant from a small piece of oval-shaped slate and engraved the four Rune-staves onto it, painted them, and drilled a small hole at its apex for a cord to pass through so it could be hung round his neck as a reminder that the powers of the Runes were *with* him. A few weeks later Paul's life was indeed transformed. This is what he told me:

> I was able to give up smoking without too much difficulty and, by cutting out the drinking and by not frequenting my old haunts, I discovered that I had created about 30 'extra' hours a week! What's more, I was saving £250 a month. That's how much my drinking and smoking was costing me.
>
> Then a job opportunity arose 'out of the blue'. I gladly accepted it for it entailed moving back to a part of the country where I spent my childhood. Property prices there were so much lower that I was able to buy a sizeable house with mortgage payments lower than the rent I was paying for my flat. That's Rune *power*!

Example 4 How Jim Developed a Shamanic Perspective

Jim had developed an interest in Shamanics but felt he needed help in integrating its principles into his practical life. He consulted the Runes through a Rune-lot and obtained this advice.

The Rune which expressed the nature of the issue was HAGAL

ᚺ, which indicated that the issue was one of linking the practical realities of everyday living with the inner reality of the Spirit – of bridging the two aspects of the self and by so doing truly experiencing the extraordinary whilst living an ordinary life.

The condition out of which this desire arose was expressed by the second Rune, KEN ᚲ, indicating a need for insight – a drive to be enlightened and to see beyond the obvious so that he could better act from the perspective of the Spirit.

The third Rune selected was JARA ᛃ, which indicated that gradual change was, indeed, taking place through inner development and that the time was now ripe for these to find outward expression.

The likely outcome indicated by the fourth Rune, THURS ᚦ, indicated a clearing away of self-inflicted barriers and impediments to find a greater sense of empowerment in taking greater charge of his own life.

Jim's attitudes to situations began to change noticeably. He became less vulnerable to the pressures of others and more confident in asserting his own qualities on conditions with which he was confronted. He began to approach every challenge as a learning experience and even found satisfaction in work which at one time he found boring and uninteresting. By changes in his attitude he recognized that the way outside situations were experienced changed, too. Then came an unexpected offer of a change of job. This provided him with the opportunity to develop the potentials he knew he had in an area of human activity which matched his own interests.

THE RUNE-SPREAD METHOD

The Medicine Wheel is a circular symbolic device for making connections at different levels of reality and for obtaining knowledge – especially about oneself. Although developed primarily through Native American traditions, the Medicine Wheel is a catalyst for all approaches that seek the discovery of the innermost Self and knowledge of the true purpose of life.

To the American Indian, the word *medicine* meant 'power' or 'knowledge' and the *hoop* represented a circle of 'wholeness'. The Medicine Wheel was thus a means of obtaining personal empowerment to enhance one's life and a way of attaining a greater sense of wholeness.

Viking and Celtic mariners, whose seafaring skills enabled them to traverse the oceans and establish settlements in North America, would have recognized the similarity between the

Medicine Wheel of neighbouring tribes and the Circle of Power or Awareness used by shamans within their traditions.

Arranging selected Runes in the pattern of a hoop or wheel with a hub at its centre is a way of confirming your own Circle of Awareness. The **Medicine Wheel Spread** can help you to perceive how the Past relates to a situation that is causing you concern, the influences at work at an unconscious level at the Present time, and the likely Future outcome if things are left as they are. The spread will enable you to recognize the challenge this experience in your life presents, so that what may appear to be an adverse situation can be turned to your ultimate good.

The question is phrased rather differently than in the Rune-lot method, which merely stated the issue at the heart of the matter of concern. In the Rune-spread the question hinges around the *effect* an experience is having on you personally, so that any harmful energies may be dispersed as a result of the consultation and the wisdom obtained in resolving the difficulty. The following examples demonstrate how the question should be phrased. The emphasized word encapsulates the effect on the individual of the question at issue.

I am *worried* about my finances.
I am *unsettled* about my job.
I am *concerned* about my health.
I am *upset* with my children.
I am *angry* with my husband/wife.

This statement is then coupled with the *intention* on the Rune-spread, which is to obtain the help and power to resolve the issue: 'I need guidance in this matter and the power to resolve it.'

Thus, it is not only *guidance* that is sought in knowing how best to deal with the situation, but the personal *empowerment* to resolve it. This is what the Runes provide. They are not only a lens through which the nature of the energies that are at work in a given situation may be discerned, but they provide access to the very *abilities* needed to deal effectively with it. A Medicine Wheel Spread does this in the following way.

Five Runes are selected at random from the Rune-bag – one for each cardinal direction and the fifth for the centre.

The *first* Rune is placed in the **East** and indicates how the problem has arisen – its source in the Past.

The *second* is placed in the **West** and indicates the influences affecting the Present and the nature of those energies.

The *third* Rune is placed in the **South** and shows how those energies are likely to manifest in the Future as a result of the conditions currently being impressed upon them in the Present.

The *fourth* Rune is placed in the **North** and reveals the kinds of *challenge* the situation is producing and what may be *learned* from it for your ultimate well-being.

The *fifth* Rune is placed in the **Centre** and shows the ability that is needed to resolve the problem and to restore balance. The power to do so is *within* you because the powers in the Runes that are inherent in Nature are inherent in *you* also. That power is brought into your conscious awareness through consulting the Runes is this way. You have thus made contact with a power, however dormant, that is at the centre of your being. You have only to *claim* that power – accept that it is *there* at the very source of your being – and you will have set it to work for you. That latent power, once activated, becomes an *ability*.

Figure 24 shows how the Runes should be arranged in a Medicine Wheel Spread.

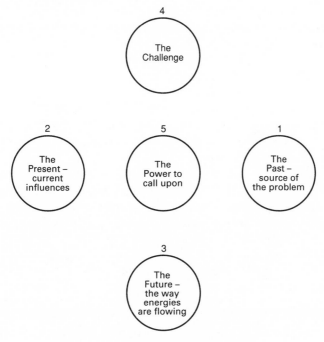

Figure 24 The Medicine Wheel Spread

Example 1   How an Unmarried Mother Learned to Cope on Her Own

Pat, an expectant mother and living alone, was worried about how she would cope on her own with a baby. She consulted the Runes through a Medicine Wheel Spread with the Runes positioned like this:

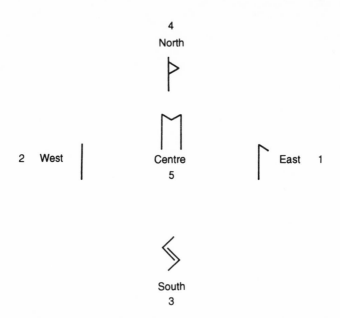

LAGU ⌐ in the **East** indicated that the source of her concern was an emotional one. ISS | in the **West** showed that her emotions and feelings of inadequacy had become so strong that the Present was a slippery surface where she felt totally insecure and abandoned. JARA ⟨ in the **South** suggested a gradual change in the circumstances of her life. Pat, now heavily pregnant, had had to give up full-time working because of her condition, so was becoming aware of the changes being wrought in her life as well as her physical body.

THURS Þ in the **North** revealed the *challenge* inherent in the situation – the need to clear away those things no longer essential in her life to make way for new responsibilities. Pat recognized that these included past emotional concerns and the ties her old job inflicted on her. The fifth Rune, in the **Centre**, was EH ⋒, which she recognized as the power of *adaptability* – the ability to adjust to changes of all kinds. This was precisely the ability Pat needed. She not only identified the Rune with the circumstances of her life but allowed herself to absorb it. She drew the Rune-stave on white card and put it in a prominent place in her home and meditated upon it at various times. She carried the Rune with her, not only to remind her of the need to adjust and adapt, but also as a recognition that she carried that power of adaptability with her. It was *there* within her to add its *qualities* to her life.

Pat now has a son and has become a devoted and responsible mother. Though life is not easy as a single parent she is coping in a manner she had not expected before, and help and support have come to her in many unexpected ways.

Example 2 How Jenny Cleared Her Anxieties

Jenny feared that further involvement in a conservation project, which defended principles that she held quite strongly, might result in attacks on her own life-style, and even persecution. She sought guidance from the Runes.

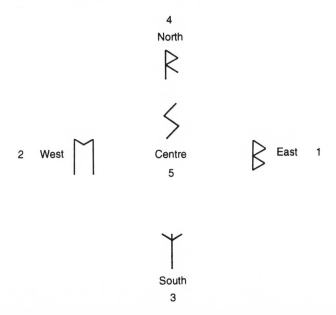

In the **East** was placed BJARKA ᛒ , which confirmed that her anxieties stemmed from her concern for Mother Earth, for this Rune is often associated with the Earth Mother. In the **West** was EH ᛗ, which indicated to her that the Present was one of transition and change, with the need to be adaptable. In the **South** ALGIZ ᛦ stressed the need for protection in future involvements and to be thoroughly grounded in practical reality. In the **North** REID ᚱ suggested that the challenge was one of *direction* so that subsequent events did not get out of *control*. The **Centre** Rune, SOL ᛋ indicated the ability to see things as they *are*. Jenny came to realize that her anxieties and fears were about the unknown: about possible and imaginary happenings rather than actual ones. SOL, like the power of light, enables us to see clearly and to disperse the mist of illusory thoughts.

Example 3 How Bill Solved His Loneliness

Bill, now in his early 30s, was troubled because he did not have a regular girlfriend. All of his old pals were either married or had a partner, and he, too, had a desire to enjoy an on-going relationship, but so far in vain. He chose five Runes at random for a Rune-spread and sought wisdom in knowing how to handle this concern.

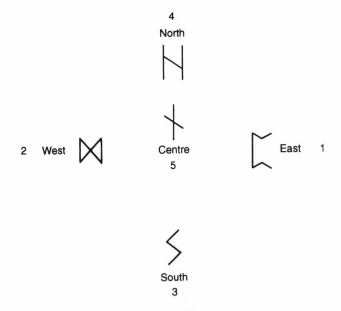

The first Rune, PERTRA ⌷ in the **East**, suggested to him that his openness in desiring a permanent relationship was the source of his problem. Girls were frightened off long before there was a chance of a firm friendship. DAGAZ ⋈ in the **West** was an indication that it was time to make changes and, like the butterfly, not stay too long in one location. Perhaps he had been trying to find a relationship through established social circles. He had to look elsewhere. And he needed to make changes within himself and in his attitude and approaches. SOL ⌇ in the **South** suggested that the future was bright if these transformations are enabled to persist. The real *challenge* this problem presented was expressed by the fourth Rune, HAGAL ᚼ in the **North**. HAGAL is the power that forges links, builds bridges and establishes partnerships. The challenge thus lay in the question or intention itself. The **Centre** Rune, NAUD ᚾ , which can be related to needs, then seemed to shout out at him. And he had been only too aware of his own needs and desires and loneliness. He had been too self-centred. Partnership involves consideration of the needs of the other person. He had been seeking a 'mother' figure, not a companion and partner. He saw this Rune was a power not to satisfy his *wants* but, rather, to enable him to discover what is *needful* in others as well as himself.

Shortly after doing this Rune-spread, Bill changed his job and moved to another part of the country. This opened up new opportunities, and as he started to make changes within himself, new friendships developed. He now has little time for loneliness.

Example 4 How Bernard Faced a Job Challenge

Bernard had held a secure job in a busy government department for eight years and was as integral a part of the office as the furniture. He was a stabilizing factor in a highly charged atmosphere, but it was leading him nowhere. He envied those whose work was aligned with their deeper interests rather than presenting a means of earning a living. He decided to consult the Runes for advice on looking for another job. Interestingly, his spread included Odin, the blank Rune, at the very centre.

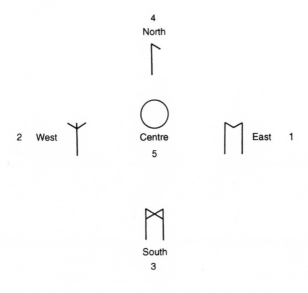

The first Rune, EH ᛗ in the **East**, clearly indicated that his decision to consult the Runes arose out of his desire to make progress in his career. He realized that his concern over his job stemmed from the constant infighting between the two seniors in charge of the office. This actually marred his own progress and development, for the lack of co-operation between the two left him in the vital role of 'picking up the bits' and maintaining a level of efficiency.

The second Rune, in the **West**, indicating current influences affecting the situation, was ALGIZ ᛉ. Bernard took this to mean the development of inner strength through the balancing of 'opposing' forces and grounding them in practical reality. The third Rune, in the **South**, was MADR ᛗ, which he took as meaning that a situation would manifest that was more in tune with his own individuality and with more compatible people. The fourth Rune, in the **North**, revealed the true *challenge* in the situation, and this was LAGU ᛚ. Bernard understood this as meaning 'go with the flow of things', become more intuitive. There was *purpose* in the whole situation – the development of an inner strength that protected him from the adverse effects of discordance and enabled him to discern the true feelings behind the words and actions of others so that a mutual endeavour could proceed. He realized that far from stagnating he had been developing 'inside' without being aware of it, and that this period of his life was a preparation for work ahead.

The fifth Rune thus held the key to all this, yet in the **Centre** Bernard had drawn a blank. What was the meaning of the blank Rune, which indicated the power to call upon in order that the issue may be resolved favourably? Odin, the blank Rune, can indicate the unexpected – that which comes seemingly from 'nowhere', out of 'nothing', or rather the 'No-Thing' out of which everything comes. The message of the blank Rune, then, is: 'There is nothing to *do*. Expect the unexpected.'

'Out of the blue' an opportunity arose for Bernard to be seconded to another department, where the work put him in direct contact with Government Ministers and parliamentary procedures – much more exciting and fulfilling work. At the time of writing it had not led to a permanent post, but it was certainly improving Bernard's self-esteem.

19 Rune-casting

RUNE-CASTING TAKES RUNIC divination a stage further from the Rune-lot or the Rune-spread. The purpose of a Rune-cast is to discover the way energy is moving in a given situation or circumstance, discern its nature and source, and consider an appropriate response to those movements that will formulate what is likely in the Future.

Again, there are many forms of Rune-casting. The method I am about to explain is one in which, through the life experience that is the subject of the Runic consultation, knowledge is provided about oneself, wisdom is obtained in facing its challenge, and understanding attained to effect necessary change.

Historically, a Rune-cast was always approached reverently, as was the *I Ching* in the Taoist tradition. Similarly, a Rune-cast today should be undertaken in a way which expresses proper respect for the Runic powers that are involved. Preparation for a Rune-cast is of vital importance. It is far more than a ritual to provide a structure in which a 'reading' can take shape. it creates the *space* for it and also the *time* in which the dynamics of movement may be stilled. A Rune-cast takes a slice of a moment in Time so that its patterns of energy may be studied.

Before I explain the preliminaries, I should point out that an essential item for Rune-casting is a casting cloth. in former times, a Runic shaman would perform divination simply by drawing a circle or circles on the ground with a staff and casting the Runes into it. Today it is best to use a casting cloth, which is simple to make for yourself.

Rune-work: Assignment 20 Making a Casting Cloth

The cloth should be about 45 centimetres (18 inches) square and preferably white, a colour of purity and clarity. The material can be linen, cotton or felt. On one side should be traced three circles, and for these a black felt marker pen can be used – one whose markings will be permanent – sometimes referred to as a laundry pen. If you have embroidery skills the circles can be formed using cross-stitch.

A dinner plate with a diameter of about 30 centimetres (12 inches) can be used for tracing the first circle, which should be centred on the cloth so there is an even amount of space between the perimeter of the circle and the edges of the cloth.

A smaller plate can be used for the second circle. This should be about 20 centimetres (8 inches) in diameter and positioned centrally within the first circle.

A mug or glass with a diameter of about 10 centimetres (4 inches) can be used for drawing the inner circle, which should be evenly positioned within the second circle.

Finally, using a long ruler, lines should be drawn from each corner to the rim of the second or middle circle (see *figure 25*).

The three circles represent the Three Norns – or Past, Present and Future. But the **inner** circle (Past) is also the Ring of Potential, indicating what is taking place unconsciously from the level of the Soul. The **middle** circle (Present) is *also* the Ring of Causation and activity that is going on at a subconscious level, bringing about conditions in life that are the result of mental conditioning and causation. The **outer** circle (Future) is also the Ring of Manifestation and indicates what is coming into physical reality and conscious activity.

Diagonal lines from each corner to the outside of the central circle create a fourfold division of the cloth into North, East, South and West (see *figure 26*).

The EAST segment is the Place of Decisions. It indicates those things or areas of life about which decisions need to be made.

The SOUTH is the Place of Giving and indicates what we need to give of ourselves or to banish. it is also the Place of the Inner Child, so this is a segment of life which holds lessons we need to learn.

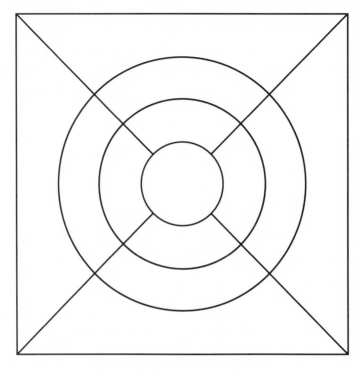

Figure 25 The casting cloth pattern

The WEST is the Place of Holding – what we are holding onto or need to retain. It shows also those things that are in need of change.

The NORTH is the Place of Receiving. It shows what is available for us to receive and shows also areas of life in which clarity and wisdom are needed.

So the circles and segments represent different levels and areas of your life – your physical life on the outside; the realm of your thoughts, ideas, and emotions on the inside; and at the deepest level, the innermost 'You' of the Soul. The pattern also enables you to see the principal areas of your life from a holistic perspective. The four segments can be identified with the Four Directions of the Medicine Wheel – with Receiving (what you are accepting into your life) in the **North**, with Giving (what you are projecting through your actions and attitudes) in the **South**, with Holding (what you are holding onto) in the **West**, and with Determining (how you are acting as a result of your choices and decisions in the **East**.)

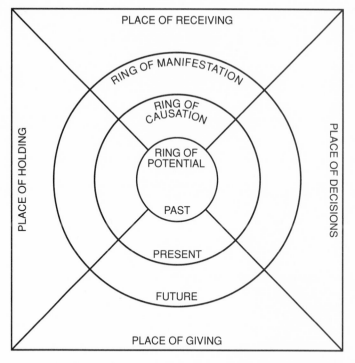

Figure 26 Locations on the casting cloth

Now you have your casting cloth you can proceed with Rune-casting.

The Rune-cast method should be preceded by the establishment of Sacred Space in the room or place where the divination is to be performed. It is more than creating a harmonious atmosphere in which spiritual work may be performed, or, indeed, providing the subconscious with a signal that a change in awareness is needed so that shamanic work may be done – though it is both of these things. The 'sacred space' is, in fact, not in the physical location at all but is outside Time, where Past, Present and immediate Future are part of a perpetually moving and ever-present NOW! Through this preparatory work the Runester enables awareness to be switched 'out of Time' in order that a 'snapshot' of Time can be obtained from a condition of timeless space.

For this preparatory work you will need:

- a candle in a holder, and matches

- a smudge-stick and pot, or incense in a holder
- a rattle
- your set of Runes in their bag
- your casting cloth laid out in front of you
- a notebook and pen

The work is best done sitting beside a table, desk, or other flat surface. It can, of course, be done on the ground or floor if you are comfortable sitting without furniture.

The candle in its holder should be placed in a central position, behind and away from the casting cloth spread out before you. On the left of the cloth place the smudge pot or earthenware bowl in which the smudge-stick can be rested and stubbed out after use. Put a little sand at the bottom of the bowl to assist in this purpose. If you are using incense instead, place the burner in a shallow bowl or dish to catch the ash.

Light the candle. Consider its symbolism. It is a 'switch' which you can use to indicate you are switched-on for shamanic work, pushing aside temporarily all your everyday concerns. Its flame also represents your Inner Light and also the Ultimate Source.

Light the tip of your smudge-stick and blow gently across the smouldering end until it produces smoke. With the stick held firmly in one hand, draw the smoke towards you with the other hand, first to the area of your chest, then to your neck and head, and then downwards towards your feet. Breathe in its pleasant aroma as you do so. Waft the smoke all around you and then over your casting cloth and surrounds, and the entire room. Follow a similar procedure should you use an incense-stick instead.

'Smudging' in this way cleanses the fibres of energy that constitute the subtle energic body or Aura, purifies the sur-rounding area and disperses negativities. It thus helps to estab-lish a harmonic atmosphere in which oracular work can be performed.

Smudging should be followed by rattling around yourself for a few minutes. A rattle is much more than a primitive means of making a pleasant sound. It is an ancient sonic device which creates an atmosphere of expectancy and gentle changes in the level of awareness when we relax into its swishing sound. The sound made by a rattle shaken gently is both physically and mentally comforting and relaxing, which is why it is possibly a baby's first 'toy'. The shaking of a rattle among native peoples symbolized the movement of cosmic forces – we might liken those forces to the movement of planets around the Sun and electrons around the nucleus of an atom. Rattling can expand and extend the consciousness so that we become more sensitive to the movement of subtle energies outside and within ourselves.

Rattling around yourself is a way of bringing all aspects of yourself into a relaxed, peaceful and harmonic unity – a necessary prerequisite for effective divinatory work. Keep up the rattling until you feel tranquil and fully at ease.

To receive counselling from the Runes on a matter of concern, first examine in your mind the matter that is troubling you. Talk silently to yourself as if you were conversing with a close friend or someone you trusted and whose advice would be welcomed. Then condense the matter into a simple question so that it can be focused into a moment of time and connected with the potencies of the Runes. As with the previous methods I have described, the question should form two parts. The first identifies the nature of the problem and should be phrased in such a way so as not to invite a simple 'yes' or 'no' answer. The second part clarifies the intention and directs it towards the innermost Self, as in the following examples.

'How can I resolve my personal finances?
I need help in knowing how best to cope.'

'What prospects does my relationship with . . . hold?
I need advice on how best to handle this affair.'

'How best can I develop my interest in . . .?
I need guidance so I can make a right decision.'

Alternatively, you may approach the Runes for a general appraisal of your life-situation at the present time, rather than for advice on a specific matter. In this case the question can be more comprehensive.

'What opportunities does my life hold for me now?
I need to be shown how I can grasp them for my well-being.'

This kind of question should also be preceded by a period of quiet contemplation as you review in your mind the circumstances of your life at the present time.

Once you have formulated your question, take all 25 pieces (the 24 Runes plus the blank) out of their bag and hold them in your cupped hands over the centre of the casting cloth – at a height of about 20–30 centimetres (8–12 inches) so the Runes are likely to fall in an even spread over the entire cloth. Ideally, none should land outside the cloth, so a little practice may be required beforehand until you arrive at a height that is right for you. Focus on the question. Repeat it silently to yourself three or four times and then let the Runes drop.

Should any Runes fall outside the casting cloth or land face down, they should be removed immediately and returned to the bag. These have no bearing on the reading. Any Runes that are inverted have a meaning contrary to that of when they are upright.

Examine each circle in turn, beginning with the inner circle.

The **inner circle** indicates the core of the problem and its underlying nature. Or it may show what potential is being activated and coming into ultimate expression. As with other shamanic work, the understanding comes intuitively, but in order to obtain that understanding the Runes must be 'read' in relation to the question and intention; otherwise the Ego-self will move in and simply interpret a set of symbols in isolation.

The **middle circle** shows what thoughts and attitudes are colouring and conditioning the situation now and also what is taking place just beneath the surface of 'appearances'.

The **outer circle** indicates what is coming into manifestation now and in the immediate future unless changes are made now. it is showing the way energies are flowing from the unseen into the seen.

The three circles can thus help you to realize how a situation has arisen, how it is affecting the present, and what is likely to arise from it.

The diagonal lines from the four corners to the middle circle provide the directional influences that indicate how the *appearance* of the problem or your current life-situation is to be perceived shamanically in order to extract from it that which can work to your ultimate good.

The top segment (**North**), which emphasizes *Receiving*, indicates what should be *accepted* from the current situation and what is to be learned from it.

The bottom segment (**South**), and the one nearest to you, is linked with the quality of *Giving* and indicates what should be given up or given out.

The left segment (**West**) is concerned with *Holding* – what is being held onto or what is to be retained.

The right segment (**East**) concerns *Determining* and brings to the surface any issues on which a decision or choice needs to be made immediately.

A Runic reading is not a question of simply relating Rune-staves with key words and interpreting them accordingly. Such key words are only indicators or categories of possible meanings. The intuitive senses must be exercised for the 'message' in the Runes to be 'felt' rather than reasoned. And I must stress again: **each Rune and each thought it provokes must be taken within the context of the question and intention that generated the cast.**

Let us examine some examples. The commentaries given are those of the individuals who conducted the readings for *themselves* and serve to illustrate the important principle that the Runes speak to each of us as *individuals*. Use the Divination Indicators only as a guide.

Example 1 Diana's Dilemma

Diana consulted the Runes for guidance about her relationship with Kevin. She has no doubt about the love they have for one another, but when the prospect of marriage is raised Kevin shies away. Diana wants her cottage to be a home for two, and to have children, but she is afraid of pressurizing Kevin into a responsibility for which he is not yet ready. Diana's Rune-cast is shown in *figure 27*. This is her reading of it.

Centre circle: There is within you a necessary ᚾ built-in protection ᛉ against things and relationships. You should rely on your own instinct and intuitiveness, which will throw up necessary considerations and cause you to be hesitant when there is a threat to your future well-being.

Middle circle: At present there are barriers ᚦ that need to be broken down if you are to *receive* in a relationship the kind of fulfilment that your heart desires. This may not be the time to make a firm decision. The relationship currently is at a standstill ᛁ.

Outer circle: Your love X of home life ⚯ is worth *holding onto*. It will come about as a result of a gradual opening up Ⱪ – like a bud coming into bloom. Be patient.

East: A *decision* should be made only when the direction ↑ is sure and you are clear Ϟ that this is the way you want to go. It will need courage and trust.

South: Allow your insight < to show you what it is you need to *give* to the situation at the present time. Perhaps you both need to talk more openly about your feelings ◇.

West: Your thoughts and aspirations ⱀ are close to the home and a partnership in the home, but it is your emotions Γ which are currently moving you Ꝝ that way.

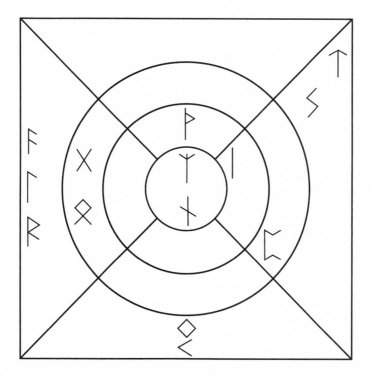

Figure 27 Diana's Rune-cast

Example 2 Jonathan's Anger

Jonathan was troubled about his anger. It welled up in him at home and turned simple domestic problems into a crisis and was undermining his marriage. At work it frequently erupted to create

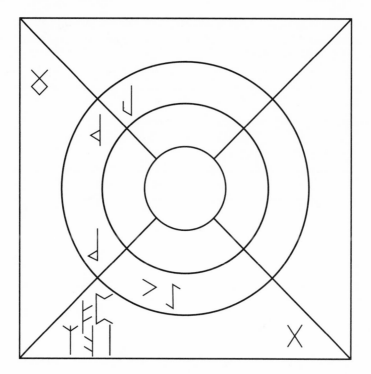

Figure 28 Jonathan's Rune-cast

explosive situations and an atmosphere that could be cut with a knife. Although Jonathan's anger, though verbal, had not degenerated into acts of physical violence, he recognized that it was causing hurt to loved ones and to friends and associates. He consulted the Runes to discover why this anger had arisen in his life, and to obtain the wisdom to deal with it effectively. Here is the understanding he received from his Rune-cast (*figure 28*).

> Five Runes fell in the **outer** circle and indicated to me what was manifesting in my life now and coming into manifestation in the immediate future unless changes were made now. Significantly, four of the Runes were inverted:
>
> Inverted UR ∪ – I feel blocked and unable to make a fresh start, both at home and at my place of employment.
>
> Inverted THURS ◁ – I am unable to remove this tendency to anger, or have the strength to deal with it.
>
> Inverted WYNJA ◁ – There is a lack of real joy and satisfaction in my life because of feelings of *resentment*. So resentment and envy are at the heart of the problem.

Inverted KEN $>$ – I lack insight to perceive another's point of view. I simply haven't been able to see why I am so provoked.

The fifth Rune, EOH $\int$, indicated that my anger was a long-standing problem, which it is.

This group of Runes in the outer ring described precisely my feelings.

Inverted UR $\downarrow$ in the **North** showed that I was blocking myself off from *accepting* what others were offering. I just did not want what they had to give. Inverted THURS $\triangleleft$ and WYNJA $\triangleleft$ in the **West** revealed that I was *holding* on to my resentments and weakness by taking control of a situation calmly. In the **South**, inverted KEN $>$ and EOH $\int$ suggested that I was not giving myself a chance to reflect on whatever issue was arising or to consider any possible long-term consequences. I was 'see-ing' with my *emotions*. I was allowing my emotions to take control of *me*. I was seeing an issue 'inside-out', like that inverted KEN $>$.

No Runes fell in the **Centre** and I took this to mean that my anger did not arise from the heart, nor was it brought into being through a process of activity. The significance of this was sudden and dramatic.

Six Runes fell in the **South**. The first was GIFU $\times$, and here my partner suggested that I need to *give* love rather than expect all the time to receive it. This struck a strong chord with me.

ALGIZ $\curlyvee$ showed me that I need to be grounded in practical reality and not allow myself to be caught up in emotional states. I need to show more my caring for others.

FEH $\not\vdash$ indicated my need to develop my sense of abundance in terms of love and friendship.

PERTRA $\lfloor$ showed that I need to be receptive to others, to listen more carefully to what they have to say, and to be more open-minded.

Inverted ASS $\triangleleft$ confirmed my lack of communication. I have been a poor *listener*.

ISS $|$ told me that I needed to *give away* those frozen-up feelings of revenge and that cruel streak in my nature. This would give a new clarity to my life.

Perhaps the most important Rune of all was the one which fell in the **West** – the Place of Change and Transition and also of *holding*. The Rune was inverted ODAL $\times$. Then it suddenly came to me. I didn't belong! Because of my background and conditioning I felt I didn't belong in this country or the country of my birth. And, similarly, I had this *conditioned* feeling that I did not 'belong' to any group of people either, or even to any situation in which I found myself. I always felt *alienated*. It is this that lies at the root of my problem. It is my sense of alienation that generates my anger.

I am sure that what happened afterwards was a healing process. I had no need to feel alienated from this country, from my partner, from my friends, or from my workplace. The simple truth is that I belong wherever I happen to be. I suppose that is true for all of us.

Jonathan's reading in relation to the problem of his anger showed the value of examining patterns that may be formed by the Runes on the casting cloth. Runes in a straight line indicate powerful influences. Clusters, as in Jonathan's case, suggest clusters of thoughts – a narrative about the issue. They can sometimes be read almost like a story, with you as the central character.

Example 3 Robin's Move

Robin had accepted a new job, which enabled him to move back to his family. It was an exciting prospect, for his career had taken him away from home and the temporary nature of his current post had made it unwise for him to bring his family to the area where he had been working. Robin consulted the Runes for advice on what lay ahead. He read the cast as a simple Past, Present and Future configuration (see *figure 29*).

Past: The central Rune in the Circle of the Past was inverted MADR ⋈ , which he saw as representing himself and the family. Its inversion suggested the loneliness he had suffered through being separated from his loved ones. Inverted LAGU ⌁ indicated the deep feelings that were involved, and unsatisfied emotions. THURS suggested the rather chaotic situation from which he wished to break free. Coping on his own had not been easy and the job itself was often confusing and disorganized. Inverted KEN > indicated that his creative energies had found little outlet. It was an accurate and meaningful description of his recent past.

Present: UR ⍊ confirmed the fresh start he was making at home as well as in his career, and PERTRA ⌊ the opening up of new opportunities and challenges. Both are positioned on the cusp of the **East** and the **South**, suggesting that there are choices and decisions to be made about what to give up. To an extent he had been leading something of a bachelor life, and, though lonesome at times, there were advantages in having the kind of privacy that is not so easily possible with a family around.

There was a line up of Runes in the **North**, with ALGIZ ⅄ and reversed ASS ⇂ in the **Present**, ING ◇ on the cusp of the **Future** and NAUD ⼍ as the sole Rune indicating the Future. ING ◇ clearly

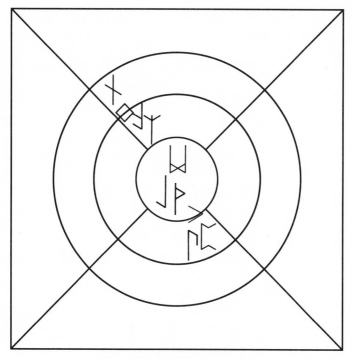

Figure 29 Robin's Rune-cast

indicated that the move was an opportunity for his complete well-being.

NAUD ᚾ was the sole Rune in the **Future** to indicate that everything *necessary* to his well-being lies just ahead. The line-up of Runes in this North-west direction suggests that though Robin's immediate future may lack the inspiring qualities he might yearn for ᚼ, it should enable him to become properly grounded in practical reality ᛏ and in a better position to fulfil his responsibilities to his family.

This book has set out to enable you to come into a knowledge and understanding of the Runes for your own personal development and cultivation. All the Rune-work in these pages has been suggested for that purpose, so that you may become better able to take charge of your own life and destiny and less vulnerable to the conditioning of others and the flow of events which may have limited and inhibited you. I have not, therefore, touched upon the reading of Runes for others – though this form of counselling can be a helpful and even vital service.

Reading the Runes for another person is, however, a responsibility which should not be taken lightly; it requires much more than what some people may regard as 'psychic' skills.

The purpose of *Rune Power* is primarily to enable you to regain your *own* power by coming into an understanding of the nature of the energies flowing through your own life and in your everyday experiences. You will then be able to connect with the energy-patterns of abilities that lie dormant within you, and can nurture them into full expression in your life.

We must each of us first become an effective catalyst for ourselves before undertaking the role of a catalyst for others. This is in the true spirit of the Runic shamans.

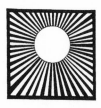

20 The Challenge

WHAT MANIFESTS IN THE UNIVERSE and in our own
individual lives is the outcome of unseen causal powers functioning from *within* the Universe, at a subatomic level, and
within *ourselves*. These sources generate energies which are
projected *outwards* and flow through a dimension we know as
Time. Everything in existence comprises energy and each of us,
like all beings, are essentially an energy-system that has come
into form and is kept in manifestation by the laws of our own
being, subject to duration, which is Time.

The Runes themselves are the patterns of these causal
sources, and in these pages we have been learning a little about
their essential *qualities* and how their movement can affect the
human condition.

We live in the Here and Now, confronted by problems
created by our own Ego-self, by situations that are imposed
upon us by others, and by demands and expectations that are
imposed upon us by the society in which we live. Life here on
Earth is thus a challenge of change and adaptation. We are each
challenged to change or be static. The choice is between
progress towards a higher quality of life, or inertia and subsequent devolution. Nature itself is *an organic process which
supports us in that experience, when we are in harmony with it*. To
come into harmony with Nature does not mean abandoning
our home and our job and living off the land in primitive
conditions. It means coming into harmony with the process of
change that is within ourselves – bringing the outside environment into harmony with our inner reality, and vice versa.

As human beings we are limited all the time by our own Ego,

which constitutes the being we *think* we are and is the lens through which we view everything. Our Ego gives us a false sense of reality, conditioning us into believing that it is the true Self and that the outside world we comprehend with our limited physical senses is the only reality and as permanent as it appears to be.

We have been conditioned into believing that Nature, and other life forms that share the Earth's environment with us, are there to be controlled, manipulated and exploited to serve our own self-interest. For many, this has also been, and still is, the way they feel about other people. And the Runes have not been excluded from this self-centred attitude.

Just as musical notes can be used to produce harmonious sounds which together create beauty and cause delight, so those same musical notes can be manipulated 'off key' to create discord and cause disharmony. I had a personal experience of this when my wife, Beryl, was at the EQ Studios in Watford, England, to record a piece of her music. She wanted a particular passage to sound ominous and threatening whilst still retaining a melody that had a familiarity and was not therefore oppressive. John Hamilton, the musical director, demonstrated how it was possible to take a passage of great beauty and, by playing notes in a different key and in discord, produce a piece of music whose mood was entirely different – though with an element of strange familiarity that was difficult to define and recognize. Though not necessarily unpleasant, the sound was certainly 'disturbing'.

It is like that with the Runes. They might be regarded as the 'silent' notes which orchestrate the Cosmos. Those 'notes' create harmony and beauty, and in a natural setting it is all around us to see and enjoy. But if those same notes are manipulated 'off key', discord results and that can create ugliness and produce unhappiness. Like musical notes, the Runes themselves are neither good nor bad. They have no moral or ethical qualities within themselves. They just *are*. Any moral or ethical qualities are what we humans may *apply* to them, which is another reason why motive and intention are so important. As I have stressed before, motive is what generates action, intent gives it direction.

The reality is that we are multidimensional beings, but our Ego limits us to the Space/Time continuum, where there is a battle going on. There are beings seeking to establish the energies of love, goodness, peace and harmony as the basics of all life on Earth; and there are beings who are dominated by the energies of greed, lust, cruelty and hatred, who exploit whatever and whoever they can for their own self-centred benefit. Their absorption in negative energies brings about such a loss of perspective that they are unable to see that in destroying the environment and others, they are destroying themselves in a far greater way.

The crisis that is occurring on a global scale is a manifestation of a crisis in multidimensional reality. The problem again is Ego. Ego locks us into horizontal thinking. That is true of both 'negative' and 'positive' Egos. Whether we come from a positive or negative perspective, whether we are concerned with our own individual problems, global problems or Cosmic problems, if we view them only through the lens of the Ego we will end up with a false perspective and not see things as they really are. It is only when we start to take a stance from the multidimensional reality of our being that we begin to tear away the veils of illusion. It is important to remember that illusion does not have to be negative to be an illusion. Illusion takes many forms. Many people seem to think that because their path is a 'positive' one they are therefore on the path of Truth.

There are beings operating in the physical universe who, at the multidimensional level, are committed to harmony, goodness and love. There are beings who have made a decision for self-centredness and all that this entails. And there are beings who are in the process of making their decision. This is why the most important thing is what goes on in our hearts. If our deep heart is set in the direction of Love and Harmony, then this is our link with our Spirit Self and through that to the Source. This is why there are ordinary people, living very normal lives, who are more evolved than many gurus, psychics and spiritual healers. To think otherwise is only the Ego playing games!

The challenge of physical manifestation for most beings is through making deep-hearted decisions for Love and Harmony to arrive at a point in their evolution where – for want of a better expression – the Soul is on 'automatic' in terms of these two qualities. When this is achieved the challenge is then to help other beings progress. In this way the Universe itself evolves and each being moves to higher and higher levels. Of course, each movement towards Love and Harmony takes a being deeper into the Source.

On the other hand, beings who have chosen self-centredness and by so doing have set themselves up as 'sources', must battle against the movement of evolution towards higher and higher levels of harmony. The real story of human history is this battle between Light and Darkness, to put it simplistically. This has always been accepted by all major spiritual traditions up to modern times. It is no coincidence that knowledge, understanding and acceptance of the reality of this battle should be at its lowest point during this time of greatest danger.

Shortly before putting the finishing touches to the manuscript of this book, I enjoyed a camping weekend with a group of my students in a beautiful forest near the village in England where I live. Apart from an opportunity to enjoy each other's company in a lovely environment, the purpose of the weekend was to establish our own personal links with Nature and to experience individually the spiritual ecology which, though 'unseen', is present behind physical appearances.

It was a hot, sunny day, and as we sat under the shade of a grove of trees enjoying a meal break, my attention was drawn to a cluster of twigs by my side. I was fascinated by it because three of the twigs formed a perfect pattern of the Rune HAGAL ᚺ and instantly reminded me of *bridging power* – the power to make *connection*. I was reminded that HAGAL might be likened to the rainbow which forms a bridge between the heavens and the Earth. I remembered as a child being encouraged, in stories that were read to me, to 'follow the rainbow to the Place of Dreams'. We, on this weekend, were endeavouring to form our own 'bridge' between ordinary physical reality and non-ordinary spiritual reality, and by so doing experience something of our own multidimensional totality and realize some of our own aspirations.

Later, as I walked beyond the perimeter of the site with a companion, we came upon a deep ditch across which the trunk of a tree had fallen, creating the clear pattern of HAGAL. I recognized this as more than a 'coincidence'. Clearly the Rune had a message for me.

I saw that although the tree trunk had formed a bridge across the two banks so that it was possible to pass from one part of the forest into another without the need to make a detour, traversing it could be rather hazardous. The trunk was smooth and slippery in places, and there were also gnarled and uneven surfaces making it difficult to walk on without losing one's balance. I needed the hand of my companion to help me across and to ensure that I did not lose my balance in the attempt. In crossing from ordinary to non-ordinary reality, too, we need help to give us courage and confidence.

As I began to make the attempt I realized that his firm hand on my left was not sufficient to ensure my safe passage. Something else was needed to *support* me on my right. My companion had with him the straight branch of a fallen tree, which he was fashioning into a walking stick. He passed me this rod, which supported me on my right as he helped me on the left, and I made the crossing safely. Then I did the same for him.

We discussed this sudden realization with much excitement. We recognized that this crossing into aspects of multidimensional reality cannot be made entirely alone. We need the help of someone to guide us on the way so we do not stumble and fall, and we need the support of Nature (symbolized by the rod) in order that we may do so with confidence and assurance. Balance and support are the two essential prerequisites.

This experience made such an impression upon us that we later shared it with the rest of the group. From the discussion arose an idea to devise a little ritual as a way of impressing a recognition of this 'bridging' onto our own subconscious, and to invite everyone to make this symbolic 'crossing' themselves. My companion decorated his staff with coloured wools and feathers to make it rather 'special' and as a means of honouring Nature. The whole exercise developed into a wonderful experience for us all.

That is what the Rune HAGAL taught me just a short time before I put these words to paper in finishing this book. That is the power of the Runes, which, as I explained in the early chapters of this book, were given to humanity *as a blessing* and are themselves a 'bridging' link between the seen and the unseen aspects of ourselves as well as those of the Universe in which we have our being.

This is the true power of the Runes. This is Rune Power.

Glossary

Aesar. The word means 'pillar' or 'support' and is the collective name of a group of 'gods' who were said to have fashioned the Earth as an abode for human beings.

Aett. Literally – eight! A division, group, or family of eight units. An octave.

Asgard. The dimension or dwelling place of the 'gods'.

Audhumbla. The word means 'nourisher' and is the name of the mythological; sacred Cow – the primeval shaping force of the Cosmos.

Aumakua. A Hawaiian word for the superior intelligence of the total being which resides in the higher dimension of the Soul and is thus sometimes referred to as the Higher Self.

Awareness. Being alert to what goes on outside and inside oneself. A registering of activity. Awareness is an activity of the Spirit.

Balance. An equal and steady relationship. Equilibrium.

Belief system. A philosophy or religion which rests upon the word or authority of another.

Bind-rune. A combination of two or more Runes superimposed on one another to make a single shape or pattern.

Chakra. A Sanskrit word meaning 'wheel' or 'disc' to describe a spiralling vortex located in the Energic Body which receives, assimilates and distributes subtle energies that are pulled into its whirlpool. A Chakra is also a gateway between different levels of energy and of states of awareness.

Chaos. An unorganized and disorderly state in which random forces prevail and in which untransformed energy moves freely and without direction in a disruptive fashion.

Chi. A Chinese Taoist word for the activating essence which energizes living beings and provides a state of 'aliveness' and wholeness. Chi is that which links spirit with substance.

Consecration. An act of setting aside for specific use, and involves cleansing, purification, dedication, and empowerment.

Cosmos. The entirety of existence.

Death. A transition from one state of being to another in a continuous cycle of change.

Desire. From a shamanic perspective, there are different kinds of desire. There is desire of the senses which is a need for physical gratification; there is desire of the mind, which exercises the Will toward self-interest; and there is desire of the Spirit, which is toward wholeness and harmony.

Divination. A way of observing energy-patterns that are in the process of moving into and out of manifestation. It entails insight from within and from the perspective of the Spirit. Its is a means of obtaining an overview of a person's life from the perspective of the Spirit.

Dwarfs. Elemental Earth spirits.

Earthing. A method of ensuring that the awareness is fully restored to ordinary reality after any form of shamanic or meditative work.

Edda. The title of ancient manuscripts that deal with Northern mythology. The Elder or Poetic Edda is a collection of poems and is dated between the years 800 and 1270 AD. The Younger or Prose Edda was compiled by an Icelandic historian, Snorri Sturluson, in 1222 AD.

Ego. A mental concept of self-identity. The personality 'I'.

Elements. Powers that generate the movement of energy and the nature of that movement. Each Element has abstract qualities which can be comprehended in human terms by relating it to the characteristics found in either physical earth, fire, water, and air.

Elves. Elemental Air spirits.

Etin. A 'giant' of mythology attributed with the powers of great size and strength.

Fetch. The Energic Body which is controlled by the subconscious Hidden Self, or what kahuna shamans called *Unihipili*.

Freewill. Liberty to learn by experience and to self-determine – that is, to have freedom of direction in determining one's own destiny.

Futhark. A form of runic alphabet in which the letters F-U-TH-A-R-K represented the first six Runes of its arrangement and which has been regarded as the most 'traditional' and magickally powerful runic alphabet.

Germanic. A linguistic term indicating language and cultures descended from a common origin.

Ginnungagap. The primal Void before creation.

God-form. A thought-form fashioned by the collective mind of a group, tribe, or culture and attributed with superhuman powers, and given expression. God-forms depend upon the continuing adoration of their adherents to keep them in existence. Without such input the god-form fades into oblivion.

Gods/Goddesses. Personifications of invisible Intelligences behind the creative and formative forces of Nature.

Harmony. A dynamic interchange of energies that resonate together in unison to create a beneficial condition.

Havamal. The second poem of the Elder Edda and meaning, 'Sayings of the High One', and containing songs of wisdom.

Huginn. Thought. Intellect. One of Odin's ravens.

Inner Guide. An 'inner' intelligence that serves as a guardian and mentor on the inner dimension of the Soul. Not to be confused with outside spirit entities and so-called spirit-guides.

Inner Light. The Spirit within that emanates from the centre of the Soul.

Inner Space. A dimension of non-ordinary reality where Time is not constant.

Intention. A clear and precise instruction to the subconscious Hidden Self (*Unihipili*) to provide a route along which energy may flow to bring about a desired result. The energy is generated by motive.

Intuition. Teaching from within. A sudden 'knowing' that transcends the reasoning mind.

Kahuna. A Hawaiian word meaning 'priest', 'teacher' or 'expert'. A shaman who acts as a catalyst.

Karma: A Cosmic Law of action and change which provides experiences that need to be lived through to further an individual's development and evolution.

Love. An unconditional, all-embracing expression of the Spirit which creates harmony. Love is also the substance of the Spirit and the bonding force which holds together that which is in existence.

Lyke. A name for the Soul Body which is controlled by the Higher Self (**Aumakua**).

Madr. An old Norse word meaning 'man'.

Mana. A vital essence that is the pure energy of Love and Harmony.

Mead. A drink brewed from honey and water and thought to be the nectar of the 'gods'.

Medicine. In a shamanic context the word means 'power' or 'empowerment'.

Medicine Wheel. A multi-dimensional symbolic device for making connections and finding direction in life. A means of coming into harmony with the forces of Nature and with ourselves. Though of apparent native American origin it is a catalyst of all other mandalas.

Midgard. A word meaning 'middle enclosure' or 'Middle Earth' – the dwelling place of human beings.

Mind. An intangible receptacle in which information is processed. Thoughts are the movement of energy-patterns within the reality of the Mind and which can be shaped and fashioned to manifest in physical reality. In shamanic understanding, the Mind should serve the Spirit.

Minni. A word meaning 'memory' but applied to the Soul and not the Mind, so it implies ancestral memory, or past lives. The name of one of Odin's ravens.

Motive. The choice of direction in which energy is generated to flow. Motive is what generates activity.

Multiverse. The many states of being that constitute the Universe.

Mystery. That which transcends the intellect and can be known only through direct personal experience.

Nature. An organic and cyclical process through which energy is transformed into matter and is enabled to revert back to energy.

Norns. Embodiment of the processes of causality and evolutionary development. There are three Norns: URD (that which is), VER-DANDI (that which is becoming), and SKULD (that which should be) – sometimes simplistically referred to as Past, Present, and Future. Each person is said to have his or her own Norns, turning their own 'wheel of life' and weaving their own web of existence.

Old Norse. A language spoken by West Scandinavian peoples during the Viking Era (800 – 1100 AD).

Odin. A word meaning 'all-pervading spirit' and having similarity with the Great Spirit concept of native Americans. The name of the principal Northern deity who was known also as 'All-Father', meaning 'Originator' – the One who 'seeded' the Universe. Odin the All-Father was attributed with 49 names – implying that different languages and cultures have different names for the same deity based on their own attitudes and beliefs. Odin was the assumed name of a political leader in the 1st century AD who led a wandering tribe from the region of the Caspian Sea through Europe to southern Sweden where he ruled with fairness and justice to maintain the right of the individual to live in peace and harmony. Odin was the name also of a travelling shaman who 'discovered' the Runes through a shamanic experience.

Ritual. A method of converting thoughts into symbolic actions in order to impress the subconscious Self (*Unihipili*) to act on an instruction.

Rune-casting. A method of Runic divination in which Runes are 'thrown' onto a casting cloth or onto casting space.

Rune-craft. The use of Runic knowledge to cause changes in the outward environment.

Rune-lore. Exoteric and esoteric teachings about the Runes.

Rune-lot: A method of runic divination in which a Rune or Runes are chosen at random.

Rune Master. A person skilled in Runic practices.

Runester. A person involved in Runic studies.

Runes. A process by which the fundamental potencies of Nature may be conveyed.

Rune-stave. The pattern or 'signature' of a runic potency inherent within Nature and ourselves.

Rune-work: Personal development work with the Runes.

Runic Counsellor. A person skilled in the Runes and qualified to provide advice to others through consulting the Runes.

Science. A systematic study and formulated knowledge of physical phenomena with principles regulating its pursuit.

Secret. A message that is concealed except for those who have been prepared in order to receive it.

Self-interest. The essence of self-interest is separateness. Self-willed energy characterized by a dedication to its own needs and unconcern for others.

Shaman. One who perceives what others cannot see and who understands that every living thing experiences its own awareness of 'aliveness', and who is able to explore non-ordinary realities.

Shamanic perspective. The application of an understanding of the holistic and holographic nature of the Universe to everyday life experiences.

Shamanics. A personal development process which incorporates the essence of universal shamanism – the ancient wisdom of the 'Wise Ones' of many cultures and traditions – into a Way of Effective Living in modern times. The word was coined by Kenneth Meadows to define the most natural and practical way of bringing body, mind, soul and spirit into harmony within the totality of being.

Shamanist. A person who applies shamanic principles and teachings in everyday life in order to further his or her own personal development and in service to others.

Skald. An Old Norse word for a poet who composes original verse.

Sleipner. A horse-like creature in mythology who conveyed Odin between the realms of spirit and matter and was symbolic of Time. According to the myths, Sleipner had eight legs, symbolic of eight directions and eight dimensions.

Sorcerer. A person skilled in magick and who is able to manipulate changes to the outside environment in accordance with the Will.

Soul. A body of energy which serves as a vehicle of the individuated Spirit within to express itself and to gain experience at conscious, subconscious and unconscious levels. A life-expression system which retains the essence of relevant life experience.

Spirit. The intelligent essence that animates a life-form but which usually cannot be seen though its presence is experienced. That which *is*. The intelligence 'within' which is aware of its own being and aliveness. Spirit is experienced as awareness of being.

Substance. That through which energy may flow in order to perform its work.

Symbol. A means of exchanging energy between different levels or planes of reality. A link between the objective and the subjective, and one level of awareness and another.

Talisman. An energy-pattern worn or carried to attract desired effects.

Thought-form. A mental pattern which, through persistence, has stability and duration, and takes on form by use of mental substance in the dimension of the Mind.

Thule. A mythical island of pre-history located in the far North which is believed by some to have been home of an Aryan race of people who were descended from the 'gods'. According to legends it disappeared under tidal waves during a natural disaster. The word means 'the place of turning back'.

Thurs. An Old Norse word for giant or 'strong one'. It is the name given to a force which shaped and fashioned Ymir from primal substance.

Unihipili. A Hawaiian word meaning 'silent spirit' or 'servant self'. May be associated with the subconscious aspect of the Mind.

Universe. A great sphere of activity and influence which functions in accordance with natural and Cosmic laws.

Vanir. A group or family of fertility 'gods' and 'goddesses'.

Viking. A word meaning 'adventurer' or 'explorer' and which characterized a Scandinavian civilization which thrived from the 6th to the 12th centuries.

Wise Ones. The visionaries of all races, cultures, and traditions who share in an ancient wisdom and understanding of life.

World. A place of ordered existence devised by the mind. Not to be confused with the Earth which is a planetary being.

Wyrd. A web of synchronicity and of cause and effect.

Yang. The masculine, active, positive, conceptual force in all that manifests. Represented in some ancient cultures as the God-power behind Nature.

Yin. The feminine, passive, receptive, nurturing force in all that manifests. Represented in some cultures as the Goddess-power behind Nature.

Yggdrasil. The word means 'Ygg's steed' or 'the carrier of Ygg – or I'.

It is the name given to the symbolic Cosmic Tree of Life which represents the structure of the Cosmos.

Ymir. A word meaning 'roarer' and the name of a mythical being, the living substance from which what is to become manifest could take form in an ordered and evolving way.

Further Reading

Arcarti, Kristyna, *Runes for Beginners*, Headway – Hodder & Stoughton, 1994

Aswyn, Freya, *Leaves of Yggdrasil*, Llewellyn, 1990

Atwater, P M H, *The Magickal Langauge of the Runes*, Bear & Company, 1986

Barrett, Clive, *The Viking Gods*, Aquarian Press, 1989

Blum, Ralph, *Rune Play*, Michael Joseph, 1987

Blum, Ralph, *The Book of Runes*, Michael Joseph, 1982

Cohat, Yves, *The Vikings – Lords of the Seas*, Thames and Hudson, 1992

Conway, D J, *Norse Magic*, Llewellyn, 1990

Cooper, D Jason, *Esoteric Rune Magic*, Llewellyn, 1994

Cooper, D Jason, *Using the Runes*, Aquarian Press, 1986

Dolphin, Deon, *Rune Magic*, Newcastle Publishing Co. Inc., 1987

Fries, Jan, *Helrunar – A Manual of Rune Magick*, Mandrake, 1993

Gitlin-Emmer, Susan, *Lady of the Northern Light*, The Crossing Press, 1993

Guerber, H A, *The Norsemen*, Senate, 1994

Gundarsson, Kveldulf, *Teutonic Magic*, Llewellyn, 1967

Howard, Michael, *Mysteries of the Runes*, Capall Bana Publishing, 1994

Howard, Michael, *The Magic of the Runes*, Samuel Weiser Inc., 1980

Howard, Michael, *The Wisdom of the Runes*, Rider, 1985

Jansson, Sven B. F, *Runes of Sweden*, Gidlunds, Sweden, 1987

King, Bernard, *The Elements of the Runes*, Element Books, 1993

Kushi, Micho, *The Book of Macrobiotics*, Japan Publications, 1986

Longland, Stella and Osborn, Marijane, *Rune Games*, Routledge & Kegan Paul, 1982

Page, R I, *Norse Myths*, British Museum Press, 1990

Page, R I, *Runes*, British Museum Publication, 1987

Pennick, Nigel, *Runic Astrology*, Aquarian Press, 1990

255

Pennick, Nigel, *The Secret Lore of the Runes and Other Ancient Alphabets*, Rider, 1991

Peschel, Lisa, *A Practical Guide to the Runes*, Llewellyn, 1989

Peterson, Dr James M, *The Enchanted Alphabet*, Aquarian Press, 1988

Terry, Patricia(trans), *Poems of the Elder Edda*, University of Pennsylvania Press, 1990

Thorsson, Edred, *At the Well of Wyrd*, Samuel Weiser Inc., 1988

Thorsson, Edred, *Futhark – A Handbook of Rune Magic*, Samuel Weiser Inc., 1984

Thorsson, Edred, *Runelore*, Samuel Weiser Inc., 1987

Thorsson, Edred, *Rune Might*, Llewellyn, 1989

Thorsson, Edred, *The Book of Troth*, Llewellyn, 1989

Thorsson, Edred, *The Nine Doors of Midgard*, Llewellyn, 1991

Tyson, Donald, *Rune Magic*, Llewellyn, 1988

Willis, Tony, *The Rune User's Handbook*, Aquarian Press, 1986

Willis, Tony, *The Runic Workbook*, Aquarian Press, 1986

Resources

Kenneth Meadows' *Shamanic Experience Drumming Tape* provides a drumming sequence to induce a state of awareness in which shamanic consciousness may be experienced. This 60-minute audio-cassette includes narrated instruction and guidance.

Beryl Meadows' unique musical work, *Powers of Love*, is a shamanic journey to other dimensions of experience, and contains much shamanic teaching in the lyrics. Its gentle melodies and sweeping orchestrations make pleasant listening for all musical tastes, and its inspirational theme has touched the hearts of all who have listened to it.

Both cassettes are available by mail order for £10 each (or foreign currency equivalent), including postage and packing, from:

Peridot Publishing
27 Old Gloucester Street
London WC1N 3XX
England

Kenneth Meadows appreciates receiving letters from readers, especially those relating to the benefits derived from undertaking the Assignments given in this book. Although he cannot guarantee to answer every letter, please do enclose a stamped addressed envelope. Write to:

Kenneth Meadows
BM Box 8602
London WC1N 3XX
England

What *is* Shamanics?

The word *Shamanics* was coined by Kenneth Meadows to describe a unique process of personal development and life-enhancement derived from distillation of shamanic wisdom from cultures and traditions worldwide. It is a process generated by the Spirit rather than the intellect to release hidden potential and creativity, extend conscious awareness and enable the individual to find meaning, purpose and fulfilment in his or her life. Kenneth Meadows considers it to be the most natural and practical way of bringing Body, Mind, Soul and Spirit into dynamic and harmonious unity, thereby extending the human potential.

Shamanics frees the esoteric knowledge of the 'Wise Ones' from racial and cultural limitations and from manipulative distortions, presenting it in a modern-day context to benefit both the individual and the community. The Runic teachings given in this book share in that Shamanics process.

The Faculty of Shamanics is an educational enterprise founded by Kenneth and Beryl Meadows to further the development of Shamanics and ways of bringing individual men and women into harmony with Nature, the Universe and themselves so that they can find fulfilment in their own individual lives. The word *Faculty* is not confined solely to identifying a branch of learning, but is defined also as 'an ability or aptitude – a potential or capacity to perform a particular skill': in this case, *life*-skill – the *craft* of Life!

The Faculty offers part-time courses and seminars on aspects of Shamanics, including Runic skills, and provides certification courses for those who may wish to teach Shamanics or practise as shamanic counsellors. Information can be obtained by writing to:

The Faculty of Shamanics
PO Box 300
Potters Bar
Hertfordshire EN6 4LE England

Index